SIGNS OF CONTRADICTION

Signs of
Contradiction
Twelve Outstanding People
Who Changed our World

David Alton

Hodder & Stoughton
LONDON SYDNEY AUCKLAND

British Library Cataloguing in Publication Data
A record for this book is available from the British Library

ISBN 0340 651644

Printed and bound in Great Britain by
Cox & Wyman Ltd, Reading, Berkshire

Hodder and Stoughton Ltd
A Division of Hodder Headline PLC
338 Euston Road
London NW1 3BH

To Lizzie, Marianne, Padraig, and Philip

Right in the middle of a contradiction,
that's the place to be.

Bono, *U2 At the End of the World*
(Bantam Press, London, 1995)

Contents

Introduction

Essentially this collection has been chosen for entirely personal reasons. Each of those selected has impressed me as an outstanding person who has successfully stood out against the odds: someone who has been prepared to act as a sign of contradiction in a hostile world.

Being 'politically correct', or running with the pack, is not a modern phenomenon: nevertheless, at many crucial moments in our history men and women have taken a stand for truth. In the words of Ben Jonson, 'Stand for truth: it's enough.' Political correctness is an insistence that you conform to certain stereotypes – and one of its first casualties has been the pursuit of truth. Political correctness has demeaned women and unmanned men. We no longer value women as women but view them as sexless persons. We now define people by their sexuality and this increasingly negative view of the value of the human being is accompanied by the flaccid language of rights shorn of personal responsibilities, duties, or obligations. Everything has the same value; what you choose for you is what is right for you.

What is wrong with political correctness, which may often have begun with a good impulse – a concern with the dignity of women, a loathing of racial hatred, a hatred of sexual discrimination – is that it can remarkably quickly degenerate into being ridiculous and even intolerant. It doesn't look at the fundamental values of society. It is often just the best cause to catch your eye on the rack at the local health shop. It is frightened to exercise moral leadership because of a fear of public opinion or fear of personal criticism. Its proponents like nothing more than to revel in the human weakness of others – especially when they fall short of the ideal they espouse. This is thoroughly corrosive of civilised values.

Being civilised doesn't simply mean knowing how to use cutlery; it particularly has a spiritual and religious dimension. The politically correct would prefer to eliminate this dimension from our lives – hence worldwide attempts to ban religious teaching in schools, to secularise school assemblies and even to ban the symbol of the cross from the classroom. Theirs has been an era of nihilism. Against this deficit, our rich spiritual culture may be weighed on the golden scales. This book is a celebration of the lives of a few individuals who have been part of that tradition.

It is these qualities of independence, personal courage and endurance – often against many besetting pressures or seemingly impossible odds – which I want to explore. What has intrigued me most about the exceptional people I have chosen has been what or who it is that inspired them to stand against the world. What price have they paid? How have they then had an effect on the people around them?

Disillusionment and cynicism with public figures are especially marked today. Over the past couple of years I have been a member of the House of Commons Committee of Privileges examining charges of ethical misconduct by MPs. To have been simultaneously writing about the lives in this book has been personally helpful to me, underlying the ability of exceptional people to soar above the messiness of our normal existence. It is even more helpful to reflect that these lives were also marred by failure and doubt and all the other human weaknesses with which we are so familiar. Before critics say it, let me freely admit that there have been thoroughly depressing periods when individuals and institutions which have claimed allegiance to higher values have failed abjectly; sometimes even inflicting terrible cruelty. But shining through it all are people who followed their conscience, pursued causes, served their community, church or nation. Self-interest was a minimal consideration. Thoreau said that if we cut down the trees there will be nowhere left for the birds to sing. As we cut down the Church, Parliament, civic institutions, the city and the individuals who serve there, we are in danger of leaving nowhere for the birds to sing.

The politics of right and left has come to interest me less and less and I have been heartened to see the debate focusing more on right and wrong. As we stumble towards a new political synthesis of personal responsibility combined with a passion for social justice, and a politics which is community-based and value-centred, the lives which are recorded in this book remind us that the common ground is often to be found on the higher ground. None of the people I have chosen settled for expediency or a lowest common denominator.

These lives show us how responsible choices may be made. Cain was offered the choice to be responsible or irresponsible; good or evil. God offers each of us life or death and He simply waits for our answer. If we look at how others have responded it can engender real hope in our lives. If we look for perfection we will deserve to be disappointed. I am always wary of heroes – you tend to find they are the same earthen vessels as the rest of us. In the lives of others though, we can sometimes see something which helps us in our own.

I have chosen twelve men and women, some dead, some still living. These portraits are necessarily brief: vignettes rather than biographies. None of them could even vaguely be described as politically correct; they have something more important to offer us than that. Perhaps, as we consider the array of problems which beset each of us and our families, our communities and countries, a glimpse into these lives will help us to make our own personal stand to be signs of contradiction ourselves. I have also used their lives to examine contemporary issues which suggested themselves in the context of the person I am writing about.

Although I take full responsibility for the text which follows, including its deficiencies and inadequacies, may I thank the following who have helped with research, encouragement, or ideas: Wilfred Wong, Christopher Graffius, Mrs Barbara Lewis, Paul Hatcher, Jonathan Bartley, and Annabel Robson of Hodder. It would be remiss of me not to also thank my wife, Lizzie, and our children for understanding when I have told them that I had to get on with the book.

David Alton
Liverpool, Autumn 1995

Chapter One

William Roscoe and the Rathbones of Liverpool

MODELS FOR GOOD CITIZENSHIP

Stand for truth; it's enough.

Ben Jonson

I want to begin this book by talking about the unfashionable concepts of duty and personal responsibility. I will return to these themes later in the book but suffice it to say here that compared with the exaggerated emphasis placed on personal choice and rights, men and women who believe in public service before self-service, and responsibilities or duties before rights, are in short supply today. This chapter is about two families, the Roscoes and the Rathbones, who were unselfishly committed to fighting for powerless people and generous with both their time and money. I have chosen them as their lives also suggest on what values human community can be rebuilt. There is no more important task in Britain today than the rebuilding of the human infrastructure, the human ecology.

Since my salad days as a Liverpool student I have represented people in the heart of the great City of Liverpool – first as a City Councillor, as Chairman of its Housing Committee and Deputy Leader of its Council, and for more than sixteen years as a Member of Parliament. All the rules of politics said that I should never have been elected. The Low Hill Ward had been part of the city's Exchange Division, once represented in

Parliament by the legendary Bessie Braddock. She earned the respect of ordinary people by her zeal as their champion. She never lost touch with their day-to-day problems and kept her feet firmly on the ground. Hers was one of the safest Labour seats in England. So was the neighbouring constituency of Edge Hill – which I went on to win in a by-election in 1979.

Not only did I find myself elected as the first Liberal MP in the city since 1926, but I became the youngest member of the Commons, and the shortest-lived! The night before my election, on 29th March 1979, Jim Callaghan's Labour Government was defeated in a parliamentary vote of confidence. During my Eve of Poll Rally at Wavertree's Lawrence Road School a piece of paper was handed to me telling me that the Government had collapsed. Having lost the vote of confidence by one vote, a general election would be held five weeks later. The way was cleared for Margaret Thatcher's 1979 general election victory.

Before that could happen the voters of Edge Hill still had to go through the ritual of electing a new MP. This they did, giving me a record swing and nearly two-thirds of the votes cast. I then found myself in the faintly bizarre position of taking my seat as everyone else was packing their bags and returning to their constituencies to contest the general election. Normally it would have been regarded as pushy to make your Maiden Speech within two hours of arriving: in my case I had little choice, certainly not without risking the ultimate indignity of becoming an after-dinner joke for the rest of my life: shortest-lived MP that never even opened his mouth! In the event, I was re-elected for Edge Hill and then, when the Boundary Commissioners abolished the seat, for the new seat of Mossley Hill – which they abolished again in 1995. All of this gave me a special sympathy for William Roscoe. He too was a Liberal, or more precisely a Whig. He was the first to be elected under these colours in Liverpool and he remained in Parliament for a mere three months, in 1807.

William Roscoe

William Roscoe, born in 1753, was a reformer, poet, historian, lawyer and banker, devout believer and MP – and a true son of his City of Liverpool. Roscoe was six years of age when he was sent to a day school in Paradise Street, kept by a Mr Martin. At twelve years of age he ended his formal education, working in his father's market garden growing potatoes; but, significantly, this was when he bought his first book. This book was to form the core of what subsequently became a world-famous library. At fifteen he worked briefly in a book store and then was articled as a clerk to John Eyes, a Church Street solicitor.

Gradually Roscoe taught himself a love of literature and the arts. He began to write and to illustrate his first poems. He began to fashion ideas and to hold political and religious beliefs. Margaret Thatcher used to talk a lot about 'self-help'. She would have liked that side of Roscoe but he also believed in mutual help and the upholding of the rights of the downtrodden and did not believe that public morality or ethics could simply be left to market forces.

In the heat of the commercial boom which hit Liverpool at the end of the eighteenth century, Roscoe became a successful banker and lawyer. But, as so easily happens, he never lost sight of his other values.

In 1790 Roscoe's family moved from Mount Pleasant, where he was born, and which is today at the bustling centre of Liverpool's main shopping area. His father had kept a tavern and a market garden there. With his much loved wife and family Roscoe moved to the nearby countryside, the Dingle, in Toxteth Park.

Where the linnet chirps his song . . .
and bending tufts of grass, bright gleaming through the
encircling wood,

> . . . grateful for the tribute paid,
> Lordly Mersey loved the Maid.

Speaking in Liverpool in 1995 at the annual Roscoe Dinner,
held in the magnificent Walker Art Gallery, Lord Rogers of
Quarry Bank said that he had little regard for Roscoe's poetry.
Unhesitatingly, I disagree.

Today's Liverpool 8 is a far cry from Roscoe's chirping
linnets. As one of the most deprived areas in Europe it is
designated by the European Community as objective one.
Roscoe's stanzas recall an age which pre-dated the industrialis-
ation of Liverpool. The evangelical preacher John Wesley
described it as 'one of the neatest, best built towns I have ever
seen in England'. Roscoe's poetry recaptures a Liverpool long
since gone. It is penned by a man born in today's busy city
centre but who was essentially a countryman. A true son of this
city, but perhaps, when he wrote these other lines, he foresaw
the destruction of Liverpool first by enemy bombs and then by
politicians and planners:

> The time may come – O distant be the year – when
> desolation spreads her empire here,
> when trade's uncertain triumph shall be o'er,
> and the wave roll neglected on the shore . . . and not one
> trace of former pride remain.

Throughout the 1960s and early 1970s the humble homes of
tightly knit communities were rased to the ground as a scorched
earth policy of urban blight was inflicted on Liverpool. The
heart was ripped out of the city and only in recent years has
there been a welcome restoration of the civic pride which was
once so strong in Liverpool. After decades of decline in
maritime activity it is only now that the port and docks are
once again a success story.

It was no exaggeration when the great historian of Liverpool,

Sir James Picton, said that no native resident of Liverpool had done more to elevate the character of the community by uniting the successful pursuit of literature and art with the ordinary duties of the citizen and man of business than Roscoe. Here was a care for his community and a profound sense of public duty.

His was a life which combined a deep commitment to a principle – however unpopular it made him – with a practical concern for the everyday needs of ordinary people, particularly their enlightenment and education. This too long neglected life, which combined a love of languages, art and poetry with a passionate commitment to political reform and human rights is worthy of serious study in an age when public duty, public service and social responsibility are too often forgotten virtues.

We give young people negative models and rarely uphold examples for them to emulate. Yet here is a man whose formal education lasted only until he was twelve. By the age of twenty he had taught himself a reading knowledge of Latin, French, and Italian. He taught himself to etch and acquired a love of the fine arts which drew him to Florence and to even write a life of Lorenzo de' Medici. His love of art and learning did not become a marginal obsession. It enriched and deepened a man who spent his life cultivating learning: learning for a purpose.

Roscoe's example, and that of other Liverpool families who were connected with him, hold inspiration for observers in and beyond his native city. It is inspiring to see how the young Roscoe shaped his ideas. It was a classic example of someone pulling themselves up by their own boot laces; translating self-help into mutual help.

Roscoe's firmest friend was William Rathbone, whose family produced many generations of politicians and philanthropists, including Gladstone's Chief Whip. The last Liberal to be elected in Liverpool before me was Hugh Rathbone, elected in Wavertree in 1926; while Eleanor Rathbone, his remarkable cousin, sat for one of the University seats as an independent.

At the turn of the nineteenth century both families were Unitarians, worshipping at the beautiful Unitarian Chapel in Liverpool's Ullet Road now regularly open to the public, thanks to the work of Andrew Lloyd-Webber's Open Churches trust. Both Roscoe and Rathbone were morally opposed to slavery: a far from popular position for a Liverpool MP then. Their Unitarianism helps to explain a great deal about their political and social positions. Like Jews and Catholics of the same period they were actively discriminated against as dissenters. Shut out of many professions, they had to band together in mutual support. This led to powerful alliances at a personal, commercial and political level.

The Liverpool historian, Ramsay Muir wrote warmly about their impact:

The glory of Liverpool in this period was to be found in a group of friends who were not content to cultivate their own minds, but who strove to diffuse throughout the money grubbing community in which they found themselves, something of their own delight in the civilising power of the arts. These men were Whigs holding unpopular politics, and very dubiously regarded by their fellow-citizens. They were enemies of the slave trade and the strenuous advocates of political and social reform.[1]

Roscoe and his friends were the creators of Liverpool's Athenaeum, a scholars' library opened in 1799: the Botanic Gardens, first established in Mount Pleasant and later moved to Botanic Road, and the Royal Institution, which was to be a place of learning with the open ideal of contradicting the lust for money which was the hallmark of the city's commercial life.

Ramsay Muir estimated that in the year of Roscoe's election some £17 million passed hands in the exchange of slaves. This would be commensurate with the wealth exchanged in the City of London today. He concluded that Roscoe and his friends, redeem to some extent the sordidness of Liverpool at the opening of the nineteenth century. Their spirit, and the spirit which has scattered over the city in a score of years schools, charities, and churches, were a fortunate augury for the new age; since they seemed to promise that gentle pities and noble dreams were not to be wholly crushed under foot by the city's march towards commercial supremacy.

The lonely stand of a few men and women against the terrible excesses of slavery is a poignant reminder that it is not impossible to speak out or to take a stand against evil however much the odds may appear to be stacked against you.

During Roscoe's few weeks in Parliament, his friend, William Wilberforce, brought forward first his anti-slavery measure. Although Parliament voted to abolish slavery in Britain it was to take more than twenty years before it was outlawed throughout the British Empire. Roscoe voted for abolition and on his return to Liverpool he was met by a hostile mob who beat him up. He was not returned in the ensuing election but spent the rest of his life campaigning for the slaves: publishing tracts and poetry highlighting their plight. He bankrupted himself as he devoted his funds to establishing schools, art galleries and botanic gardens. Having given away all his wealth he ended his days in penury, living in Liverpool's Lodge Lane, where more than a century later the Toxteth riots began.

Liverpool's prosperity was based on the slave trade. Visitors to the city today will gasp in admiration at the city's buildings, its architecture and at the sheer scale of the South Docks but these tourist attractions have their genesis in Liverpool's pivotal role in the slavery triangle. The slaves were not brought directly to Liverpool. Manufactured goods were shipped from Liverpool to Guinea. These cargoes were exchanged for slaves who were then taken directly to the West Indies and sold into slavery. Raw materials were then shipped back to Liverpool and turned into manufactured goods in the Lancashire hinterland.

In the Liverpool newspapers of Roscoe's day there were many advertisements urging Liverpool gentlemen to try their luck and to amass their fortunes in this trade of human misery. It would have been easy for Roscoe to turn a blind eye to these lucrative, evil practices. The slave trade dominated Liverpool and it was highly unpopular to speak out against it. Yet Roscoe and William Rathbone – the scion of another great Liverpool family, who was equally detested by the slave traders – were two of the few who did.

Roscoe went further and joined with the Quakers and political leaders like Fox and the Christian political reformer, Wilberforce, to challenge the slavery laws. In 1787 and 1788 he published tracts and poems attacking the inhumanity and evil of slavery. In his outstanding epic poem, 'The Wrongs of Africa', are lines which retain their strength and poignancy to this day:

Blush ye not to boast your equal laws, your just restraints, your rights defended, your liberties secured, whilst with an iron hand ye crushed to earth the helpless African; and bid him drink that cup of sorrow, which yourselves have dashed, indignant, from Oppression's fainting grasp?

Alex Hayley's memorable book, *Roots*, traced the lives and travels of African slaves who were cruelly uprooted and transplanted. It adds graphic detail to the ordeals which Roscoe's poetry recounts. In coming to terms with the inhumane and barbaric way in which blacks were treated, we need to heal our own past. Roscoe was an exception in a society which largely baptised the slave trade or indifferently refused to question the basis on which it was conducted. This need to heal the past and to honestly seek forgiveness for unrequited actions of the past is a subject which Professor Kenneth McAll admirably addresses in his book *Healing The Family Tree*.[2]

Just like our forebears we count ourselves as great champions of liberty and rights but, too often, like them we turn a blind eye when the iron hand of oppression crushes those who enjoy none of the same liberties.

Roscoe showed admirable courage as he shunned popular acclaim, vigorously admonishing his Liverpool readers and reminding them that for all of us there comes a time of reckoning: 'Forget not, Britain, higher still than thee, sits the great Judge of nations, who can weigh the wrong, and can repay.'

In 1807, when he was elected to Parliament, he had his chance to do something about the utilitarianism which said 'It's my right to own another as my slave.' He ignored the hatred which his position engendered and from across the floor on the other side of the House of Commons chamber he strongly supported Wilberforce. After he had cast his vote for emancipation, other abolitionists told him his vote in the House had been worth twenty cast by anybody else. In his case, however, there would be a price to pay.

The received wisdom in politics today is to check the opinion polls before you open your mouth and on no account say anything which might upset anybody. In the nineteenth century, W. S. Gilbert satirised this phenomenon when he wrote of MPs that 'they always voted at their Party's call and never ever think for themselves at all'. In the twentieth century MPs have become too obsessed with opinion polls, toeing the Party line, and with serving vested interests. I am always deeply suspicious of MPs who do not use their position in Parliament to pursue causes but are there to advance themselves or their vested interests. Causes, conscience, constituents, Country. That should be the stuff of politics, not commercial lobbyists and financial interests. During recent years I have served on Parliament's Committee of Privileges. If I previously had any doubts about wrong motives in politics I have none now. The reputation of politicians is at an all-time low and public cynicism at an all-time high. We need an urgent return to the politics of conscience.

Roscoe always put conscience first. After just three months in the House of Commons he returned to Liverpool and was assailed by enraged slave traders. In the general election which followed, Liverpool returned a Tory in his place. Undaunted by public opprobrium his determination to put principles and conscience first was summed up by what he had told the House of Commons: 'I consider it the greatest happiness of my existence to lift up my voice on this occasion, with the friends of justice and humanity.'

Roscoe showed similar courage in supporting the ideals – though not the fanaticism – of the French Revolution. From his political position as a Whig, he bitterly attacked Edmund Burke, who changed sides and became an opponent of political reform. By keeping alive these ideals he and the Whigs paved the way for the reforming legislation of the 1830s and probably helped avert a bloody revolution. He was a reformer who believed that if institutions were to survive then they needed to change. During the same period he once again faced public opinion when he opposed the Napoleonic Wars.

Roscoe was not a revolutionary bent on destroying institutions and structures; but he passionately believed that revolution would become inevitable if injustice was not addressed. As in contemporary Britain, there was a need for a new civic reckoning. Roscoe believed that only moderate reform of atrophied institutions could fend off their wholesale destruction.

In 1790, he penned these lines about the revolution in Europe: 'Too long had Oppression and Terror entwined those fancy-formed chains that enslave the free mind ... Seize then the glad moment, and hail the decree that bids millions rejoice, and a nation be free.' Words which might contemporaneously be applied in South Africa or Eastern Europe.

Roscoe fought against slavery and championed individual liberty. He was adamantly opposed to the Test Acts which debarred and discriminated against Dissenters and Roman Catholics – another unpopular cause in the Liverpool of his day. It would be another twenty-five years before the influx of Irish-Catholic immigrants to Liverpool. In arguing for 'general toleration' he was ahead of his time and certainly not in line with the more fervid adherents of Whiggism in Liverpool. In 1746 they had burnt to the ground the only Roman Catholic chapel in the town, and the home of a Catholic widow.

As a Dissenter himself he refused to compromise when offered the position of the Deputy-Lieutenancy of the County (which the law said could only be held by a member of the Established Church). Even though he was assured that the law would not be invoked against him he held that bad laws should be repealed, not ignored. Roscoe clearly saw the difference between right and wrong and never shied away from a fight when an important principle was at stake. Nor was Roscoe simply long on words and short on actions.

He supported every project calculated for the public good. The extent of his private charities was considerable. He knew that there was nothing wrong with wealth or privilege *per se*; failure to share it and make it work for others constituted the wrong. His commitment to his city and his family was legendary. He lived at Liverpool's Mount Pleasant, Dingle, Islington, and Allerton Hall and he died in 1831 at his home in Toxteth's Lodge Lane. Although he often wrote about the city he loved he also wrote for his family. His children's poem, 'The Butterfly's Ball', captivates me more than any of the others, not least because it shows Roscoe's ability to communicate with his own children through the unusual medium of poetry.

Written for his son Robert it describes some of the guests at revels in the insect world:

Come take up your hats, and away let us haste
To the Butterfly Ball and the Grasshopper Feast;
The trumpeter, Gadfly, has summoned the crew,
And the Revels are now only waiting for you . . .
And there was the Gnat, and the Dragon fly too,
With all their relations, Green, Orange and Blue;
And there came the moth with his plumage of down,
And the hornet, in jacket of yellow and brown.

Many fathers today must surely wish they had the capacity to write verse for their children – or that they were even able to talk to them. In our age of mass communications, when a modern form of Trappism overtakes our television couch potatoes, we have lost many of the gentler arts of personal communication such as verse and even conversation. King George III liked 'The Butterfly's Ball' so much that he had the poem set to music for his three daughters, the princesses Elizabeth, Augusta and Mary.

Roscoe's family gave him enormous comfort. This must have been a great boon when he found himself and his ideas spurned. Thankfully, history sometimes reaches a kindlier verdict than contemporaries. I am always struck, in Westminster Hall, by the plaque commemorating the life and works of Thomas More. History has treated him in a kindlier way than it has treated Henry VIII, who sent More to the block.

It is also surprising how a person's influence can reach out beyond the grave into the lives of friends and descendants.

William Rathbone and Eleanor Rathbone

One of Roscoe's closest friends was William Rathbone. His family were allies of Roscoe and Wilberforce. Rathbone and Roscoe were two of the eight subscribers to the London Committee for the Abolition of the Slave Trade. William Rathbone died in 1809 but he was succeeded by several generations of

Rathbones who epitomised the early spirit of public service established by their progenitor. I recently met William Rathbone the tenth who is still involved in important philanthropic work and who, through the work of the Eleanor Rathbone Trust, takes extremely seriously his social responsibility to the disadvantaged.

The Liverpool librarian, George Chandler, writing in 1953[3] about Roscoe and Rathbone described their political beliefs as 'the inevitable result of Christian moral philosophy'. These were ideals which were handed down within the Rathbone family and which were to come to influence another famous Liverpool family, the Gladstones (who were, at that time, engaged in making their wealth from slavery).

Chandler continued: 'Freedom, equality and toleration were ideals which followed only in so far as they were not used to justify doing harm to others.' For them 'there was no short cut to the Kingdom of Heaven on earth'. The measures they supported 'were not those of violence but of persuasion, self-discipline and individual effort'. Both men were guided by the 'inner voice'.

Roscoe and Rathbone brought like-minded people into their circle. Edward Rushton was one of these. He was a blind poet who had been a sailor on a slave ship. His *West Indian Eclogues* may not be great poetry but they quiver with righteous detestation of slavery and with a love of liberty. Another was James Currie, a young Scottish doctor who risked his practice and reputation by denouncing the trade which gave the wealthiest men in the town their wealth.

They fashioned their arguments and stood their ground against slavery's apologists. The Reverend Raymund Harris, a Spanish Jesuit, was paid £100 by the Liverpool Corporation to publish a tract in favour of slavery. Having received his commission he stated that slavery is in 'conformity with the principles of natural and revealed religion delineated in the sacred writings of the Word of God'. Roscoe and Rathbone were having none of it and published their own *Scriptural Refutation* in response.

Rathbone shared Roscoe's liberalism and his non-conformism. Together they bravely spoke out against the iniquities of a trade which brought Liverpool a flood of wealth but also brought with it responsibility for one of the most enduring acts of barbarism of the modern centuries. The wounds which it created are still unhealed to this day. Etched in my mind is the comment of a young black woman in the aftermath of the 1981 Toxteth riots who told me, 'We came here 150 years ago and since then we've moved half a mile up the road.' The slave trade in England ended on lst May 1807. The last slave ship to sail from Liverpool on a slaver's mission was captained by Hugh Crow. The *Mary* picked up its human cargo of 400 blacks and they were sold by English merchants to work as conscripts on the plantations of the New World.

William Roscoe and William Rathbone understood the responsibilities which go with privilege. They had a concept of citizenship which we badly need today. Their belief in public service and public duty – so often scorned as paternalistic do-goodery – seems to have been given to their families along with their breast milk. Another Rathbone persuaded the City Council to open Liverpool's first public wash houses in 1842 and was to become Lord Mayor of Liverpool; another, Member of Parliament for Liverpool and Gladstone's Chief Whip. He was also responsible for launching the public appeal, initiated at a town meeting in 1879, which led to the establishment of Liverpool University – to which the family ultimately gave their home and land. He also established the Liverpool Training School and School for Nurses, after taking advice from Florence Nightingale.

His daughter was the formidable Eleanor Rathbone, elected to Parliament in 1929 where she served until she died, aged seventy-three in 1946. His nephew, Hugh, became MP for Liverpool Wavertree from 1923 to 24.

It is worth saying something more about Eleanor Rathbone because in many ways she was the final heir to the legacy of public service and conviction politics bequeathed to Liverpool by her great-grandfather and his friend William Roscoe. Eleanor Rathbone is one of the outstanding figures of inter-war-year politics and like Roscoe she has been too long neglected.

Sitting as an Independent for one of the now abolished University seats, Miss Rathbone pioneered the reforms which set up family benefit, championed the rights of women to have the vote, travelled to India and highlighted the plight of Indian women, and in her home town of Liverpool she established committees to oversee the distribution of aid and relief. She supported Winston Churchill in his isolated stand against Nazi Germany and at the end of the Second World War she was actively involved in the cause of refugees and the creation of a Jewish homeland. She, too, was a reformer not a revolutionary.

Eleanor's father had strong opinions about the use of wealth and privilege and the whole conduct of his life had its roots in strong religious faith. Like many of his forebears he was a Unitarian; his wife an Anglican. Eleanor summed up her father's approach as 'a belief that whatever ought to be done can be done'. While he was propounding his belief in the power of the individual to engage in direct attacks on social evils, Karl Marx was publishing *Das Kapital*, which said individuals should be seen as 'the personifications of economic categories, embodiments of particular class relationships and class interests'. This mechanistic approach to life would have been an anathema to these reforming Liverpool families.

Eleanor and her father inevitably remained implacably opposed to Marxism and its collectivist State-led approach. Her father's practical Christianity and inborn inheritance of Rathbone conscience and Rathbone sensitivity to other people's distress sustained her through her life. She saw Christianity as 'a guide for life' but while applying each of its strictures in her own life she appeared to derive few of its comforts.

After her father's death, in 1902, at the age of eighty-three, Eleanor plunged herself into practical philanthropic work. Having graduated from Oxford in 1896, she immediately returned to Liverpool where she became a visitor for the Liverpool Central Relief Society, a manager of the Granby Street Council School, and Honorary Secretary of the Liverpool Women's Industrial Council. By 1904 she had become secretary of the Victoria Women's Settlement, where she met her lifelong friend, Elizabeth MacAdam. In 1909 she highlighted the plight of dockers' families by publishing *How the Casual Labourer Lives* and in 1913 she published *The Condition of Widows Under the Poor Law in Liverpool*. In her early advocacy of motherhood – as an occupation as worthy of financial support as any other – lies the germ of the case for family allowances. In an age when women are made to feel inferior because they have chosen the most crucial task in any country, forming, rearing and encouraging our children, Eleanor Rathbone's views have a new relevance and importance. Eleanor's sense of justice also led her to insist that where a woman and a man were doing the same work they should receive the same recompense.

This same sense of justice also led her to accept the post of Parliamentary Secretary to the Liverpool Women's Suffrage Society – and she was very soon organising, writing, pamphleteering, and speaking. She crossed swords with Lloyd George and Winston Churchill (then Home Secretary and strongly opposed to women's emancipation) although she overcame this early antagonism to Churchill during the inter-war years. By then he was one of the few voices to oppose appeasement and Eleanor Rathbone, one of the women whom he had tried to deny the vote, was by then elected to Parliament and staunchly sharing his anti-Hitler views.

Above all else she deserves to be remembered for the way in

which she championed the family and pioneered family allowances. In 1924 her *The Disinherited Family*[4] became a textbook on the subject and in 1940 she published *The Case for Family Allowances*[5] – a measure which reached the Statute Books in 1945, a year before her death.

Goethe once put the following words into the mouth of the Devil: 'I am the Spirit of Negation – and rightly; because everything that comes into existence is worthy only of destruction. It were better therefore than nothing had existed.' Like William Roscoe, Eleanor Rathbone viewed this nihilism and evil pessimism as defeatist and she utterly opposed those who argued that because there was poverty and pain in the world it would have been better not to have been born. She held to her father's obstinate belief that if life for many was not good, it could and should be made so. This had been the philosophy which spurred the earlier Rathbones and William Roscoe into opposing the slave trade. Eleanor was remembered as tenacious, courageous and independent as a politician and as a humanitarian crusader. She never received, nor sought high ministerial office. Disdaining partisan politics her successes were the successes she secured rather than the portfolios she might have had. Sir Herbert Samuel, also born in Liverpool, former Home Secretary and leader of the Liberal Party, gave her memorial lecture in 1953. He described her as 'always in deadly earnest, persistent and insistent'.

These great Liverpool familes are redolent of an age when people could be passionate about causes and where words were not measured in soundbites and opinions were not shaped by pollsters but by a sense of justice and by a sense of duty. They had a clear idea of what it meant to be a citizen. If this is what people mean when they talk about Victorian values then we should try to rediscover them. The lives and work of William Roscoe and the Rathbones are an example to us all.

Chapter Two

John Wesley

FEARLESS AGAINST THE ESTABLISHMENT

I design plain truth for plain people.

John Wesley in sermons on several occasions

John Wesley knew the Liverpool of Roscoe and the Rathbones, and had admiring words to say about its buildings and well-appointed streets. But he also understood how its wealth had been generated, forthrightly condemning the slave trade. I have chosen him because of his trenchant adherence to his beliefs; because of his zeal in promoting and advancing those beliefs; because of his refusal to conform to the prevailing climate of the times. It goes deeper than that. Wesley promoted renewal within the life of the Church and the nation. Renewal led to revival which, in turn, led to political reform. As Wesley helped men to change, the nation changed.

As a child I had a jigsaw puzzle. On one side was a man; on the other, the world. For a young boy it was very hard to get the world right. It was much easier to get the man right. The great thing about the puzzle was that once the man was right, turn the puzzle over and the world had come right too. Wesley knew the simple truth that he had to get the man right before the world would change. Christian political reformers, touched by the revival in faith which Wesley led were to spearhead social change in everything from the slave laws to the Factory Acts. A new tolerance led to the extension of the franchise and emancipation of Catholics and Jews. John Wesley's remarkable life and work created the set on which the English Victorian age would be acted out. It also offers an opportunity to reflect on what Wesley would make of contemporary Britain and our response.

Robert Van de Weyer in *Island Vision: Prophets, Pastors and Pilgrims of the English Church*[1] says

> John Wesley was the most influential – and possibly the most extraordinary – Christian that England has ever produced. In the course of his ministry he travelled a quarter of a million miles on horseback or as he got older, in a simple coach; he delivered about forty thousand sermons, typically preaching three or four times a day; and he wrote two hundred and thirty-three books and tracts, mostly composed in the saddle.

Robert Van de Weyer is just one of many who have marvelled at Wesley's ability to cram so much activity into his ministry. John Capon, in *John and Charles Wesley: The Preacher and the Poet*[2] says

> John Wesley's principle of striking a blow only where he could follow it up is nowhere better illustrated than in his phenomenal literary output. Had he done no more in his lifetime than travel a quarter of a million miles and preach forty thousand times, he would have achieved in fifty years what few men could in five hundred. But in addition to his travelling and preaching he also published some four hundred books and booklets.

The imagination fails when attempting to comprehend how he found the time for such a prolific output. His three activities – travelling, preaching, publishing – were interrelated in so far as some of his published works were sermons, while others were accounts of his travels. The many hours he spent travelling also gave him time for writing, as well as reading. But allowing for those slender advantages the scale of his written work remains literally incredible.

Not only its scale, but also its scope. No two-year period can ever be typical, but a glance at Wesley's publishing programme for 1743 and 1744 gives some indication of the range: the latest selection of his and Charles's hymns; a three-volume thousand-page anthology of *Moral and Sacred Poems*; a small book of family prayers; another containing Methodist Society rules; his blistering Oxford sermon of 1744; his Journal for 1739–41; a book of *Instructions for Children*; numerous pamphlets including one aimed at soldiers and another recommending celibacy; abridgements of religious classics by Scougal, Bunyan, Law, von Zinzendorf and others. Standing head and shoulders above these was his *Earnest Appeal to Men of Reason and Religion*, a fifty-three-page tract which attacked those whose Christianity was a pretence and 'clergy who were indifferent to the spiritual needs of men, and sought to persuade professed unbelievers of the reasonableness of the Christian faith . . .'

Not many Christians have been credited by historians for averting a bloody revolution by their ministry and Wesley is one of those few. His long life of zealous ministry is a testimony to how God can work wonders through a person who is willing to sacrifice all for Him. My principal reason for choosing him as one of my signs of contradiction is that he stood firmly against the spirit of his times. Moreover, he was extraordinarily effective in the challenge he mounted. His influence is on a par with that of St Benedict, St Francis, Luther and St Ignatius. In our times the men who have a comparable impact are Billy Graham and Pope John Paul II.

Wesley's Early Life

Wesley's parents came from Nonconformist families but had rejoined the Church of England. His father, Samuel Wesley, was rector of Epworth in Lincolnshire. His mother, Susanna, ruled her children with an iron rod and had strong views on their upbringing. She believed that, 'The first thing to be done is to break their wills and bring them to an obedient temper.' Whenever they misbehaved she insisted they should not cry when beaten but only 'murmur softly'. Although she thought that it was a worse cruelty to spoil a child than to give them the rod, she was ready to give praise and encouragement whenever needed.

John was the second son in the family, born in 1703, and until the age of ten was taught by his mother. He then studied at Charterhouse School in London and at sixteen went to Christ Church College Oxford, to study for a Bachelor of Arts degree. Whilst there, he worked hard at the classics and logic and also spent hours in reading a wide range of topics outside his course work. He was no bookworm and also devoted a lot of his energy to tennis, swimming and boating.

Wesley took his degree in 1724 and his father encouraged him to become a clergyman. He complied, and settled down to five years of rigorous theological study. Around the beginning of Holy Week in 1725, John's mother wrote to him, urging 'Enter now upon a serious examination of yourself, that you may know whether you have a reasonable hope of salvation by Jesus Christ, that is, whether you are in a state of faith and repentance or not.' She wrote that to stay always in this state of mind and soul was the essential condition of salvation. Examining himself as his mother had suggested, he wrote down a list of his temptations. They have a fastidiousness which sounds strange to less innocent modern ears:

a. Too much addicting myself to light behaviour at all times;
b. Listening too much to idle talk, and reading vain plays and books;
c. Idleness; and lastly
d. Want of due consideration in whose presence I am.

From which I perceive it is necessary
a. To labour for a grave and modest carriage;
b. To avoid vain and light company; and
c. To entertain awful apprehension of the presence of
   God;
d. To avoid idleness, freedom with women, and high-
   seasoned meats.

In his zealousness he was determined 'to resist the very beginnings of lust, not by arguing with, but by thinking no more of it or by immediately going into company'.

This same workaholic approach to Christianity also led Wesley to systematically delve into the literature of the Christian mystics and spiritual writers, reading the medieval classics as well as more recent Catholic and Protestant devotional literature. Three books which particularly impressed him were, Thomas à Kempis' *The Imitation of Christ*, Jeremy Taylor's *Holy Living* and William Law's *A Serious Call*. However, some of *The Imitation*'s strictness initially annoyed and perplexed Wesley. He wrote to his mother, 'I can't think that when God sent us into the world he had irreversibly decreed that we should be perpetually miserable in it ... Another of his tenets is that all mirth is vain and useless, if not sinful. But why then does the Psalmist so often exhort us to rejoice in the Lord?' Most of us who, upon first reading, have been repelled by *The Imitation*'s detailed strictures would share Wesley's later observation: 'I began to see that true religion was seated in the heart, and that God's law extended to all our thoughts as well as words and actions.' The young Wesley nurtured his faith with further reading and began to work on the method which would give strength and direction to his faith.

Holy Living inspired him to keep a diary, a forerunner of his famous Journal, in order to help him keep a check on his own feelings and motives. Wesley strongly believed that true faith should be nurtured and strengthened by a disciplined life. His daily self-analysis of his own actions and motives helped him to keep his sense of purpose. *A Serious Call* convinced Wesley that it was not possible to be 'half a Christian' and he resolved 'to be all devoted to God – to give him all my soul, my body and my substance'. The strict religious discipline which this book advocated appealed to Wesley's uncompromising character, and he began to fast regularly, and to spend much time each day in prayer and meditation. Wesley also believed in frequent communion and began to attend Holy Communion in the cathedral at Oxford every Sunday. It is hard not to make comparisons with the approach of the founder of the Jesuits, St Ignatius Loyola, and his Spiritual Exercises. Yet despite Wesley's strictness in religious observance, he was still inwardly restless and continued to feel he was not 'in a state of salvation'.

Wesley was ordained in Christ Church Cathedral on the morning of Sunday 19th September 1725. On the night before his ordination, he wrote, 'Boasting, greedy of praise, intemperate sleep, detraction, lying – Lord have mercy – heat in arguing.'

The Methodists

On March 17th 1726, Wesley was elected a fellow of Lincoln College, Oxford, where he lectured in Greek. It was a position he held until the end of his life. At about the same time, he started in his diary an hourly introspection of his behaviour, and kept it up for four days, then abandoned the first notebook and began another, reverting to twice-daily reports and a Saturday-night appraisal. When his mother learned of his system, she said, 'There's nothing like a clear method to save both time and labour in anything.'

In 1729, John's brother, Charles, started a small group who met for theological discussion and prayer. They were soon nicknamed the 'Holy Club', 'Sacramentarians' and 'the Godly Club'. The name which stuck was 'Methodists' for their methodical religious observance. A few months later, John joined them, assuming the leadership of the Club. He made the rules stricter and added a social ministry to its activities, visiting the local prison and providing clothes for poor children. They also sometimes helped a debtor gain discharge and adopted three or four poor families, visiting them regularly, reading to the sick and aged. Wesley urged 'method and order' on members of the club, so that every hour of the day had its proper use, whether study, devotion, exercise or charity.

When Wesley told his father about the charitable work of the club, the old rector said, 'None but such as are out of their senses would be prejudiced against your acting in this manner.' He was mistaken. It was not long before vociferous criticisms were being made of the Holy Club's activities as a whole and especially its charitable work. Wesley had to learn early how to take a stand against hostile criticism. Wesley prepared a careful written response to the serious critics and taught his disciples to ignore the jeering, or to see it as helping them to be more worthy of God's favour and more Christ-like. He had also resolved to 'make the Scriptures my study'. The Bible now constituted the main portion of his reading in Divinity.

To give himself more time for such constructive activities he shook off his 'trifling acquaintance' and was very careful how he used each hour. He offered prayers at intervals throughout the day, including the ejaculatory prayer on the first second of every hour. He also trained himself to rise at five o'clock or even at four. Early rising became a hallmark of the Methodists. To save on coals or logs and sometimes to inflict a penance on himself, Wesley sat in a fireless room unless he had company. To deepen their humility and to save on the hire of horses, the Wesley brothers even took to walking all the way to Epworth, about 150 miles away. Ever conscious of not wasting time, the two would read as they walked.

John Clayton, a tutor of Brasenose College, and who was intending to take holy orders, approved of the religious observances of the Wesleys and urged them to keep the fasts of the primitive church, which were enjoined in the Book of Common Prayer but had lapsed from general use. The Wesleys agreed to do so and began to fast every Wednesday and Friday. John Clayton also introduced the Wesleys to the writings of the Church Fathers. Wesley would spend hours in the Bodleian Library discovering new strands of Christian thought. He also bought two huge volumes of texts culled from the Fathers by the late Bishop William Beveridge. From the Fathers, Wesley learned about asceticism and ideas of Christian perfection. This strengthened his belief that true Christianity could not be fully experienced by simple souls, though all must start on the path.

For nearly six years Wesley would try to reach Christian perfection, and there would be many diversions before he realised he was moving in the wrong direction. In 1735 John and Charles set sail for Georgia, purportedly to evangelise the Indians. But John wrote that his chief motive 'is the hope of saving my own soul – I hope to learn the true sense of the gospel by preaching it to the heathen'. However, this was not to be the case and he returned in even greater spiritual turmoil, writing, 'I went to America to convert the Indians, but oh, who shall convert me?' He was entering his dark night of the soul.

Justification by Faith

Shortly after returning to England, Wesley met Peter Bohler, a twenty-six-year-old German on his way to be a missionary in South Carolina. Peter had come by a sudden experience into a clear understanding of Christian salvation. Peter was a Moravian minister and his happy faith was a contrast to Wesley's own turmoil. At one point, Bohler contended that a true faith in Christ always brought two fruits: 'dominion over sin, and constant peace from a sense of forgiveness'. Wesley wrote that he was, 'quite amazed, and looked upon it as a new gospel. If this was so, it was clear I had not faith.' He vigorously disputed

Bohler's contention, arguing that forgiveness and peace must be earned by unceasing effort. He admitted that he groaned under the heavy yoke, and that the more he tried to be holy, the more he sinned. Bohler replied, 'Believe and you will be saved. Believe in the Lord Jesus with all your heart, and nothing shall be impossible to you! This faith, like the salvation it brings, is the free gift of God. Seek and you will find.' He added, 'Strip yourself naked of your own good words, and your own righteousness, and go naked to him. For everyone that comes to him he will in no wise cast out.'

Gradually, by detailed reference to Scripture, Bohler managed to persuade Wesley that he was right. Wesley decided to seek 'the free gift' of faith of which Bohler spoke, by 'absolutely renouncing all dependence, in whole or in part, upon my works of righteousness'.

Wesley was converted on May 24th 1738. That afternoon he attended evensong at St Paul's Cathedral. The choir sang Purcell's anthem, 'Out of the deep have I called unto thee, O Lord'. He was very much encouraged by the lines of the song, which included the words 'O Israel, trust in the Lord, for with the Lord there is mercy, and with him plenteous redemption. And he shall redeem Israel from all his sins.' He then went to a religious meeting in Aldersgate Street and what followed is described in the most well-known passage in Wesley's journal:

In the evening I went very unwillingly to a society in Aldersgate Street, where one was reading Luther's preface to the Epistle to the Romans. About a quarter before nine, while he was describing the change which God works in the heart through faith in Christ, I felt my heart strangely warmed. I felt I did trust in Christ, Christ alone for salvation; and an assurance was given to me that he had taken away my sins, even mine, and saved me from the law of sin and death.

He then testified to all there what he had first felt in his heart. However, he adds, '. . . but it was not long before the enemy suggested, "this cannot be faith; for where is the joy?"' He then realised that faith does not depend on feeling; joy might be given or withheld. His description of how the spiritual enemy tries to blunt or destroy the new buds of faith helps to remind us that our spiritual progress is never going to be easy.

Now began Wesley's extraordinary ministry. He found himself growing daily in spiritual strength 'so that though I was now assaulted by many temptations, I was more than conqueror, gaining more power thereby to trust and to rejoice in God my Saviour'. On the first Sunday after his conversion, he preached at St George's Bloomsbury on justification by faith. He was told in the vestry afterwards that he would not be asked to preach there again. No doubt he felt hurt and rejected but this unpleasant experience forced upon him a new approach which was to become the hallmark of his ministry.

He was so often refused a pulpit that he resorted to preaching in the open air. He soon realised that this was more effective as it enabled him to reach ordinary working-class people who would never have entered a church. He created Methodist Societies wherever he preached, so that new converts could meet for Bible study and prayer. He formed the members into 'classes', each with a class leader to care for their spiritual welfare. He appointed lay preachers to share in his evangelistic work, and stewards to look after the material assets of the societies; and he organised local 'circuit meetings' of preachers, stewards and class leaders to regulate the societies' affairs. The societies ensured that the preaching and evangelising would have a lasting effect. As a model, this 'field' church movement has echoes in today's rapidly expanding house church movement and all denominations should pay attention to the successful Wesleyan approach.

Wesley's days passed in ceaseless activity – proclaiming the Gospel in private houses, preaching in any church still open to him, speaking with converts and helpers, and drinking large amounts of China tea. Field preaching inevitably involved preaching in other men's parishes, for all England was subject to the parish system. As a fellow of an Oxford college, Wesley had a general licence to preach, but this implied the permission of the local incumbent, and Wesley preached regardless of whether or not he was invited. He told an old friend who objected to this practice: 'God in Scripture commands me, according to my power, to instruct the ignorant, reform the wicked, confirm the virtuous. Man forbids me to do this in another's parish; that is, in effect, to do it at all; seeing that I have now no parish of my own, nor probably ever shall. Whom then shall I hear, God or man?'

He then coined the phrase which was to be inscribed, long after, on his memorial in Westminster Abbey: 'I look upon all the world as my parish.' This is a classic confrontation between a proponent of Christianity and the stuffy world of Churchianity. He later defined this phrase as meaning that wherever he was in the world, 'I judge it meet, right and my bounden duty to declare, unto all who are willing to hear, the glad tidings of salvation. This is the work which I know God has called me to.'

As John Pollock points out in his admirable biography of Wesley,[3] he was reviving the long-discarded practice of preaching friars of the medieval Church when he spoke from market crosses and on commons and hillsides, often with a boy to play an oboe for the hymns. In all his preaching he aimed 'to invite; to convince; to offer Christ'. His sermons included much Scripture and frequent anecdotes, and were informed by the vast range of his reading in Christian and classical literature. Yet he put across his message so clearly that even the simplest person could understand. John Fletcher, a disciple of Wesley, wrote of him in his old age,

Of the two greatest and most useful ministers I ever knew, one is no more. The other, [i.e. John Wesley] after amazing labours, flies still, with unwearied diligence, through the three kingdoms, calling sinners to repentance. Though oppressed with the weight of near thirty thousand souls, he shames still, by his unabated zeal and immense labours, all the young ministers in England, perhaps in Christendom. He has generally blown the gospel trumpet, and rode twenty miles, before most of the professors who despise his labours, have left their downy pillows. As he begins the day, the week, the year, so he concludes them, still intent upon extensive services for the glory of the Redeemer, and the good of souls.

Wesley's great strength was that while men like Whitefield drew converts, who were described as 'melting like a rope of sand', Wesley's methods and organisation secured long-term conversion. His genius lay in attracting the poor and uneducated, in reaching people who had never heard the Word of God and in giving people convictions in an age of reason, where very few people professed any religious belief.

Wesley remained a loyal Anglican all his life, despite the opposition of many bishops and clergy, and ensured that Methodist meetings did not clash with services at the parish church. However, not long after his death in 1791 at the age of eighty-seven, the Methodists split from the Anglican Church and became a separate denomination. Perhaps one of the sadnesses of religious revival and reform is that it has frequently led to new separate denominations. In achieving one set of objectives new obstacles of denominational rivalry inevitably appear. Wesley saw his initiatives not so much as a new denomination – that was where his followers took it – but as a renewing movement for the whole Church.

Lessons from Wesley's Life

I agree with Robert Van de Weyer's assessment of John Wesley, that it is his life itself, rather than the texts of his sermons which spellbind the onlooker. There are so many lessons that we can learn from his inspiring example. Wesley was a man on fire for God and his theology, like Augustine's, was beaten out on the anvil of hard experience. His apostolic zeal clashed with a Church that had at that time grown quite complacent and lost sight of some of the essentials of the Christian message, such as the issue of justification by faith, the importance of proclaiming the Gospel to all and the duty to help through good works those who are less fortunate than us. He suggested that meat would not be so scarce and dear if the nobility and gentry would stop the 'amazing waste' allowed in their kitchens and eat less enormous meals. He urged Methodists to relieve and evangelise the poor systematically and gave most of his own income away to help the poor or support the spread of the Methodist movement. Wesley was a well-rounded Christian, who showed by his example that concern for the poor was to be tied in with evangelism and demonstrated that such issues were in no way mutually exclusive.

He was also not afraid to speak out against injustices. He raised his voice against the slave trade, which at that time was almost universally condoned. In 1774 Wesley wrote *Thoughts on Slavery*, becoming the first voice of importance to be raised in England on this issue and was uncompromising in his approach. He wrote:

> Give liberty to whom liberty is due, that is, to every child of man, to every partaker of human nature. Let none serve you but by his own act and deed, by his own voluntary action. Away with all whips, all chains, all compulsion! Be gentle toward all men; and see that you

invariably do with every one as you would he should do
unto you.

John Newton, the former slave trader, who was a Christian,
read Wesley's pamphlet and had his eyes opened to the crime
in which he had been engaged before and after his conversion.
He became determined to make amends and eleven years later
was one of the chief influences on the young Member of
Parliament, William Wilberforce, who as a boy had known and
admired him, and had turned to him at the crisis of his own
conversion. Wilberforce was joined by men like Roscoe in
finally ending the slave trade.

As John Pollock points out, the long campaign for abolition
belongs to Wilberforce's story, which I have written about
elsewhere.[4] But in its early stages Wesley advised and encouraged all who were involved in the struggle. Shortly before his
death, Wesley wrote to Wilberforce, to encourage 'your glorious enterprise in opposing that execrable villainy which is the
scandal of religion, of England, and of human nature ... O be
not weary in well doing! Go on, in the name of God and in the
power of his might, till even American slavery (the vilest that
ever saw the sun) shall vanish away before it.'

I believe there is a great deal that we can learn today from
the example of John Wesley. He is a man who is very relevant
to our present situation because although the problems faced
in eighteenth-century England may not all be similar in their
specific details to our present situation, there is a broad
resemblance to the pressing issues that modern British Christians have to grapple with. For instance, more than 200 years
after Wesley's time, we still have widespread poverty in this
country, which demands a response from the Church. In my
own city of Liverpool we have seen the return of poverty-
related diseases, such as tuberculosis and rickets. But material
poverty is nothing in comparison with spiritual poverty. Some
200 years after Wesley's death, there is an even greater number

of people in our society who have yet to hear the Good News of Christ. Wesley did not wait for them to come to church, he went to the unreached to evangelise them wherever they were. With the increasing secularisation and aimlessness of our society, there is a crying need today for a man like Wesley. His preaching, though the spark of a great revival, was often violently opposed, and it was fairly common for him to be physically attacked. However, this did not deter him from his mission and he carried on despite the violence. This is what our country needs today, people willing to preach and practise the undiluted Gospel, regardless of the opposition they encounter.

The Church in Britain in Wesley's time was facing problems which sound familiar. They had lost sight of what was important and had fallen into a comfortable rut of complacency. They were out of touch with the poor and the silence of the Church over slavery was deafening. We have our own forms of slavery – abortion, eugenics, euthanasia, drug abuse and pornography. Once again parts of the Church are often conspicuously silent. In some cases, such as Dr Habgood's support for destructive experiments on human embryos, it has given succour by actively promoting such laws.

Following Wesley's example, there are some contemporary Christian groups which are trying to deal with the pressing issues of today and offer a prophetic voice. One such group is the Maranatha Community, an interdenominational group committed to the Christian healing ministry and to working for Christian unity and renewal of faith. It is led by Dennis Wrigley, himself a Methodist lay preacher and a great admirer of Wesley. Maranatha has engaged in many activities dealing with the myriad problems of this nation, such as abortion, the rise of the occult and New Age beliefs, child abuse and the increasing exposure of children to unhealthy influences. They also have a ministry to prostitutes and homeless people.

Maranatha has produced the book, *What on Earth Are We*

Doing To Our Children? which has alarming information on just how bankrupt our society has become.

One in five children conceived in the United Kingdom is aborted. (Movement for Christian Democracy)

7 in every 100 girls aged 15–19 become pregnant. One-third of them have abortions. (*Independent* 26.10.93)

750,000 British children have no contact with their fathers following the breakdown of marital relationships. (Family Policies Study Centre Survey of Lone Parents)

There has been a 600 per cent increase in marriage breakdown since 1961. (Movement for Christian Democracy)

1,626 children died from abuse or neglect from 1974 to 1984. (NSPCC)

An estimated 38,600 children and young people were on the Child Protection Register in England at 31st March 1994. (Department of Health)

Two-thirds of 15–35 years olds 'are not sure any more what is right and wrong'. (Mori Poll 10.10.94)

Alcohol is now a major social problem directly affecting young people. Every hour 243 people are admitted to hospital for alcohol-related problems. (Alcohol Concern)

More than 160 babies have been born addicted to purified cocaine in one year in the United Kingdom. (*Sunday Times* 10.7.94)

75 per cent of 15–16 year olds in 116 British schools in 1987 had used cannabis leaf. (Health Education Association)

In 1992 47 per cent of North West adolescents had tried an illicit drug. (Manchester University Research Project)

More than 40 per cent of parents are now concerned that their children are being exposed to bad language, sex

and violence on the radio according to the
Broadcasting Standard Council. (*The Times* 8.12.94)

Dennis Wrigley and the Maranatha Community's initiative in
highlighting this issue led to a full-scale debate in Parliament.

Another contemporary example of people living out the
Wesleyan approach to their faith is the Reverend Kevin Logan,
an Anglican vicar who is one of a small band of tireless
campaigners struggling to alert the Church and our society at
large to the explosion of occult activities. Despite years of
warnings by activists such as Kevin Logan, the Church appears
ill-prepared to handle the growth of the occult; and in some
cases has even allowed itself to be influenced by it.

This makes for depressing reading and raises questions of
what the Christian community in our country is doing to tackle
these issues and whether we can do anything constructive. I
believe we can. Wesley demonstrated that ordinary Christians
can change society for the better and even alter the course of
history. Wesley has been credited by some historians for
preventing a revolution in Britain similar to that which
occurred in France. The great revival he helped to bring about
had a profound influence on the hearts and minds of the
working class, where the seeds of revolution would have been
sown. Simultaneously he did what he could to relieve their
distress and helped to bring the rich and the powerful to a
more just approach in facing poverty.

I mentioned at the beginning of this chapter that in our own
times Billy Graham and Pope John Paul II have had a
comparable impact to Wesley. I have had the privilege of
meeting them both and am convinced that they will go down as
two of the great men of the twentieth century. Like Wesley,
the Pope has encountered vociferous opposition even from
within his own Church simply because he has taken a vigorous
stand in upholding Christian teaching and dares to be a sign of

contradiction in the compromising times in which we live. In Tad Szulc's biography of Pope John Paul II,[5] he writes:

> To coin an expression, John Paul II believes in 'aggressive tolerance', religious and political, starting with his readiness to denounce violations of human rights wherever they occur. He does not believe in compromise over principle, be it in his theological and moral positions or in his views of human rights and political freedoms. In fact, he holds that all these views form a comprehensive whole.

Thinking about the miles he has travelled, his unwavering faith, and his grounding in Scripture, there are further parallels to be drawn between the two men. So, too, are the similarities in their spiritual methodology. A glimpse of the Pope's spiritual life is given by the following passage from Tad Szulc's biography:

> Wojtyla [the author usually refers to Pope John Paul II by the name he had before he became Pope] is said to pray as many as seven hours a day: at his private chapel at dawn, sometimes prostrate before the altar, then with invited guests before breakfast, often in his study next to his bedroom, at Masses and services in Rome or on the road, aboard the plane, and on the back seat of his black Mercedes limousine. The Pope has a power of concentration that wholly insulates him from his temporal surroundings as he slides into prayer or meditation, even facing huge crowds at an outdoor Mass. The expression on his broad face is otherworldly, he shuts his eyes so tight that he seems to be in pain, and occasionally, his lips move lightly in silent prayer. Then, the moment passes, and Wojtyla is alert again, the happy smile is back on his face, and his eyes scan the clergy and the rows of faithful in front of him.

There may be a temptation to dismiss people like John Paul II or John Wesley as a 'one-off' and to think it would be unrealistic for our present society to produce anyone similar, but I disagree. We should recognise that Wesley had many of the human weaknesses which we find all too familiar, like being fond of praise, given to imperious behaviour and a hot temper. He struggled with his lack of faith and had a very unhappy marriage. However, he was a man determined to give his all for God and to allow himself to be used and changed by God. It was God who made Wesley's ministry so extraordinary, but naturally he had to put in a lot of effort as well. Like St Paul, he kept his eye on the prize and completed the race. Like St Paul, he exchanged the opportunity to be a part of the establishment and live a quiet life for uncertainty, ostracism and persecution. He was self-disciplined, efficient, committed, single-minded and a good organiser. Wesley also made good use of his time and read widely on a whole range of topics, constantly seeking to improve himself.

Above all, he remained a spiritual man. The simplicity of the small closet where he prayed at his City Road home is deeply revealing. His 4 a.m. start for prayer and his religious fasting were apostolic and monastic in approach. His extempore prayer avoided the dead hand of formalism. His knowledge of the Christian mystics, the use that he and his brother, Charles, made of music in worship, and his love of the Eucharist were all part of his spirituality. Nor was he a bigot, despising other denominations or narrowly hiding inside a fortress of prejudice. When his nephew, Samuel, became a Catholic, he wrote to Charles not to worry as the heart mattered more than opinions. He said that external disunion need not prevent a union in affection. In a 'letter to a Roman Catholic' (1749) he wrote: 'help each other on in whatever we are agreed leads to the Kingdom ... fall not short of the religion of love'. Christians who talk today about not being seen to work publicly with Christians from other traditions lest it upset their 'constituency', or because they think it will upset some minor theological sensibility should take note.

Wesley's single-mindedness is reflected in the following prayer which he wrote:

> Fix our steps, O Lord, that we stagger not at the uneven motions of the world, but steadily go on to our glorious home; neither censuring our journey by the weather we meet with, nor turning out of the way for anything that befalls us.
>
> The winds are often rough, and our own weight presses us downwards. Reach forth, O Lord, your hand, your saving hand, and speedily deliver us.
>
> Teach us, O Lord, to use this transitory life as pilgrims returning to their beloved home; that we may take what our journey requires, and not think of settling in a foreign country.

Here was a man who contradicted the world. In every generation such men and women are needed. If a person is willing to commit his life to God as Wesley did, with all the sacrifices that entails, God can use such a person as He used Wesley. God has no favourites. If He could raise such a person in our country more than 200 years ago, why not today as well? Wesley's example should continue to inspire.

Chapter Three

Jacques Maritain

THINKING THE UNTHINKABLE

> Act well thyself, who can
> Counsel others;
> And truth shall deliver,
> Thee have no dread.
>
> Chaucer *The Ballad of Good Counsel*

Jacques Maritain was born in 1882 and died just over ninety years later. A French Christian philosopher, probably one of the greatest thinkers of our times, I have included him in this collection because he dared to think the unthinkable, to contradict and to refute Nazism and Marxism alike – while offering a view of humanity which was to help shape the thinking of the post-war Christian reformers who built the European Community and who set about the work of reconciliation and political renewal. Maritain also had a fundamental impact on the Church, in shaping encyclicals and the thinking of the Second Vatican Council, as well as deeply influencing Pope Paul VI and Pope John Paul II. Maritain's fearlessness in contradicting the prevailing political and philosophical views no doubt cost him preferment, and it led to his exile in the USA after the Nazi invasion of France, but he lived to see his views vindicated and widely accepted. His life is an icon for those who feel trapped by ideologies or teachers who try to subvert the intellect or human personality. Most of us have been caught up in such vanities from time to time. Maritain was not. Somehow he not only held fast to the truth but led an unblemished and virtuous life.

Not to drift along with the opinions of the day requires enormous courage. Young people in particular are intimidated into thinking that their ideas are outmoded and irrelevant if they challenge contemporary culture. In the world of academia it often leads to ostracism if you step out of line. The British political philosopher David Selbourne, whom I will mention later in this chapter, lectured at Oxford. At the time, he was a Marxist but had expressed some offbeat views about the parameters which the State might have to set. He began writing in the reviled Murdoch press and when *The Times* moved to Wapping – a move which led to huge industrial confrontation – his students told him he must stop expressing his opinions in that newspaper. Preferring, as he saw it, to address the unconverted and recoiling at the intellectual intimidation which followed – his lectures were picketed – he bluntly refused. Some years later he told me that it forced him to realise that they 'would have clubbed a new idea to death at first sight'.

Selbourne left Oxford and took his family to Italy. He subsequently published his pessimistic work *Spirit of The Age*[1] and then his seminal *Principle of Duty*,[2] one of the most exciting books of the past decade.

His journey of intellect fascinates me because as he has travelled from Marxism towards a new appreciation of civic duty, he has also rediscovered something of his Judaic roots. His powerful advocacy of the importance of the community and the responsibilities of the citizen are themes which have simultaneously been taken up by the Chief Rabbi, Jonathan Sacks, especially in his book *Faith In The Future*.[3] Politicians, too, are beginning to embrace this new thinking and to understand the need for a new civic reckoning. Selbourne has been crucial in initiating this change of heart.

Like David Selbourne, Dr Sacks believes that because we have abandoned most of our traditional beliefs we are a nation simply living off our moral capital. His book is a declaration that the faith communities in Britain have something significant to say in the debate about the rights and responsibilities of a citizen. It is also a sharp repudiation of the bizarre and silly notion that democracies can reject all that is old and wise merely because it hasn't been freshly minted. The spiritual gold reserves are full of riches. Principal among those treasures are the ideas of Jacques Maritain; ideas, as Selbourne and Sacks recognise, whose time has surely come.

A Truly Human Life

In the years leading up to the Second World War, Jacques Maritain condemned the pagan empire of Nazism and Fascism and the attendant evils of anti-Semitism and nationalism. But he also warned that victory over these forces would not necessarily prevent their re-emergence: 'War was unleashed because the world was too sick and this kind of sickness is not cured at one stroke.' The end of the Cold War and the subsequent nightmares in Rwanda and Bosnia graphically illustrate the truth of that today. International attempts at peace-making have been a dismal failure.

Quoting Isaiah, Maritain warned the world not to expect too much from the peace: 'Behold, in peace is my bitterest bitterness.' To avoid that bitter sense of defeat Maritain offered remedies which were not always palatable to his audience. He believed that the challenge for post-war Europe would be to create 'a truly human life'. He had in mind our attitudes to the human personality and the conditions in which family life, community life and international co-existence might flourish. In this 'true humanism' justice would be a necessary foundation for common life and civic friendship. If barbarism were to be avoided, society had to recognise the centrality of the human person, not the old forms of 'anarchic individualism' or the collectivism of Fascism and Communism.

Maritain's vision of post-war Europe was that it should be 'the age of the people, and of the man of common humanity –

citizen and co-inheritor of the civilized community – cognizant of the dignity of the human person in himself, builder of a more human world directed toward an historic ideal of human brotherhood'. He took an active role in implementing his vision by participating in the framing of the United Nations Universal Declaration of Rights of 1940, which significantly upheld the greatest of all rights: the right to life itself. He was one of the midwives of the European Community and a leading inspiration at the Second Vatican Council, which set out to renew the life of the Church. Christian Democracy, which has shaped most of the post-war Western democracies, and which through the European People's Party remains one of the two principal players in the European Parliament, draws much of its inspiration from Maritain.

At one level – in the reconstruction of Western Europe, the creation of the European Community, and the flowering of liberal democracies – it is possible to see how many of his hopes have become reality. But at another, deeper, level – the upholding of the dignity of the human personality – society is still today every bit as base as the one which Maritain vilified.

Many of the ideas of Maritain and his contemporary, Emmanuel Mounier, which were paraphrased in rather ugly language as 'personalism' and 'communitarianism', have recently been revisited by American political thinkers, such as the exotic-sounding Amitai Etzioni, founder of the American Communitarian Movement, as well as David Selbourne. This thinking has been having a profound effect on political parties on both sides of the Atlantic. Etzioni is an advisor to President Clinton and has met Tony Blair and Paddy Ashdown. Conservatives, such as David Willets, have also been publishing pamphlets based on the same ideas.

Mounier said of personalism that, 'It is not fundamentally centred in political action, but is a total effort to comprehend and outgrow the whole crisis of twentieth-century man.' Crucial to this is the Christian conviction that every person is of inestimable worth; that rights must be balanced by responsibilities; that civic institutions and democracy must serve God and man: all find their finest expression in Maritain's writings. Dorothy Day, of the American Catholic Workers' Movement, was a follower of Maritain and in opposing rugged individualism said, 'We are personalists because we believe that man, a person, a creature of the body and soul is greater than the state.'[4]

Maritain's Beliefs and Convictions

The formation of Maritain's beliefs began during his childhood in France. His mother's family, the Favres, were one of the great political families of France, and Maritain had inherited a passion for freedom from his grandfather. During his youth he was fascinated by the works of Leon Bloy, who called Christians to live above the level of mediocrity. Bloy published *Salvation Is From The Jews*, which the Maritains paid to have reprinted. In 1906, two years after he married Raissa, who was Jewish, they were received into the Catholic Church. His wife later introduced him to the works of St Thomas Aquinas. According to Maritain, 'Thomism is the only philosophy whose peculiar characteristic is that it is peculiar to nobody, absolutely universal.' The communal emphasis of Thomism became the basis of Maritain's philosophy.

Maritain, like Aquinas, believed that man must be recognised as a person, 'as a unity of spiritual nature ... made for a spiritual end'. He strongly believed, as I do, that without a fitting respect for personality, as distinct from individuality, civilisation cannot function. In *Christianity and Democracy*,[5] Maritain wrote that the pagan empire was seeking to liquidate 'Christianity and democracy at the same stroke ... freedom's chances coincide with those of the evangelical message'. His understanding of Thomism and the principles which it lays down about the relationship between faith and reason helped him to develop his understanding of the relationship between science and philosophy.

Noting how science and genetics had been warped by the eugenicists of the 1930s, and in a stirring and prophetic passage from *Christianity and Democracy*, Maritain states that:

> The Christian spirit is threatened today in its very existence by implacable enemies, fanatics of race and blood, of pride, domination and hate. At the core of the horrible ordeal, everything indicates that in the depths of human conscience a powerful religious renewal is in preparation, which concerns and will restore to their vital sources all the persecuted, all the believers of the great Judaeo-Christian family, not only the faithful of the Catholic Church and those of the Protestant Churches, but also those of Judaism, whose abandonment to nameless suffering and iniquity and to the sword of vile exterminators would be an unbearable scandal for the soul if we did not see in it a terrible reminder of the promises of their God . . . a common action will bring forth common fruits.

For Maritain, democracy and Christianity, though not dependent upon one another, were always at their best when moving forward together.

'Democracy, too', he continued, 'is threatened in its very existence, and by the same enemies.' Erroneous ideologies and aberrant tendencies had subverted democracy but Maritain remained confident. With democracy, too, he said, 'a great renewal of the spirit is taking place which tends to restore democracy to its true essence and purify its principles'.

The sickness which Maritain diagnosed, and which degraded and abused humanity, is still waiting to be cured. What on earth would he have made of a purportedly civilised country like our own which permits the mass manufacture of human embryos and their subsequent freezing, manipulation, and destruction? What would he make of a government which aids and abets – in countries like China – the forced abortion and sterilisation of women? What would he make of doctors who kill handicapped babies and European governments which legalise euthanasia?

What would he make of a country – our own – where over a decade, more than 1,000 children have died of abuse or neglect; where 750,000 British children have no contact with their fathers following the breakdown of marital relationships; or a world, in which there are now more than 10 million child prostitutes; in which 250 million copies of child pornography are in circulation; in which 17 million children die each year from starvation; or a prosperous and affluent late twentieth-century country where rickets and tuberculosis are again emerging in the homes of the poor?

What would he make of our culture of violence, the indifference which is so often shown towards the poor; the rejection of the elderly – 1 million of whom do not see a friend or a relative during an average week; the plight of the unemployed; our obsession with rampant materialism? Truly, in peace we often experience the bitterest bitterness.

In contrast to many of the attitudes of the present day, Maritain's theory of rights combined a dislike of individualism with affection for the community and the common good. He believed in pluralism in the democratic society and that society should be vivified, animated and guided by Christian thought which would serve as the core of ethical values as a basis for living. Each human being has a responsibility to the next and we must hold together in community. Tom Paine's Rights of Man are not enough. We need to spell out his responsibilities too. We are our brother's and sister's keeper, and responsible people must care for one another. Any truly humane civilisation also requires a culture that nurtures spiritual development. We can't do without God. Democracy must have a soul.

Maritain also affirmed that pluralism produces diversity, civil tolerance, independent regional social units, a multiplicity of political parties, a representative body and an independent executive branch. Thus, co-operation between states will require a reduction in individual states' sovereignty. His ideas of shared sovereignty and subsidiarity were among the core beliefs which led to the formation of the European Community.

Yet Jacques and Raissa Maritain were never cold intellectuals without the capacity to meet people wherever they were. They were famed for their hospitality and their friendships. In their own lives they believed their first priority was to develop their friendship with God and then to see Him in everyone they encountered. Nor were they fairweather friends. Stories abound of the little acts of kindness and consideration which they showed to people over long periods of time.

During the 1920s a succession of scientists, artists, and composers visited their home and joined in the intellectual pilgrimage of applying the ideas of St Thomas to contemporary problems. This opportunity for serious philosophical study and inspiration drew people to their study circles. The age of couch potatoes languishing in front of their television sets, the stultifying introversion of Internet conversations, and the inability to engage in the refreshing quest for ideas, or even in a sustained conversation, stand in mocking contrast to their enlivening company. Built on this foundation of solid friendships was a refreshing new view of the role of the laity in the Church. Clericalism had an inhibiting effect on the development of lay action and the Maritains helped fashion a new vocation for the laity which came to fruition in the documents of the Second Vatican Council.

The basic idea behind Maritain's theory was that society would dramatically benefit from a renewal of Christian political activity and that a loss of faith would jeopardise the success of any enterprise as well as any government. His true humanism, suitable for modern man, arose from an appreciation of historical man. For the modern world Maritain did not want to serve up a dishevelled form of medieval Christendom but, rather, a society which is 'vitally Christian rather than one which is decoratively so'. Thus, Maritain emphasised the need for pluralism and personalism. Pluralism accepts that there will be diversity of belief, variety of opinion, and differences in the way we live. It accepts this in a spirit of tolerance. Similarly, without a proper respect for the person – as distinct from the individual – Maritain believed that a new civilisation could not function.

Maritain's Relevance to Today

The failure of many Christians to embrace a distinct view of society and their indifference to the barbarous conditions which existed during the rise of capitalism allowed Communism to forge ahead; just as indifference to the rise of Nazism allowed anti-Semitism and eugenics to form the cornerstone of Hitler's State. In a more modern sense, Christian isolation from civic affairs induces others to substitute new faiths in place of the Christian faith in the public arena. By employing a policy of isolationism and indifference, and by privatising their faith, or by opting out, Christians lose influence because they have no public philosophy to guide their political activities and organisations.

Christians have conceded the argument to those who believe that unfettered personal choice is more important than an ethical foundation for government and its priorities. G. K. Chesterton put it well when he said that 'to admire mere choice is to refuse to choose'.

All choices carry consequences. This is palpably as true in questions of medical ethics as it is in decisions concerning resources. A country that chooses to use finite resources without regard for the consequences is depriving underdeveloped nations of opportunities and denying future generations any choice. Unfettered personal or corporate choice is not compatible with the concept of a responsible society. The words 'my right to choose' are all murderously loaded and could be the epitaph of this generation. Choices not only carry consequences but are always made at someone else's expense. The Christian thinker and social democrat, R. H. Tawney, said that, 'freedom for the pike is death for the minnow'. We have to decide whether we are on the side of the minnow or the pike.

Maritain and Mounier, and men like Dr R. W. Dale, the Congregational minister in Birmingham who upheld 'civic faith', all understood the need to be on the side of the minnow. However, they differed in one crucial respect from the secular conclusions of Etzioni and Selbourne. In understanding the thinking of Tony Blair and New Labour, it is a crucial question. It concerns our ultimate reliance on ourselves and our ability to dispense with God.

While at Oxford, Tony Blair was deeply influenced by a Scottish philosopher, John Macmurray, who wrote *Persons in Relation* and *Self As Agent*.[6] The similarity to Maritain's ideas is striking.

Blair also became friendly with a radical Australian theologian, Peter Thompson, who said, 'The idea of community started there (with Macmurray), and it wedded beautifully with our concept of religion.'[7]

What, then, is that concept of religion? Is it simply ethical socialism, as some proponents have argued? Is it purely about social justice? Or, as Maritain believed, is it something more central? Is faith something for the private moments of our lives or is it part and parcel of the way you live out every aspect of life? If it is not simply a private matter is there something here for the whole community? Is it a convenient form of shorthand to highlight those concerns which correspond to Gospel values but to be dispensed with when you rub up against other Gospel values which are politically awkward?

Maritain's approach was that faith was the starting point and that everything else derived from it. Jonathan Sacks, in his two admirable books, *Persistence of Faith*[8] and *Faith In The Future*,[9] convincingly argues for this alternative view, that faith is indispensable. True civic values are based on the marriage of the soul and the social community. This is the antidote to the fevers of our age. Dr Sacks says that prophecy and priesthood are 'both necessary to the civil order. Without the matrix of institutions within which individual responsibility and the moral sentiments are nurtured, no freedoms are secure for long.' He adds that democracy is 'the least unreliable form of government, which is itself only a framework of human flourishing, not the flourishing itself'.

The politicians who now argue for new values must address these questions. They must come clean about whether they share the view that political life and religious faith should converge, as only with such a convergence will the politics of the common good supplant the politics of power. The upholding of the dignity of every person must be based on justice and based on the rule of law. If their creation is recognised as ordained by God it will bring about a real revolution. Without such a convergence, the new civic reckoning will be about as worthless as the rhetoric surrounding John Major's 'Back To Basics'.

Genocide, murder, abortion, euthanasia, the sale of arms and indifference to the poor, are all part of our anti-life, pro-death secular culture today. They all represent the destruction of the unvalued person. The relatively powerful exert their will, their lethal dominion, over the relatively weak. This is radically subversive of justice and done at great cost. All the more reason, therefore, to know precisely where our leaders stand and how deep their convictions lie.

I have come to admire Tony Blair on a range of issues. His backing for my amendment in Parliament to reform the law on video violence was significant (he told me I had 'powerful support' – that of his talented wife). What then is his reason for voting for abortion up to birth on disabled babies, and for destructive experiments on human embryos?; why has he not abolished the infamous Emily's List, which promotes women candidates in his Party on condition that they support abortion?; why does he believe that these supreme human rights questions can be reduced to a matter of choice?; and why did he not condemn the intolerance and denial of free speech which led to the Labour Life Group being banned from even having a stall at Party Conferences? If an embryo is human we cannot say that the law should treat it any differently from that governing the adult. From the first minute life must be protected. If it is wrong to sell a man as a slave it must be wrong to sell a human embryo.

These issues and Tony Blair's decision to fight for Sunday trading, including the opening of shops even on Easter Day and Christmas Day are not fringe concerns. They go to the very heart of the debate about how you perceive the person, of what Macmurray called 'persons in relation', and what Maritain called 'personalism'. They go to the heart of the debate marked out by Etzioni and Selbourne about how you reconcile rights with duties and obligations, and how you protect the vulnerable, families, workers and communities against exploitation.

These issues also illustrate the clash which is under way between modern liberalism and the search for a more authentic human culture. It was a question to which Maritain devoted much of his intellectual power. It is also a question which is central to the emerging democracies in Eastern Europe.

With the fall of Communism, the countries of Central and Eastern Europe are now looking to the West for help in their transition to free political orders and market economies. But the problem is that along with Western freedom come Western consumerism and materialism. As paradoxical as it first appears, Western liberalism in the long run may present a more serious threat to the Church, and, indeed, to authentic human culture, than Communism did. Communism appealed to power and was explicit about its ideology of Marxist materialism. Liberalism, on the contrary, appeals to appetite, and does so only in the name of freedom. It creates a society that will satisfy wants and desires, but in so doing it claims to impose no world-view ideology. It merely provides material goods in abundance, and says that one is now free to choose. But with the objects of our appetite there comes a 'way of life': a materialist and consumerist vision of the good life.

Western liberalism, as Stratford Caldecott, at the Oxford Centre for Faith and Culture, has pointed out, is therefore pernicious in a way that Communism is not, because liberalism fills culture with its vision so imperceptibly and invisibly.

Cultures embrace Western freedom, only to discover that they've been made unfree by Western consumerism. People know they've lost their freedom when they've been run over by a tank. They are not so quick to notice the loss of freedom that comes from enervation of the soul and slavery to appetite: hooked by our desire for bigger, faster, better and more. In a parody of the Gospel message, people 'do unto others' before they do you, grab whatever they can, and devil take the hindmost. The whole basis of this kind of society must be challenged.

Maritain was one of the first to subject liberalism and democracy to theological – philosophical and spiritual – discernment. There is much at stake here: the welfare of thousands and even millions of human lives. Christian leaders in the nations of the former Communist bloc and, indeed, elsewhere have come increasingly to view liberalism as the only way forward – the only way which is both moral and realistic. Yet as I saw myself in St Petersburg in 1995, the replacement of a Communist command economy by the Mafia is a funny kind of progress.

Maritain passionately believed capitalism becomes sterile when it has a contempt for the poor or when it enslaves man in materialism. In the ideal community, people can use the community to achieve an independent life inspired by the preservation of both property and political rights. This can be achieved ethically.

The opposite of this is our constant desire for self-gratification and exaggerated individualism, spurred on by the false values promoted by television advertising and the demand for individual rights. Sound democracies are comprised of diverse local communities. The medieval idea of service to God and humanity is infinitely superior to the modern myth of self-fulfilment and individualism or simply making money.

Maritain opposed the liberal open society because it does not produce truly free communities. The only truly free person is one who isn't enslaved to sin. Freedom of choice does not constitute the essence of moral actions. Choice is not an end in itself; it's simply a vehicle. Freedom of expression is not an absolute right; just because something has been conceived by human minds does not make it justified. We only become free by struggling to be free of sin. Obedience to God is not slavery; rather, it confers real independence from materialism. According to Maritain, freedom of religion and the right of conscience are the most important rights because both are vital to ensuring justice and the common good.

In *Man and the State*[10] Maritain lists his goals – equality, justice, civil friendship, religious freedom, reverence for and understanding of the communities' heritage on the local as well as international level. He believed that faith is a public matter; the rights of the unbeliever demand respect and protection in the private sector. Maritain also refuted the idea that Christianity and democracy are incompatible; rather, democracy tends to build on Christianity and is at its strongest and best when there are deep religious roots. In such democracies the citizen is more easily able to make good or bad choices.

Alexander Solzhenitsyn recognised this need to distinguish between right and wrong and the consequences when we fail. He writes in *East and West*

The same old atavistic urges – greed, envy, unrestrained passion, and hostility – readily picked up by respectable pseudonyms like class, race, mass or trade union struggles claw at and tear apart our world ... This attitude creates millions of victims in ceaseless civil wars, it drones into our souls that there exist no lasting concepts of good and justice valid for all mankind.[11]

Solzhenitsyn and Maritain both rejected relativism and Solzhenitsyn echoes Maritain's call to a new understanding of community and the need for an examination of the consequences of individualism.

We must understand the seriousness of the challenge posed by 'disintegrative consumerism'. What Pope John Paul II memorably described in his encyclical, *Evangelium Vitae*[12] as a 'culture of death' increasingly threatens the vital structures of the family and community. At its most lethal, 'consumerism' undermines respect for human life in its most vulnerable forms – particularly that of the unborn child. Tampering with the unborn or with their genes to create people with pre-determined properties is the ultimate obscenity of consumerism and liberalism. It is a terrible abuse of power.

It is not feasibility, or practicality, which are the issues but respect for life itself. How can we countenance the standardisation and the programming of a new child even before its first smile? As life comes scratching softly at the door it deserves a warm embrace: not gene manipulation, eugenics, experimentation or abortion. Against this new age of barbarism, as Maritain would have described it, against this anti-civilisation, the consumer society, by its very nature, has fewer and fewer defences. Maritain perceived this and argued that our civic life and our democracies would only deepen when Christian inspiration and democratic inspiration recognised one another, reconciled, and united. Beyond the politics of left and right we need a politics of life.

It is hard not to conclude that we must look beyond piecemeal solutions to some more radical alternative to our entire social system. The way forward, it seems to me, must lie partly with a more profound analysis of the problem. Every society expresses a particular set of concepts and assumptions. If, as Maritain did, we can put our finger on the root ideas that shape our own society, and see where they are distorted, it will be easier to see whether and how things might be set right.

In affirming free human creativity in the economic sector, circumscribed by a strong juridical framework, equal attention must be paid to human needs which find no place in the market. There must be a level of justice which occupies the ground above the fair exchange of goods beyond the savage face of capitalism – monopolies, wage slavery and plutocracies.

Naked consumerism, is clearly linked to ecological destruction, to social alienation, and to eugenic practices. In turn, these practices lead to genetic manipulation of animals, to designer babies and to the weeding out of human beings because of handicaps, ability, gender or race – and, if American scientists are to be believed, to elimination in the future on the grounds of sexual orientation. They are creating a new caste system based on human genes and embryology. Just because something is scientifically possible or because the consumer demands it, does not necessarily make it right.

A consumerist society is oriented primarily to demands devoid of ethical implications and to economic growth in which the market is not subordinated to human and spiritual questions. As Maritain foresaw, such a society is unChristian because its forms of social organisation, production and consumption make it more difficult to offer the gift of self and to establish genuine social solidarity and a sense of community. Everything is reduced to questions of choice – a word which derives from the same Greek root as the word heresy. Unbounded personal choice is the apotheosis of modern liberalism. It is a modern heresy.

It is impossible to find a compromise between unfettered consumerism, Marxism and Christianity. In moving beyond all that was short-lived in Marxism, and all that is shallow in a consumerist society, present circumstances are leading to a reaffirmation of the positive value of an authentic theology based on the human personality and the community. Not the individual and its demands, not the State, but the human personality and its basic needs. In economic terms this must lead to a more equitable sharing of property and wealth, what G. K. Chesterton called 'distributism'.

The very deepest assumptions on which a society rests, and which determine its fundamental direction, are theological in nature. Bound up with a doctrine of God there is always a doctrine of man. Theology and anthropology must walk hand in hand.

Maritain attempted to construct a Christian anthropology. He believed that Christ reveals man to himself. This anthropology immediately poses a challenge to any so-called 'liberal' society that wishes to elevate freedom of choice (or even creativity, initiative, and enterprise) into the position of a supreme value. Christianity recognises the nature of true human freedom and creativity as entirely founded on love, formed by love, and for the sake of love. We must receive love – the love of God above all – before we are ourselves free to love.

The Christian concept of love – that is, love as re-defined by the life and death of Christ, and lived out in every authentic Christian community – is capable of transforming the assumptions of a liberal culture, whilst at the same time integrating its most authentic values.

My mother is an Irish speaker from Mayo. I have always been struck by the emphasis that Celtic theology and Irish people place on the importance of authentic human values and the living of life in community – the most basic of which is the family: '*Is ar scath a cheile a mhaireann na daoine*' – it is in the shelter of each other that the people live. Human beings, not individuals; communities not bureaucracies.

What stands in the way of such re-ordering of our liberal society is a distorted idea of human nature, fulfilment and motivation. Life-styles and structures of power matter, too. We must address those structures of sin by which moral failures take on a social dimension. Among these are many of the patterns of behaviour and institutional forms associated with consumerist capitalism. A failure to recognise a need for the radical reform of structures is one expression of that separation of faith from culture which is the tragedy of our time.

An evangelical return to the Gospel, of the sort favoured by Maritain, makes us face our own darkness, our own guilt and that of the world we live in; the places in yourself and in the world that make you want to cry or despair; the things which make you feel a hypocrite or a fraud. As Maritain says, Christ's cross 'quells the war in our hearts and offers an alternative to the wars of men'.

It is worth briefly re-stating the values of the cross. They are summed up in the first eight lines of the Sermon on the Mount: reality and spiritual strength for Christ are named in tears, in poverty of spirit, in persecution. Not in terms of power, prestige or possessions: all the staple fare of politicians.

Who can doubt that Christ was on the side of all that our shallow society despises: the insecure, the mentally ill, the handicapped, the addict, the low achiever, the inadequate, the poor? That is the reverse of everything that our consumer society holds dear. As Maritain recognised, allegiance to Christ's values puts you on collision course with the world. Maritain never feared such a collison and tried to find a way to reconcile the competing claims of self-interest and the wider good.

Ethical Investment

In *Freedom in the Modern World*,[13] Maritain says that the animosity between the rights of ownership and demands of communal need is perpetual. He links property and inheritance rights to the responsibility to preserve the family. He insists that ownership and consumption should always serve the good of the community. In our own day this could be facilitated by the encouragement of ethical investment – a concept lucidly set out by Russell Sparkes in *The Ethical Investor*.[14] Maritain's philosophy could transform the way in which we handle and use money and how we bank, too. Opinion polls have consistently demonstrated that ordinary people want their money to be used ethically and that many are even prepared to forego some return if they know that their money is being used well. For Christians this is not really an optional extra.

Christ's parable of the talents reminds us that we mustn't dig a hole and bury our money because we are frightened of it. Nor does the parable berate us or make us feel guilty for having the money in the first place. The story is about using money wisely and creatively. Profit and privilege are not evil in themselves. How they are used is the issue. A personalist approach puts money at the disposal of people and encourages a wider distribution of personal property.

There is little point letting off steam about disintegrative consumerism, the exploitation of workers, the destruction of the global environment, or fair trade, if we simultaneously allow investors to use our money at their own discretion. Is the money being used wisely, is it being used creatively? Is it being used justly? On a whole range of questions, from the role of banks and credit unions, to the provision of a new model of companies, a personalist approach offers an ethical application of capitalism.

I was especially taken with Sparkes' account of the Mondragon Co-operative in the Basque country and the role which the Church played in its establishment. Quoting Pope Leo XIII, 'Men always work harder and more readily when they work on that which is their own.' His personalist and distributist ideas sit easily alongside ethical investment. Together they form a socially just approach and a capitalism which serves the community.

This would also have implications for the way in which banks handle our money. The disappearance of banks from the community – like the Liverpool-based Martin's Bank, which was swallowed up by Barclays – illustrates how centralised our capitalist institutions have become. Personalists and distributists for seventy years have opposed centralising bureaucracy, supported subsidiarity and been imbued with a strong sense of the value of place, of environment, and of cultural diversity. Centralisation of banking in Britain reached its present concentrated structure as early as 1918, with five major clearing banks becoming dominant. This followed a century in which the number of banks in Britain declined very rapidly from 715 in 1825. The consolidation process was the result of legislative, technological and economic factors. Only the Trustee Savings Banks retained a strong local presence, until they were regionalised in the mid-1970s, then consolidated and privatised in the mid-1980s. The results have been all too predictable.

The British financial sector has become overwhelmingly based in London, the home of thirty-nine of the largest fifty banks. The only areas of the United Kingdom with a significant local financial sector are Scotland, and to a lesser extent, Northern Ireland. The only major financial institutions with a strong remaining regional presence are the building societies, which are increasingly controlled from London or Leeds–Bradford. The credit union movement, which is locally based, is very small in the UK except in Northern Ireland. Since 1982 the top six banks in the UK have closed about one in three local branches (some 3,000 bank branches).

Local resource availability has been critical for most of

human history to a civilisation's prosperity. Hence the Nile's riches and those of the Tigris and Euphrates fed the development of the earliest cities in ancient times. Liverpool in the nineteenth century was well served by the same principle. Today, such a link between resources and the servicing of Maritain's concept of civic advancement is rarely seen.

Financial control is centred in the square mile of the City of London in whose reflective glass skyscrapers almost a trillion pounds' worth of sterling, marks, francs, dollars and yen are feverishly moved around the globe. Less than five per cent of this beggar-my-neighbour speculation is linked to world trade or any other real economic activity. Only doorways away from these dealing rooms are growing armies of homeless people, slumped in doorways, begging for pennies. You will find their American counterparts not far from Wall Street.

As Maritain urged, an ethical use of our resources could link our economies to human need. It would not create voids in inner cities where the banks have been replaced by pawn-brokers and moneylenders, charging from 60 per cent to 6000 per cent for loans on an annual basis. Credit unions might fill part of this gap but without their active promotion by government it is hard to see how they will rapidly expand from their meagre presence in only 1 per cent of British households.

Legislative and other reasons also handicap credit unions by preventing them from providing development credit for small businesses and housing needs. Their American counterparts, the Community Development Loan Funds and a number of fully fledged community banks, have mushroomed over the past decade: and over the past five years they have invested $120 million (in aggregate) in low to moderate income communities.

There are straws in the wind in the UK that such an approach might take off here. Ethical investment, as measured by the take up of socially and environmentally screened unit trusts, investment trusts, and personal pensions has doubled in the

UK in less than two years to over £800 million. The potential is vast; and the lead given by men such as Richard Harries, the Bishop of Oxford, extremely welcome. *Which* magazine says that more than one in three households want to invest ethically. People must be encouraged, and enabled, through access to proper information and transparency in financial institutions, to vote with their feet. But we must reform the structures to do this.

The handy acronym 'Deposit', suggests seven words which might accelerate the process of ethical investment:

Disclosure
Education
Protection
Other regional financial institutions
Stock Exchanges at a regional level
Information
Trusts – new forms of financial institutions called regional
    trusts.

DEPOSIT would encourage an environment where money is used responsibly and where – as Maritain argued – it serves the people, instead of making us its slaves. In a country where consumer debt is now larger than national debt, who can doubt the need for such an ethically led approach?

John Ruskin once said: 'Above all, a nation cannot last as a money making mob; it cannot, with impunity – it cannot with existence – go on despising literature, despising science, despising art, despising nature, despising compassion and concentrating its soul on pence.' Maritain also knew this.

Although the academic world ultimately fêted and honoured Maritain, his ideas have not always been given the credit which they deserve. The Church has done rather better. Two Popes, John XXIII and Paul VI drew substantially on his ideas in framing their great social encyclicals, *Mater et Magistra*[15] and

Populorum Progressio.[16] The then British Overseas Aid Minister, Arthur Bottomley, said of the encyclical on the development of the peoples that it 'proclaimed in loud and clear tones what everyone's responsibilities are in a world where two out of every three persons live in conditions which we in this country would not wish on our domestic animals'. Our priorities concerning animals and people have remained largely unchanged.

After fifty-six years of marriage Raissa died in 1960 after suffering a cerebral thrombosis. In 1973, at the age of ninety-one, Jacques followed her. Yet, the quality of their personal lives and the depth of their thinking still have a great deal to say to us today. His writings remain central to the re-opened debate about rights and responsibilities, the balances to be struck between the prerogatives of the individual and the desirability of strong communities, and the conflicting impulses of self-help and mutual help.

Chapter Four

Thecla Merlo

MAKING THE GOOD PRESS

The Truth shall set you free

John 8:32

At the end of summer 1995, I visited the church of St Paul in Rome. It is close to the ancient basilica of St Paul outside the walls, where the body of the greatest of all the evangelists is laid. In the newer church are the earthly remains of a man and woman of our own century who modelled their lives on that of Paul. Thecla Merlo and James Alberione, and the Daughters of St Paul and the Society of St Paul which they founded, took on a Church establishment suspicious of evangelisation, wider dissemination of Scripture, and of the new technologies of mass communication. Today, next to the crypt where their bodies rest is a huge printing and publishing house, a college for media studies and the administrative centre of worldwide operations. What inspires me most about this extraordinary achievement is that it was based on a vision way ahead of its time. Yet it was also true to the earliest traditions of the Church. Thecla Merlo's story also challenges the way we use mass communications today and this is why I have included her in this collection.

St Paul, knowing that he had a good story to tell, let nothing inhibit him. He criss-crossed the ancient world, starting the occasional riot here and there as he went. Standing in the remarkable ruins at Ephesus, today's visitor can almost still hear Paul's words reverberating around the amphitheatre.

Indifferent to his own safety, he challenged the materialism and wealth of the cult of Diana and sparked off the silversmiths' riot. The same giants are waiting to be slain in contemporary society but who can doubt that today Paul would make straight for the television studio, the radio station, and the newspaper publishers. He would be setting up satellite broadcasting opportunities; sending radio signals over the heads of the despots and dictators who curtail religious liberties; and his trusted friends, Luke, Barnabus and Timothy would be commissioning film-makers to transmit the Gospel stories via television and video.

In our own times a remarkable woman, Thecla Merlo, born at the dawn of the new age of mass communications, understood the opportunities and the dangers which the modern media offered. She is doubly remarkable because she overcame the prejudice which existed against women. Through the prism of her life, we can explore the impact of the modern media and how some of its more malign influences might best be contradicted.

Thecla's Early Life and the Daughters of St Paul

Born in 1894 at Castagnito d'Alba, in Italy, the young Thecla – or Maria Teresa, as she had been baptised – was brought up in a family of poor but self-sufficient farmers. On completion of her elementary education she was offered training in one of the limited avenues open to girls in pre-World War One Italy. She chose embroidery and sewing. Having acquired this skill she returned to her home and became involved in the teaching of catechetics.

In 1905 Pope Pius X had published his encyclical, *Acerbo Nimis*[1] where he said that many Christians 'live in an extreme state of ignorance of those matters which are essential for their eternal salvation'. He said that every week the children of each parish should spend an hour being instructed in the faith. Pius

X then published his universal catechism, setting out the framework of basic teachings. In the diocese of Alba, where she lived, young women like Maria Teresa were quickly enrolled as catechists.

It was through this work that she met the remarkable priest, Fr James Alberione, who was to recognise her qualities and gifts. James Alberione's life has been commemorated in a biography by Luigi Rolfo.[2] He had gathered a small group of men around him and urged them to feed the minds of the people: 'In the same way that others are feeding them with illusory promises, let us give them the Gospel and let us do so with the same instruments that they use for the communication of ideas.' To achieve this, James Alberione began an association 'for the good press'. This subsequently developed into the Pauline Family – men and women who have dedicated their lives to using every modern means of communication for the discussion of moral ideas.

Fr Alberione met Maria Teresa in 1915 and told her of his intention to create a congregation of young women alongside the group of young men, as active partners in their new work. She and two other young women came together to form the Daughters of St Paul. She chose to take the name Thecla – after one of St Paul's earliest followers – and over the next six years they established a tiny lending library, 'The New Book Shop'. They also trained as compositors, and launched a diocesan newspaper, *La Valsusa*.

In 1922 Thecla had so entered the spirit of this vision that she was invited to become the first Mother General, or Prima Maestra, of the small nucleus of women who had gathered around her. The purpose of the Order was 'the proclamation of the Gospel through the printed word and by other means offered by the advance of modern technology'.

Their early efforts drew fierce criticism and hostility. The local bishop was asked by some opponents to stop them in their tracks. Others wrote to the Vatican asking for their suppression. They were criticised for enticing young men and women into a risky project and for drawing them away from existing religious orders; but the project was blessed from the start.

They laboriously worked to hand print, sheet by sheet, extracts from the Gospel and simple lives of the saints. In his biography of Thecla Merlo,[3] Dominic Agasso described how they began to revolutionise their operations: 'At Sesto San Giovanni near Milan a business which specialised in pornographic and anti-clerical publications had gone into liquidation. Fr Alberione was among the first to hear about this and he immediately rushed over. They quickly agreed a price, paid for the equipment, dismantled it, and moved it back to Alba.'

Thecla Merlo was appalled that so few families had a family Bible or had access to Scripture or spiritual works. She said: 'No book of ours ought to be more frequently read than the one given to us by the Church. We do not seek to imitate the life of this Saint or that, only the life of Jesus Christ Himself.' With their new presses they set about the mass production of the Scriptures and then began their distribution to every corner of Italy. The picture of the Daughters of St Paul, arriving by twos in remote villages and towns, armed with heavy suitcases full of publications, is redolent of the early Christians receiving their Great Commission and going out, two by two, to spread the Gospel.

Yet their enterprise was not without its problems. In 1923 James Alberione became seriously ill. Tuberculosis was diagnosed and he was given eighteen months to live.

Some of the sparkle had also gone, as so often happens once a movement or a new enterprise is launched. Not everyone stays the course or is prepared for the hard slog. We hear Thecla Merlo urging everyone on: 'It is up to us to set an example of boundless energy and enthusiasm in all our activities. Yet here we are, resigning ourselves, losing our grip and our passion, without considering the seriousness of the account we must render to Our Lord ... We lack that extra eagerness. And short-lived enthusiasm isn't enough.'

James Alberione recovered and the work continued. They backed up their distribution of the Bible with instruction and Bible courses. This was followed by a decision to open book shops in major Italian cities. The first group of women to run a shop were sent off to Salerno, south of Naples, in November 1928.

This was the time of the Great Depression but despite extremely adverse economic conditions the venture did not falter. Sales were not always what had been hoped but Fr Alberione offered a dual mandate: 'If you can't leave a book you can at least leave a good word, something to cheer people up, a smile.' He also believed that ventures which start in humble, inauspicious surroundings can successfully grow from an unlikely beginning: 'Everything starts at Bethlehem,' he said.

From these small Italian beginnings Thecla Merlo travelled the world, setting up shops and centres everywhere she went. The Daughters of St Paul now have operations on every continent, in fifty countries. Despite meeting local opposition – usually generated by a fear of the unknown – she persevered and gradually made Christ's teaching accessible to millions of people. It would also be difficult to calculate how many people who although they might feel unable to venture over the threshold of a church have felt able to enter these high street access points.

By 1963 the Second Vatican Council – a year before Thecla Merlo's death – had embraced the vision which had been so controversial half a century before. The Council proclaimed that the Church's 'task involves employing the means of social communication to announce the good news of salvation and to teach men how to use them properly'.

Violence and the Media Today

In the 1990s we are beset by every possible 'means of social communication'. That we still have to learn 'how to use them properly' is self-evident. What does Thecla Merlo's life have to say to us about how the media is used?

The latest venture of the Daughters of St Paul is to establish parish video libraries – where families will be free to hire family entertainment which will not contain pornographic or violent material liable to cause offence or distress to those who see it. This is a real sign of contradiction in a media world which has grown rich on producing violent material.

There have been many signs in recent years that people are becoming tired of the diet of violence which pours into their homes.

In the early 1990s I began to question Ministers in Parliament about the links between what people see and how they behave. I have never suggested that this is the only factor involved in the increase in violent crime in Britain, but I have been equally adamant in dismissing the suggestion that it plays no part. The issue became particularly controversial after the case of James Bulger – the two-year-old murdered by two boys on Merseyside.

In the aftermath of the verdicts the trial judge remarked on 'the striking similarities' between scenes in the video, *Child's Play 3*, and the attack on James Bulger. Just twenty-two days before his death this video was one of three hired out by the father of one of the convicted boys. He had hired 440 other videos in the previous few years, including soft pornography, violent horror and necrophilia. The two-year-old was murdered and mutilated on a railway line. His face, like the doll's in the video, was splattered with blue paint. In the video the doll abducts a young military cadet and tries to kill him under the wheels of a fairground train, only itself to be mutilated and killed. In Manchester, a chant from the same film was used by the torturers of the teenager, Susan Capper, to taunt her while she was subjected to the most brutal and horrifying assault. She eventually died.

A Midlands woman reported that her six-year-old child had seen *Child's Play 3* and that he had 'become possessed' and tried to kill their pet dog.

During the week when the measures I initiated, which placed tighter curbs on gratuitously violent video material were finally ratified by Parliament, there were two more straws in the wind.

In Norway, the children's programme *Power Rangers* (which is shown in the UK on Saturday mornings) was withdrawn. A link was suggested between the killing of a little five-year-old girl by her six-year-old friends and an episode which had occurred in the programme. GMTV and Sky broadcast the programme. Channel Four had rejected it because of what they said was the unclear line between real and fictional violence.

During the same week the Lincoln coroner, Roger Atkinson, said that an episode of the ITV series *Cracker*, in which two characters were stabbed to death, could have led to the murder of a midwife twelve hours later. Granada Television dismissed the coroner's remarks as only his 'opinion'. Regardless of opinions, the 1990 Broadcasting Act imposes an obligation on the broadcasters not to 'give offence to public feeling' and not to 'transmit programmes likely to incite to crime or lead to disorder'.

It is not that every child who sees gratuitous violence will go on to behave violently but those who are living on the edge, who may be predisposed to maladjustment, can certainly be tipped over the precipice. The drip drip drip effect of desensitisation of the rest of society should not be underestimated either.

In one typical week on British television there are more than 400 killings screened; 119 woundings and 27 sex attacks on women. Vicious weapons are wielded, foul and abusive language is the norm. A common defence of the broadcasters is that this simply reflects real life. The 400 deaths which occur in an average week in the name of entertainment compares in reality with fourteen killings each week in real-life Britain.

Violence in Britain and America – where it is considerably worse – has become gratuitous and random. It is ingrained into the very fabric of society. Violent films such as *Natural Born Killers* and *True Lies* are typical box-office hits. In *True Lies* Arnold Schwarzenegger throws a meat hook into a man's stomach; hurls a pointed instrument at his torturer which sticks in the man's eye; breaks a man's neck with his bare hands; and a driver is shot through the head and blood splatters everywhere. Gruesome, violent death, mutilation, serial killing: all become an art form which can be turned on or off with the flick of a switch.

Violence is now *everywhere*. Perhaps our contemporary attitudes have been formed by the bombing of civilian populations at Hiroshima, Nagasaki, Dresden, Hanoi, and more recently in Iraq. Then by the legalised killing of the unborn; now, the infirm and dying. Television violence reflects all this and nurtures it too. People complain incessantly that the younger generation do not have our values. Isn't it more the case that they *have* adopted our values and are simply expanding upon them? *That* is the problem: and *that* is where our culture of violence has evolved.

Violence has also invaded the music industry through violent rock and rap singers like Wu Tang Clan and Onyx, with lyrics about masochism and murder. The techno-punk band Nine Inch Nails produced a video for the song 'Closer'. It is littered with violent imagery and had to be edited extensively to be given air time. The lead singer is portrayed as decapitated, as his head spins around on a platter.

The climate of violence – real and imagined – has led to ordinary citizens living in fear. People no longer feel safe in their homes, let alone in the parks or streets or at night time on public transport. Security companies and the alarms systems which they sell for personal use, their cars, their homes, their offices and their work-places are a booming industry. Meanwhile, the entertainment industry seems to be in the throes of a passionate love affair with violence, embracing it at every opportunity. We are becoming emotionally deadened by the horrors which we witness and have come to accept violence as normal.

According to a study for the Broadcasting Standards Council (BSC) women's fear of male violence can be reinforced and even increased by watching television programmes that depict violence against women. The then chairman of the Council, Lord Rees-Mogg said: 'Television is an extremely powerful reinforcement agency in most of the areas in which it operates.' A Mori Poll, in 1994, found that 93 per cent said their concern about crime had increased over the previous few years; 57 per cent of women said they were afraid of being raped; among women under the age of twenty-five the figure rises to 78 per cent and 67 per cent of women said they were afraid to go out at night alone. Two years ago the BSC found that the overall rate of violence had risen from 2.9 scenes per hour in 1992 to 4 scenes per hour: a 40 per cent increase; that violence occurred most often in light entertainment (11.2 scenes per hour), national news broadcasts (8.8 scenes per hour) and films (8.2 scenes per hour). By comparison, in factual and fiction programmes violence occurred relatively infrequently (3.7 and 4.6 scenes per hour respectively). Violence occurred less in programmes which started before the 9.00 p.m. watershed. Before the watershed 164 programmes (54 per cent) contained 938 violent scenes and after the watershed 142 programmes (71 per cent) contributed 866 violent scenes occurring at a rate of almost seven scenes per hour.

British academics continue to agonise over what the connection is between what we see and what we do and about the real effects of video and TV violence. American experts tell me they are puzzled that we are still debating the effects rather than admitting the damage already done.

The American Psychiatric Association linked television to 50 per cent of the crime in the USA and suggests that it may play an important role in teenage suicide as well. The research came on the heels of an FBI report which showed that violent crime in America had increased for the sixth year in a row.

Dr Brandon Centerwell, psychiatric researcher formerly with the University of Washington, claims that it is the young children exposed to TV violence in the 1950s and early 1960s who later fuelled the initial dramatic increase in murder and property crime. He says that without TV violence there would have been 10,000 fewer murders, 70,000 fewer rapes, 1,000,000 fewer motor thefts, 2,500,000 fewer burglaries, and 10,000,000 fewer acts of larceny in the USA each year. Rates of crime would have been halved.

By adolescence, a young American will have seen an average of 100,000 acts of violence and 8,000 murders on television and Centerwell says their effect cannot be ignored.

Whether or not you accept these dramatic conclusions there is a growing body of research which convincingly challenges the British establishment view – usually put by Michael Howard, the Home Secretary, Michael Grade of Channel Four, and their hired 'experts' – men like Guy Cumberbatch – that there is no proven correlation between real-life violence and that which is broadcast.

What is most certainly true is that real crime in Britain has been rising inexorably. One in three of those born in the 1950s in the UK had a criminal conviction – in a third of the cases involving violence – by the age of thirty-one. Half of those in Britain's prisons are doing time for acts of violence and in each of the past ten years between thirty and eighty young children have been killed in the United Kingdom.

Professor Elizabeth Newsome and nearly thirty child psychologists, child psychiatrists and pediatricians published a paper – which I had asked them to write – courageously stating that they were 'naive' in previously underestimating the links.

In Sweden, Professor Inga Soneson of the University of Lund followed 200 children in Malmö, southern Sweden, aged six to sixteen. The material showed that among boys in particular there was a pronounced correlation between emotional disturbance and intensive television as six-year-olds developed more aggression than their contemporaries, and later in life continued to watch violent films. This often led to behaviour problems such as vandalism, hooliganism and theft.

Professor Soneson also found that girls were strongly influenced by horror films. They lost their ability to concentrate and had frequent nightmares.

The study showed that in all, 14 per cent of the children who watched more than two hours' television a day at six were rated as being much more aggressive than their classmates by their teachers in fifth grade. In the eighth grade these children were the most aggressive in their class, and watched considerably more video violence than their classmates.

The Parliamentary Office of Science and Technology tells me that there are now video recorders in 68 per cent of British homes and that material classified as '15' or '18' is routinely seen by younger audiences, whether due to failure at the retail outlet, lack of parental control, or evasion of rules (for example, by televisions and video recorders in younger people's bedrooms). The Office goes on to say that 'studies show that the threshold of tolerated violence is raised in groups who have watched violent films'.

The Royal College of Psychiatrists has also pointed to media violence as one area where tighter controls could help protect vulnerable children; calls which have been echoed by the NSPCC and professional bodies representing teachers.

The Professional Association of Teachers (PAT) spoke to 1,000 teachers in different parts of the country when my amendment to curb video violence was before Parliament. The response of teachers does not support in the least the view that children are cynical sophisticates able to reject those aspects of the adult world for which they are not ready. One teacher said: 'I am very disturbed by the totally unsuitable films and TV programmes which are available to young children. They often talk of nothing else and revel in tales of blood, cutting off of limbs, disembowelling etc. This is the norm so that children who do not have access to this material often feel they are missing out.'

Increasing numbers of parents are using videos and video games as their electronic baby-sitter, allowing children to play with the games or to see violent videos so that they will not themselves be disturbed. Many parents simply do not seem to understand the harm which inappropriate entertainment can do.

More than 90 per cent of the PAT respondents believed that children's emotional, social and moral development is being damaged, sometimes irrevocably, by what they see. Three-quarters of teachers also believe that there is a link between over-exposure to computer games and factors such as tiredness and inattention, heightened levels of aggression and a tendency to act out fantasies.

The *TV Times* has published a survey of viewers' opinions, and 59 per cent of those interviewed felt that there were links between television and real-life violence. Some 85 per cent said that the TV companies are not careful enough in monitoring screen violence. Lady Howe, who succeeded Lord Rees-Mogg as Chairman of the Broadcasting Standards Council, confirmed in 1993 that violence on TV was the main concern of viewers and she warned against a distressing trend towards sensational techniques used in crime reconstruction programmes. Lurid techniques – such as heavy use of incidental music and slow-down dramatisation of violent attacks – were American-style devices increasingly used in Britain.

National paranoia has led us for years to tilt at imaginary Spanish windmills and at French farmers while remaining indifferent to the Americanisation of British values and our way of life. British culture has been increasingly dictated by American tastes in everything from what we eat to what we watch. Some of the least attractive aspects of life in modern Britain, drug dependency, street crime and mugging, screen violence and the disintegration of family and community life were all manifesting themselves in the States years before they were washed up on our shores.

What is particularly distressing about this is that there is no shortage of British talent available to contradict the values of Hollywood. David Puttnam has been one of the most important voices raised against the values of Hollywood. He was good enough to send me some of his thoughts about screen violence.

Commenting on the Newsome report he said:

> What proof are we looking for, I wonder? Are we going to wait a decade or two to see if there is a fresh outbreak of gruesome murders before deciding perhaps *Driller Killer* wasn't the thing to show the kids after all? Does the railway company wait for someone to be killed by a train before fencing off the railway line – on the grounds that there is no proof that a speeding train is dangerous or that children can be silly enough to wander onto the line? So far as the railway is concerned, common sense has always provided the proof that is necessary. The next step is action.

Puttnam continued:

> Human society has been wrestling with the responsibilities of child care for rather longer than it has been thinking about the problems of speeding trains. Why is it then, that we so readily apply common sense in one case but seem to find it so difficult to trust our instincts in the other?
>
> Does common sense not tell us that it is foolish to debate whether watching sadistic pornographic films

makes children into dangerous psychopaths? Leaving aside the impact this influence may or may not have in future for the rest of us, what is abundantly clear is that, for them, as immature human beings, watching sadistic pornographic films has to be a very bad idea.

Disputing all this has been Guy Cumberbatch who, over the years, has usually been 'the expert' who pops up on programmes to tell us that this is all bunk. But the arguments have sounded increasingly dreary and facile.

Visual images are incredibly powerful. They have a terrific impact on the consciousness of a small child. Film-makers share the opportunity of advertisers. They both deal in the currency of heightened reality. An artificial and often attractive world of images is manufactured and this power brings with it a responsibility to deal sensitively with our hopes and dreams as well as our fears.

Certainly the people who make the advertisements which fill so much of the TV airtime have never been in any doubt about the influence of TV. If they didn't think it was affecting anyone why else would they spend nearly £4 billion a year trying to sell us their wares on television?

The Chairman of Unilever is reputed to have said that he knew that half of his spending on ads was a complete waste of money ... the only problem was that he didn't know which half.

One of the most disturbing lines now being trotted out by Home Office officials is that even if there was a link 'only 30 per cent of British homes now have children in them'. Therefore, this does not justify the limitation of the 'freedom' of the 70 per cent to provide 'protection' for the 30 per cent. What a revealing aspect of the anti-child culture which is on the increase in Britain today.

However, there are some signs that the programme-makers are beginning to recognise their responsibility in these matters.

The BBC – in contrast to satellite television – have been deliberately monitoring and reducing their output of violence. Nor have the BBC yet removed the inspiring inscription which the pioneers of the Corporation placed above their doors at the inception of radio transmissions:

> This temple of the Arts and Muses is dedicated to Almighty God by the first Governors of Broadcasting in the year 1931, Sir John Reith, being Director General. It is their prayer that good seed sown may bring forth a good harvest, that all thoughts hostile to peace and maturity be banished from this house, and that the people, inclining their ear to whatever things are beautiful and honest and of good report, may tread the path of wisdom and uprightness.

There are echoes here of the principles that were at that very time taking Thecla Merlo and her friends into the inspired work of founding their 'good press'. In the intervening sixty years the Paulists have continued to offer an alternative approach to the use of media technology.

Sadly, the BBC's foundation principles have not always been similarly matched by their deeds. Take, for instance, one evening's offerings from BBC2 – supposedly the up-market, quality arm of television broadcasting. In an orgy of programmes presumably broadcast to coincide with Hallowe'en Night 1994, BBC2 offered the following 'beautiful and honest' programmes, no doubt intended to be sown as good seeds to reap a good harvest.

First came *The Vault of Horrors: What's Behind The Door Mummy?*, followed by *Tales from EC* which was billed as an inspirational programme because it traced the history of comic strips which have 'inspired horror writers and film makers'. Next came *Creepshow* followed by a programme about horror make-up effects. Then came *The Unholy Trinity* and *The Curse of the Werewolf*. By 3.10 a.m. the BBC was excelling itself, and perhaps giving the game away, with a programme entitled *Prime Evil*. This was a discussion of the Evil Dead saga.

The night was yet young and concluded with *Terror of the Page*, *The Bride of Frankenstein*, *The Horror of Sex* – a discussion of sex in horror – *Dario's Friends* (showing impeccable European credentials, some imported Italian horror) and *Deathline*, a subtle little tale about the everyday life of some cannibals on the London Underground.

In case none of this appealed to the viewer, and not to be outdone, BBC1 staged a Screen One Special entitled *Ghostwatch*. Some of the scenes were so macabre and horrific that the Corporation switchboards were jammed with complaints from parents whose children had been frightened and distressed by a programme which carried no warnings.

By contrast, the following day was one of the great days of the Christian calendar: All Saints' Day. There was no screening of Zeffirelli's life of St Francis; or a recital of the poems of Titus Brandsma, who was detained by the Nazis at Scheveningen; or a celebration of the life of C. S. Lewis; or a discussion of the impact of Christian reformers, such as Wilberforce and Shaftesbury. There was no discussion of the lives of contemporary saints such as Lord Cheshire or Mother Teresa – although Channel Four was on hand to provide a negative and destructive programme aimed at destroying this great woman's reputation.

The BBC countered the criticism by stating that it broadcast two 'religious' programmes that day. *Songs of Praise* was one. The programme's host opened by telling viewers that it was a special day because the words All Saints College were to be dropped from the title of the new Middlesex University, which replaces it, and from where the programme was broadcast. Later came *Everyman* which told us it was celebrating the beginning of the pagan Celtic new year. *Songs of Praise* had gone one better by including a hymn praising Hindu gods.

Tolerance of other faiths has its place but this is simply syncretism. Where is the proper celebration of this country's values, heritage, and witness?

The need for the media to use its power properly – as Thecla Merlo perceived – is an urgent one in Britain today. Parents may soon be able to rule violent TV programmes out of bounds. A 'V' chip is being developed in the United States. It is a microchip which will allow parents to block the reception of violent programmes when children are left unsupervised. Every programme classified as violent would be tagged with an electronic signal. The 'V' chip would detect the signal, and if chosen, block transmission.

This would be a start, but what about the programme-makers and the people who run the industry? Last year a video was being sold to children in school playgrounds in Manchester which had been produced in America and pirated for illicit sale in the UK. It contained more than an hour of material culled from police videos and uncut and unused news material. It showed real people being killed or mutilated. It showed terrible scenes of unspeakable violence against the person. It had been manufactured as a sick form of entertainment. The doctor who showed it to me said it was the worst thing she had ever seen. But was this worse than the simulated violence that has become the hallmark of so many film productions today? Yes, parents should no doubt do more to protect their children but the film-makers, broadcasters and governments must play their part too.

Some of the most notorious video nasties are already illegal, as they have been for several years, but children continue to have access to them. Backstreet shops – like those exposed in a 1995 *Panorama* programme – will continue to peddle it for as long as they think they can make money and avoid prosecution. Until government departments enforce existing legislation and courts impose the exemplary penalties now available this aspect of the problem will not be solved.

Values and the Media

Parents must also stop and think about what is happening to their children. In a recent National Opinion Poll, commissioned by CARE (Christian Action Research and Education), and followed up by Rob Parsons in his highly readable *Sixty Minute Father*,[4] over half the fathers interviewed said they spent less than five minutes a day with their child on a one-to-one basis (15 per cent spent no time in the week with their child). In the same survey some children were found to spend at least two hours every day watching TV, some watch over five hours a day. Many children are simply being dumped in front of a video – with the TV as surrogate parents and programmes taking the place of conversation.

Last year Strategic Marketing And Research Consultants published a report, *The Class of 94*. It found that four in ten boys and 28 per cent of girls aged between seven and seventeen watch TV past the watershed during the week. This rose to half the boys and 41 per cent of the girls at the weekend. They confirmed the NOP findings claiming that children watch an average of two to three hours of TV a day. Two-thirds of the children had TV sets in their own bedrooms and a quarter also had video recorders. These findings cast grave doubt on the ability of parents to effectively ensure that children do not see unsuitable material.

The absence of fathers hardly helps matters. Some 750,000 children in Britain have no contact with their fathers and 150,000 children are caught up in divorces every year. One in five British children can now expect to experience the divorce of their parents before they are aged sixteen. Also 48,000 children are on Child Protection Registers. Many live on sink estates where it may appear that basic material needs are met – but their homes are often a spiritual hell. Children devoid of love, discipline, hope or help. Into this situation we pour this diet of violence and materialism.

The insidious campaign to persuade us to buy more and more luxury goods attacks family and community life at its core. It is every bit as destructive as the violent and nihilistic programmes which it helps to finance. Their message leads to financial bondage which cripples and destroys family life. Money problems are now named as the major issue in over 70 per cent of divorce cases. Consumerism destroys quality time which families need together. It creates debt and stress, both of which destroy relationships, builds up personal pressure and ruins lives. Consumerism and materialistic values are the opposite of all that Christianity upholds: especially charity and mutual help. To Eastern Europe we are exporting the same creed with Karl Marx being replaced by Marks and Spencer and power politics being replaced by *Power Rangers* and their like.

It was to contradict this culture that Thecla Merlo and her companions dedicated their lives. They appreciated that it is not enough to deplore or to condemn. Alternatives – the 'good press' – must be developed. Their family-based popular newspapers, published in many parts of the world, have been a particularly constructive contribution; so will their parish family-video libraries in due course.

The Thecla Merlo approach has been based on clear values. Perhaps when broadcasting companies come to apply for their franchises they should be required to publish a values statement defining what criteria they use when selecting the programmes to screen. The treatment of sex and violence could be outlined and if the franchise selectors thought a given company was not living up to its values statement it would not get the franchise again.

I believe that all TV broadcasters, whether satellite or terrestial should have to reapply every five years. The management board of the BBC should also have to submit to such a process.

To those who complain that I am in favour of censorship, I

would simply say that I want these programme selection policies to be more democratic. The decisions about what programmes to screen are always made by broadcasters; and this amounts to a form of censorship. All I am asking is that these decisions should be made more democratically. They should not simply be made by unelected bureaucrats behind closed doors.

If the electronic media needs to become more responsible and discerning, the same must surely also be said about the tabloid press. I have regularly argued for greater freedom of information allowing public access to information which they are entitled to see. Even the gardeners at Hampton Court Palace are required to sign an Official Secrets declaration – presumably because someone is fearful that they might divulge the secrets of the compost heap, or why their begonias grow to such an impressive size.

This obsession with secrecy in some areas of our national life is mirrored by an intrusion into matters which are legitimately private. Reconciliation between certain well-known estranged public figures might have been easier if they had not been under the constant glare of tabloid attention. Some of the more gross invasions of private life are completely unacceptable and in France, for instance, would lead to prosecutions under their privacy laws. Parliament has been reluctant to introduce legislation here – because of the fear that powers might be draconian and might be misused. If the tabloids are to avoid legal curtailment they will need to achieve a better balance between what should genuinely be in the public domain and that which is legitimately private.

There is a challenge here to those who buy and read newspapers or watch television or videos. Consumer power is not to be underestimated. For instance, after Channel Four screened *The Last Temptation of Christ*, I tabled a motion in Parliament simply listing the companies who had advertised immediately before, during, or after transmission. Among these were Tesco, Vauxhall and World Vision. None of them had been asked for or given permission for their advertisements to be screened in conjunction with this film. Apologies had to be issued to them and, in the case of Tesco, compensation was given. Asking the Chairman or board members of companies who advertise alongside offensive material whether it is their policy to do so can create a perfectly legitimate pressure point from consumers.

Another way is to follow the Pauline model of creating an alternative media. During the 1920s they ran a series of newspapers, *Il Giornalino* (The Little Newspaper), a weekly illustrated newspaper for children, and *L'Aspirante* (The Aspirant), a lively weekly which became very popular among young people. In 1926 *La Domenica Illustrata* (The Sunday Illustrated) followed and subsequently changed its name to *Focolare* (The Hearth). But their great success story was *Famiglia Christiana* (Christian Family), born on Christmas Day 1931 with eight pages and a run of 18,000 copies. Today it publishes with up to 200 pages, has a run of 1.2 million, and is probably the Christian magazine with the largest press run in the world. It is imitated in many countries and along with the Italian edition, Spanish and Portuguese editions are produced on the same printing presses in Alba.

In London the advent of Premier Radio – which has a distinctly Christian ethos – is yet another example of creating your own media, and the nationwide network of bookshops and alternative journals and newspapers all deserve to be supported and encouraged.

Thecla Merlo's life, alongside that of James Alberione, are fascinating examples of someone who saw a need and met it. Their vision was an evangelistic one and it inevitably ran into opposition. Local jealousies, and even fear among clerics who were nervous of the empowerment of the laity through mass distribution of Scripture and teaching, all played their part. Fear of new technologies and their impact on the traditional strengths of the family and the community created another form of uncertainty. But Thecla Merlo saw the need to harness mass communications and to use it just as St Paul had used the facility of the Ephesian amphitheatre.

However, it is with another ancient, Aristotle, that I will conclude. He might have had our video and film industry, our tabloids and television stations in mind when he rendered his own version of what the 'good press' might be:

> Shall we just carelessly allow children to hear casual tales which may be devised by casual persons, and to receive into their minds ideas for the most part the very opposite of those which we should wish them to have when they grow up?
>
> We cannot ... Anything received into the mind at that age is likely to become indelible and unalterable; and therefore it is most important that the tales which the young first hear should serve as models of virtuous thoughts ...
>
> Then will our youth dwell in a land of health, amid fair sights and sounds, and receive the good in everything; so that beauty and good works shall flow into the eye and the ear, like a health-giving breeze from a purer region, and insensibly draw the soul from the earliest years into likeness and sympathy with the beauty of reason.
>
> There can be no nobler training.

Used in a responsible way, and placed in responsible hands, Thecla Merlo's life was part of that noble calling: to use modern technology in the service of truth.

Chapter Five

Maximilian Kolbe

GREATER LOVE HATH NO MAN

To love truth for truth's sake is the principal part of human
perfection in this world, and the seed-plot of all other virtues.

John Locke, letter to Anthony Collins, 29 October 1703

To sacrifice your life for someone else is something which most
of us hope we will never be called upon to do. To do it for one
we love is at least within the range of normal human emotion;
to do it, as Maximilian Kolbe did, for someone he did not even
know is the folly of which greatness and great acts are made.
Maximilian Kolbe's place in this book will need no justification
or explanation once his story has been told. He is also included
here because his life's account enables me to say something
about anti-Semitism and the hatred which may so easily displace
civilised values.

'Love each other'

In His parable of the vine and the branches, recorded by St
John in the fifteenth chapter of his Gospel, Jesus uses one of
the most memorable of His rich illustrations to describe His
relationship with each of us. He is the vine and we are His
branches. As His father has loved Him so He loves us. Instead
of servants we are His friends. And here, too, are His most
important command and His prophecy of what would await
Him: 'Greater love hath no man than this, that he lay down his
life for his friends . . . This is my command; Love each other.'

In the next paragraphs John goes on to record Jesus's warning that adherence to His teachings would lead to a contemptuous response from the world: 'If the world hates you, keep in mind that it hated me first ... If they persecuted me, they will persecute you also. They will treat you this way because of my name, for they do not know the One who sent me.'

In recent years Western European Christians have escaped hatred but have been treated to something far worse, indifference. It would be a good test for English churchgoers to consider for a moment how many people hate them: hate them for what they believe and for Who they follow. Or is the world completely indifferent?

There is a cosiness about Church life which can quickly degenerate into pietism and a narrow concern for personal salvation – which is all a long way from that great command to love one another. Loving others, and not just yourself, in a self-congratulatory spasm of religious narcissism.

The privatisation of faith, and opt-out churches which have settled for a regulated and non-controversial role in society, are an easy option. But Christ came into the world; He didn't try to escape it or avoid it – even when He knew the risks of rejection and condemnation. Being 'affirming' and 'nice' people is no doubt important but the word 'nice' appears nowhere in Scripture.

In the Old Testament the priest offers David a sword and he says: 'If thou wilt, take this, take it, for there is none other but this.' Like that sword Christ comes to the heart of human history. The Christian believes that there is none other than this; no other but Him. The sword is the love of Christ and it is to be wielded against the giants who loiter at every turn of the path. David was an outlaw in his own country and to some extent, we too, if we are to be faithful in our secularised society, must also be prepared to be outlaws. The outlaw must be prepared to live outside the citadels and make daring raids. It is a dangerous life, one which can cost you everything.

Now the sceptic has the right to ask how well Christians have measured up. The truth, of course, is that we often fail abysmally. What is mildly depressing nowadays is the assumption, therefore, that it is not even worth trying to live up to a noble ideal.

The purpose of this chapter will be primarily to look at the life of one man who not only lived his life faithfully – albeit with blemishes – but who took his Master at His word through his willingness to lay down his own life as an act of love. Maximilian Kolbe gave his life for someone he did not even know. In the mire of hatred of World War Two concentration camps this solitary action helps redeem what is otherwise an overwhelming sense of shame.

Maximilian Kolbe was by no means the only Christian to take a stand against Nazism, but I fear that because we are so familiar with the names of those who did speak out, it sometimes disguises the millions who did not. There were not many people who were prepared to be outlaws.

The Holocaust

Pre-War Europe was largely occupied by Christians who had retreated into church buildings and tribal nominalism: a Sunday service form of Churchianity. Religion was a family matter, something to be passed down, not to be taken too seriously, but a useful regulator for births, deaths and marriages. It was not concerned with politics and often indifferent to ethics. It chose a quiet life and hoped that when the bad days had passed it would be there to pick up the pieces.

These were not inherently bad people. Many simply opted for that quiet life, fearful that if they spoke out there would be serious implications for their own children and families. Without being in that situation it is impossible to know whether we would have responded so very differently. Never allowing ourselves to forget what occurred during the years from 1925 until 1945 is at least a salutary reminder of the consequences of opting out. Through it all glimmer the rays of hope that rescue us from our own failures.

In the Book of Genesis the promise is given to Abraham and his people that:

> I will bless those who bless you,
> and whoever curses you I will curse,
> And all people on earth
> will be blessed through you.

Jewish culture, community and family life, history, and religion have enriched the world to a degree which is completely incommensurate with their numbers. The promise of Genesis that the world would be blessed by the descendants of Abraham is a promise which has been kept. These blessings have frequently been repaid in persecution and anti-Semitism.

The Hebrew Bible has at its centre a respect for the ideals of justice and the rule of Law. This has been a part of the Jewish contribution to civilisation ever since. Few religions have placed a respect for the Law and its proper dispensation so prominently. The Ten Commandments, given by God Himself to the assembled Israelites at Mount Sinai are the perfect manifestation of this love of law and an ordered society. In the Book of Amos, and the other prophetic writings, this theme of justice is returned to again and again: 'Let justice roll down like a river, and righteousness as a never-ending stream.' And yet the Jewish people have themselves rarely been dealt with justly.

From Judaism springs our Judaeo-Christian belief in the sanctity of life, the dignity of the human person, the importance of individual and collective conscience, the requirement for personal and communal responsibility, and our accountability before man and God. This special genius, these momentous insights, have been the staple fare in civilised societies ever since they were first revealed through the Jewish people.

Yet the jealousy and the vilification which have afflicted generations of Jews – often at the hands of at least nominally Christian people – have been extraordinary. It came to its conclusion in the destruction of the Holocaust, the Shoah. In the nightmare kingdoms of the concentration camps the Jews faced extermination but they also renewed their covenant with God. Rabbi Elchanan Wasserman said before he was killed: 'The fire which destroys our bodies is the fire which will restore the Jewish people.' Our own Chief Rabbi, Jonathan Sacks, sees in the persistence of faith, even amidst the greatest adversity, the long-term ability to conquer evil: 'The Jews of faith, who were able to sanctify death *in* the Holocaust, turned out to be the most determined to sanctify life *after* the Holocaust.'[1]

It has become unfashionable today to speak of good and evil. Everything has been given a relative value. Yet who can doubt that in the ideologies of Hitler and Stalin the world was confronted by the overthrow of justice and righteousness and the imposition of unrelieved wickedness?

Dealing with the evils of the Soviet system Alexander Solzhenitsyn said, and it might just as easily have been written about the Third Reich:

Depending upon the circumstances, any act, including the killing of thousands, could be good or bad. It all depends upon class ideology, defined by a handful of people. It is considered awkward to use seriously such words as good or evil. But if we are to be deprived of these concepts, what will be left? We will decline to the status of animals.[2]

No people have better cause than Jews to fully understand the consequences of what happens when society loses those concepts of good and evil. Standing, as I did again two years ago, at Yad Vashem, the Jerusalem memorial to the victims of the Holocaust, I was struck once more by our seemingly unlimited capacity for evil and the silence of the majority in the face of what was done in their name. At Yad Vashem there is a chamber of broken lights – which seem to break into infinity – as the visitor listens to the names of individual children being read constantly from a record of remembrance. These are not mind-numbing statistics but human beings bursting with all the attributes of childhood and life. Little children cruelly cut down. At the Nuremburg Trials a guard at Auschwitz told the court how, at the height of the genocide, as ten thousand Jews were daily being turned into ashes, children were thrown into the furnances alive. Chamber music was played over the cries of these burning children.

These times of monstrous inhumanity do not come about all at once; we slip into them gradually. People often ask, where was God at Auschwitz? We are each given the gift of free will to choose life or death, right or wrong. The more appropriate question is to ask where man was during the horrors of Auschwitz.

This year, 1995 was the fiftieth anniversary of the liberation of Auschwitz. It was a time for recalling the shadows which passed over Europe. It has also been a time, perhaps especially in the context of the ethnic cleansing in Bosnia, to ask whether we will respond differently as this evil fanaticism, driven by racial hatred and nationalism, visits us again.

It is not possible in the space of one chapter to do justice to the sheer enormity of the evil which the Holocaust involved but perhaps a recollection of this one camp and of this one life which was surrendered there will help to illuminate the darkness.

On 1st September 1939 Warsaw was bombed by Hitler's air force. A few days later Warsaw was encircled by the German army. The siege of the city, which lasted for several weeks, saw brave resistance by Poles and Jews who fought alongside each other. Almost immediately the Nazis began their extermination of the Jewish population.

The first phase involved the isolation of the entire Jewish people in particular cities and they installed local Councils of Elders who were invested with 'the complete responsibility ... for the precise and timely execution of issued directives'. Then began the process of relocation – ethnic cleansing – with an order from Himmler that all Jews from Pomerania, Poznan and Upper Silesia should be relocated to the so-called General Gouvernement, an area of central Poland. Several thousand Christians and Jews were transported in unheated stock cars, without food, to Lublin, Krakow and Kielce.

Those Jews not yet removed were required to wear a white armband with a blue star of David. Many were subsequently put in forced labour camps. Mortality rates were appalling, the regime unbelievably cruel, the methods frequently sadistic.

In the two cities with the largest Jewish populations, Warsaw and Krakow, ghettos were created. People were living as many as twenty to a room. The population of the Warsaw ghetto reached a staggering 500,000 people. Hygiene and sanitary conditions were unspeakable. Starvation and despair stalked the ghettos.

All of this was to achieve Himmler's *Generalplan Ost*, the extermination of the Jews and the forced resettlement of 50 million Slavs, among them about 20 million Poles, who were to be forcibly resettled to Siberia after Germany defeated the Soviet Union. The Polish intelligentsia was to be annihilated.

The decision on the 'final solution' to the Jewish question was made in Berlin in January 1942. Cold-bloodedly the minutes of the meeting, under the head of the *Reichssicherheits-hauptamt*, state that 'During the final solution to the European Jewish question about 11 million Jews need to be considered ... The practical execution of the final solution will comb Europe from West to East.'

The complete liquidation of the ghettos began and under the

pretext of further resettlement extermination camps were created at Treblinka, Sobibor, Belsen, Auschwitz-Birkenau, and Majdanek.

The Allied governments and the Churches were increasingly aware of what atrocities were under way but the world was slow to react. At one of the most moving ceremonies of 1995 the memory of 1,000 Jewish orphans was recalled. They were sent to Auschwitz after being denied sanctuary by Britain in 1942.

General Vasili Petrenko, the Russian commander who finally liberated the camp attended a London meeting at which the wartime British Government was accused of failing adequately to protect European Jewry.

Fred Barschak, a member of the Holocaust memorial committee of the Board of Deputies of British Jews told the meeting that the American Government persuaded the Vichy regime in France to temporarily suspend their own deportations and to offer the British Government 1,000 children aged four to fourteen: 'The British Government could send a ship under seal of safe conduct to any port under their control and they could take the children.' Jewish organisations promised to fund the entire operation.

Government ministers said there was a law prohibiting the entry of anybody from enemy-occupied territories. There were to be no exceptions. The Minister, Herbert Morrison, vetoed their entry – partly on the grounds that no-one could prove that the children were actually orphans. The children were then sent to Auschwitz and died in the camp.

The Pope of the day, Pius XII, has also been criticised for not speaking out early enough in denouncing the Nazi massacre of the Jews; although the Holy See was instrumental in directly saving the lives of countless Jewish refugees.

Lord Rees-Mogg, writing in *The Times*, believes that the Church should, however, have been more active:

There is, I think, no doubt that his first priority was to protect and preserve the Catholic community in Europe ... and by the end of 1940 almost all of Europe's Catholics outside Ireland, and the British minority, were under Nazi or Fascist power ... He tried to follow a policy of covert assistance for Jews, rather than open denunciation, which he believed would provoke further retaliation. His policy did in fact save many Jews. Perhaps half a million or a million were helped to survive by Catholic agencies and support of one sort or another ...

Yet I think the thrust of the criticism is justified. Pius XII failed the Jews and thereby failed the Church. He took too narrow a view of his responsibilities. He was faced with evil incarnate and tried to evade rather than confront it ... It would have been better if the Catholic Church had accepted the risk of martyrdom in the Nazi period. Prudence and prayer were not enough. Human affairs require a more active courage.[3]

Martyrdom and active courage were, however, to be the marks of individual Christians such as Maximilian Kolbe.

Kolbe's Life and Work

Maximilian Kolbe was born in 1894 in a village outside the city of Lodz (which then had a substantial Jewish population), the son of an impoverished weaver, and was given the baptismal name Raymund.

In her excellent account of his life, Mary Craig describes Raymund's family background as devout.[4] All three children were given a basic education and a grounding in their faith. Raymund and his older brother, Francis, both asked if they might join the Franciscan junior seminary and at the age of thirteen he left home and travelled to Lvov. When their third son also left home Raymund's parents each decided to enter the religious life themselves, his mother as a Benedictine sister and his father as a Franciscan.

Raymund had been brought up as a patriot by his father and reared on the romantic stories of the knights of the Polish Legion. He had been tempted to turn the romance into reality by joining the army but ultimately took vows as a Franciscan. With a certain twist of irony he took the religious name Maximilian after the third-century Christian martyr who had been executed after refusing to be conscripted into the Roman Legion.

During his subsequent training and study in Rome he had his first encounter with Freemasons, who were celebrating their bicentenary. They held a demonstration in St Peter's Square, unfurling banners of Lucifer. Vitriolic slogans: 'Satan Must Reign in The Vatican'; and 'The Pope Must Be His Slave' were accompanied by equally virulent anti-clerical pamphlets and propaganda. Showing his willingness to confront the enemy and not to dodge a fight, the young student organised a committee to oppose Freemasonry and Satanism.

A year later, in 1918, Maximilian Kolbe was ordained priest and returned to teach philosophy and history in Poland (restored by the Treaty of Versailles as an independent state at the end of World War I).

Although plagued by frequent bouts of serious ill health the young Maximilian immediately plunged himself into his work. He realised that the new methods of communication had to be harnessed, and as Thecla Merlo and James Alberione were developing their Good Press in Italy, Maximilian Kolbe began the same work in Poland. He perceived the growth of secularism and the need to give ordinary people access to good information and knowledge about their faith. His publication, *Knight*, began with a circulation of 5,000 and, despite the criticism of many of his own compatriots, within three years it had reached a circulation of 45,000. Within another two years it had risen to 60,000 copies and by the autumn of 1927 an entirely new friary had been established at Niepokalanow, just outside of Warsaw. They bought the finest printing machinery available. Within ten years the small community of two priests and seventeen lay brothers had increased to a phenomenal 762 friars, the largest religious community in the world.

For six years, between 1930 and 1936, Maximilian stayed in Japan, where he established a brand new house and Japanese publications (and by 1936 there were twenty young Japanese studying for the priesthood). Poor health once again took its toll and another proposed new venture, this time in India, had to be abandoned.

There were, however, other reasons why he was needed at home. At Niepokalanow a daily newspaper was produced which now had a circulation of 230,000 and everything from a sporting journal to illustrated spiritual magazines were being turned out on their state-of-the-art machines. On his return Maximilian also established a radio station.

Anti-Semitism had become an increasing feature of Polish life during the years of economic hardship. Although Fr Kolbe had written from Japan to voice his concerns, some of the Polish friars undoubtedly shared those anti-Semitic sentiments. 'When talking about Jews, I would be very careful not to stir up, or deepen hatred towards them in people who are already sometimes ill-disposed or openly hostile,' warned Fr Kolbe.

It would not be long before Jews and Poles would discover the need for solidarity in the face of a common enemy. Within nineteen days of the German invasion and the siege of Warsaw Fr Kolbe and those of his friars who had not been despatched to join the Red Cross were arrested by the Nazis and their presses were silenced.

On 8th December they were unexpectedly released and Fr Kolbe and a small band returned to Niepokalanow. They began to provide relief for refugees. They cared for more than 3,000 deportees, including 2,000 Jews.

By the following December Fr Kolbe had gained permission

from the Germans to once again publish *Knight*. Signing his own death warrant he fearlessly published an editorial denouncing the evil empire of Nazism:

> No one in the world can change Truth. What we can and should do is to seek Truth and serve it when we have found it. The real conflict is within. Beyond armies of occupation and the hecatombs of the extermination camps, two irreconcilable enemies lie in the depths of every soul. And of what use are the victories on the battlefield if we are defeated in our innermost personal selves?

The Gestapo arrested him in February and on 28th May he was herded into a cattle truck and transported, along with 300 others, to Auschwitz, near Krakow.

Branded with the number 16670 he was stripped of all that makes a man human. Priests were singled out for especially brutal treatment by their sadistic keepers. They were forced to do some of the most gruelling work and were treated to particularly demeaning humiliations.

On one occasion Father Kolbe was ordered to lie face down on a pile of logs and was given fifty strokes of the lash. Unconscious, he was left for dead in the mud. Under the cover of dark he was taken to the camp hospital and gradually regained his strength. All around him men were dying, sometimes three and four to a bed.

Stories abound of his concern for others, even while he was himself chronically ill. Secretly he celebrated Mass and dispensed the sacraments, bringing hope into the lives of desperate men shrouded in hate. Fellow prisoners collected grapes or berries which were crushed to make wine. Others kept crumbs of bread and Fr Kolbe then celebrated the Mass for them.

Mary Craig quotes many instances of the comfort and encouragement which 16670 brought to his compatriots. There was the story of Joseph Stemler. Ordered by the SS to report to the camp hospital he was told to remove corpses. One was the body of a young man who had been disfigured and cruelly tortured before being killed. Stemler was overcome and unable to comply. The SS guard began hurling curses and Stemler stood frozen to the ground. 'Then, I heard a voice say quite calmly: "Shall we take him together, my brother?" The other prisoner guided Stemler through his task: 'When I heard his whispered "requiescat in pace", I knew it was Father Kolbe.'

Another survivor, Zygmunt Ruszczak said:

Every time I saw Father Kolbe in the courtyard, I felt within myself an extraordinary infusion of his goodness. Although he wore the same ragged clothes as the rest of us, with the same tin can hanging from his belt, one forgot this wretched exterior and was conscious only of the charm of his countenance and of his radiant holiness.

But these were not the stories by which the world would remember Maximilian Kolbe.

At the beginning of August 1941 a group of three prisoners escaped. The Nazis killed ten men for every one who escaped. The death was a long and slow starvation. The condemned men were simply buried alive in an airless underground concrete bunker.

The deputy camp commandant, Karl Fritzsch, accompanied by the Gestapo chief, Gerhardt Palitzsch, passed down the lines of prisoners. Fritzsch selected his victims.

As the ninth man was chosen he cried out: 'My wife, my children, I shall never see them again.'

It was at this moment that the unexpected and the unprecedented happened. A man stepped forward and stood before Fritzsch and calmly asked, in correct German, if he might take the place of the condemned man. 'Who are you?' asked Fritzsch. 'A Catholic priest' was the straightforward reply.

The reprieved man, Franciszek Gajowniczek, was ordered to return to his place in the line. The condemned men were then sent to be stripped of their rags and to be buried alive.

What happened next was recounted by Bruno Borgowiec, an assistant janitor and interpreter in the underground bunkers. He described the atmosphere in cell 18 as resembling that of a church. Fr Kolbe led the prisoners in prayer and hymns as they prepared for death. Gradually they died, one by one. After two weeks only four remained alive and Fr Kolbe was the only prisoner who remained conscious.

The authorities wanted to use the bunker for a new batch of victims and so the head of the camp hospital, Hans Bock – a common criminal – injected each of the men with carbolic acid.

When Borgowiec returned to the cell he found Father Kolbe 'still seated, propped up against the corner, his head slightly to one side, his eyes wide open and fixed on one point. As if in ecstasy, his face was serene and radiant.' It was 14th August 1941, the vigil of the feast, greatly celebrated throughout Poland, of the Virgin's Assumption into heaven.

In that underground cell good overcame evil; the voluntary surrender of a life, on behalf of another, overcame death. It was the definitive answer to the megalomania of the Nazis; it was the victory of love over hate. It was the outlaw taking on the giant's might.

Franciszek Gajowniczek, the Jewish prisoner whose life was purchased by Maximilian Kolbe, survived the camps. During the last days of the war his two young sons were tragically killed on the streets by Russian shells. He was present when another Pole, John Paul II, the former bishop of Krakow, canonised Maximilian Kolbe as a martyr-saint in October 1982.

John Paul described Fr Kolbe's life as offering a wonderful synthesis of the sufferings and hopes of our age but it also offers a warning: 'It is a cry directed to man, to society, to the whole human race, to systems which hold human life and human society in their hands ... This martyred saint cries aloud for a renewed respect for the rights of men and nations.'

The story of Maximilian Kolbe is a story which gives some comfort to those who wonder aloud about the failure of the world to respond to the plight of the Jewish people. If this comfort instils a sense of complacency then the sacrifice will have been in vain and the story worthless.

'I did nothing'

At the end of the Second World War Pastor Niemoller reflected on the failure of Christians to speak out and to act politically. 'First they came for the Jews and I did nothing' are words which ring down the pages of history. Then it was the trade unionists, gypsies, homosexuals, Catholic and Protestant dissenters. But people generally did nothing. The terrible truth is that most people did comply and very few repudiated Nazism.

Nazism had begun in the 1920s when the German medical establishment, even before the Reich, had condoned eugenics. Experiments on humans, abortion, and euthanasia were a natural extension of an ideology which cared nothing for the sanctity of life. Then came wholesale massacre of races and groups of people who were deemed to be inferior.

Nazism was spawned by the philosophy of Friedrich Nietzche, the German philosopher. He maintained that the one great freedom was freedom from God. To him Good was everything that heightened the feeling of power in man; Bad was every form of weakness, especially Christian self-sacrifice, which he saw as no better than suicide. He would have had a special loathing for a man like Maximilian Kolbe.

Under the influence of Hegel, Nietzsche dreamed of a higher sort of man, the Aryan Superman. He claimed that Christianity, with its upholding of the weak – and erroneous belief in meekness, forgiveness or mercy – had constantly sought to undermine the creation of this perfect human. Condemning the

Church he said: 'How a German could ever have felt Christian is beyond me.' The hatred of gentleness, the worship of perfection and power, and a world in which man himself became a god inevitably led to Dachau, Belsen and Auschwitz. To what else could such a monstrous ideology lead?

The idea of destroying a life which has lost its social usefulness springs from weakness, not from strength. The right to live is entirely divorced from questions of social utility. In God's sight there is no life which is not worth living – for God is the Creator of all life. Each life has a distinct and unique value. It is of infinite worth and is not to be squandered like surplus raw material. Nor is it to be belittled or reduced in status for reasons of racial origin, gender, or ability.

Europe's crimes against the Jews remind us where an anti-life mentality leads. Judaism contributed richly to the world of pre-war Europe. The Talmudic academies, the courts of Jewish mystics, the masses of Yiddish-speaking people, the synagogues, the flourishing Jewish townships, the customs and characters – brought so vividly to life in scenes from *Fiddler on the Roof* – all were wantonly destroyed in an orgy of hatred. This catastrophe relied on the fears and indifference of millions of responsible people. They failed the Jews.

But out of death must come new life. *Lo amut ki echyeh*, says the Psalm: 'I will not die, but I will live.' In the life and death of Maximilian Kolbe we see what should have been the Christian response to the Shoah. We see the triumph of authentic living over the dead hand of ideology and fanaticism.

In another context Martin Luther King once said: 'Cowardice asks the question, "Is it safe?" Expediency asks the question, "Is it politic?", Vanity asks the question, "Is it popular?" But conscience asks the question, "Is it right?"' Maximilian Kolbe was unhesitating in delivering his verdict. The troubling question today is whether we would do the same.

Chapter Six

Edmund Campion

'COME RACK, COME ROPE'

Rather than love, than money, than fame, give me truth.

Thoreau, *Conclusion, Walden*, 1854

Edmund Campion's story is one to capture any schoolboy's imagination – as it did mine at eleven years of age. It is the story of an Englishman who 400 years ago stubbornly but bravely clung to his beliefs despite the scaffold that might await him. It no longer has to be told as a polemic in favour of one denomination against another. It is part of our collective history and just as the Catholic must understand the positions taken by Luther, Latimer or Cranmer, so it behoves the Protestant to understand why More, Fisher and Campion held to theirs. The bloody reigns of Henry VIII, Mary and Elizabeth I shaped the attitudes of protagonists and apologists for the Catholic and Protestant positions for generations. Even today there is still a residue of snide remarks, bitter resentments, and sectarian rivalry. 'See how these Christians love one another.'

When Anne Widdecombe became a Catholic I remember a BBC interviewer on *Woman's Hour* asking how it felt to be 'part of a religion of Italian waiters and Irish navvies'. Perhaps she should have replied that a religion which has its roots among Galilean fishermen and Palestinian peasants can find room for the Irish, the Italians and even the English! This sort of question, however, betrays not only a deep-seated prejudice but a woeful ignorance of history.

Like Maximilian Kolbe, Campion paid the ultimate price. But

I have included his story here because it opens a more honest debate about the wrongs we have inflicted on each other; it might also help shed some light on why divisions run as deep as they do and why some choose as their right to cling to traditions that trace their origin to the arrival of Augustine in England – sent by another Italian, Pope Gregory.

Our Christian Heritage

In 1962 my parents sent me to Campion School in Hornchurch. It was a boys' grammar school inspired by a Christian ethos and named by its Jesuit founders after a sixteenth-century English martyr. Coming from an Irish Catholic tradition I had no personal links with the story of English Catholicism, but I had always been interested in history. I thrilled to the stories told about Campion, the image of the hunted priest, the willingness to pay the ultimate price for his beliefs.

Some time later I found a rare copy of Campion's biography by Evelyn Waugh, perhaps the most inspiring book he ever wrote. In its pages I found a copy of 'Campion's Brag', an open letter addressed to Elizabeth I and her Council. The letter was written in haste in East London, with the horses saddled at the door for a missionary journey and the threat of capture, torture and death close at hand. Yet Campion wrote in those few minutes a foundation document for the persecuted Church that echoes to our own day. Writing of the young Englishmen exiled to the Colleges abroad Campion reminds the Queen that: 'Many innocent hands are lifted up to heaven for you daily by those English students, whose posterity will never die, which beyond the seas, gathering virtue and sufficient knowledge for the purpose are determined never to give you over, but either to win you heaven or to die upon your pikes.' Campion School, and those who are formed in faith within its walls, are part of that posterity. I am conscious that but for the sacrifices made by men and women whom we have almost forgotten, places such as Campion School would not exist. I do not need any convincing about the importance of allowing Christian schools and I am not surprised that secularists within the political parties now have them within their sights.

It saddens me that the story of the Catholic and Protestant martyrs is not comprehensively taught in all our schools today. Understanding what has been done in the name of religion engenders a determination to resist repetition. We need a suitable mixture of shame and pride, sadness and inspiration, never forgetting that this is English history, not some other nation's. These were English men and women and what happened to them happened in London, Lancashire and in every corner of the kingdom, not some faraway land which has nothing to do with us. Campion's story is part of this nation's history.

I write this in my Commons office high above the great bulk of the medieval hammer-beamed Westminster Hall. It was in that very Hall in 1582 that Campion faced his fellow Christians who were to condemn him to death for his faith. In our ecumenical age it seems an embarrassment to recall that both Catholic and Protestant once persecuted each other but it would be a tragedy for us to forget. The persecutions of the Reformation period remind us of our fallibility as Christians. Our forebears persecuted others because they believed it was their duty under God. In a more tolerant age we have the opportunity to atone for their errors by the love we bear for each other.

The history of the Church echoes the story of Christ. The blood of martyrs, the 'seed of the Church', has played a central part in the evangelisation of the world. We live in an age of martyrdom and elsewhere in this book I record the lives of some modern martyrs. More Christians have given their lives for Christ in our own time than ever before. From Latin America to Eastern Europe, from the Middle East to China,

Christians daily risk their lives and liberty, and each sacrifice mirrors the crucifixion.

> Listen, I am sending you out like sheep to the wolves ...
> For My sake you will be brought to trial before Rulers
> and Kings ... When they bring you to trial do not worry
> about what you will say, or how you will say it; when the
> time comes you will be given what you will say. For the
> words you speak will not be yours; they will come from
> the Spirit of your Father speaking through you. (Matt.
> 10:16–20)

We should treasure the stories of our martyrs for through the candlelight of the torture chamber, the smoke of the Smithfield fires or the noise of the crowd at Tyburn, God's grace shines through, redeems and makes all well.

Campion's Story

The watchers at Dover had been warned in advance. Reports from the Government's spies on the continent had been circulated giving the descriptions of two Catholic priests, both wanted by the Government, who would attempt to slip through the Channel ports. In the event, the port authorities stopped the right men but failed on both occasions to make an arrest. The first, Robert Persons, sometime fellow of Balliol College, Oxford, and now the superior of the new Jesuit English mission, came through disguised as a soldier returning from the European wars. Halted by the searchers he bought them several rounds in the local tavern and then hurried away to London. The second, Edmund Campion, disguised as a jewel merchant was less fortunate. He was interrogated and then placed alone in a room. Arrest must have seemed imminent when orders arrived to let him go. When an angry Government ordered an investigation the excuse of the watchers was that they had released Campion because he seemed such a 'mild-mannered' man.

It is that charm, courtesy and gentleness that combined with his scholarly background which seemed to make Campion so unfit for the mission of the last two years of his life. The Elizabethan age was dominated by heroes: it was the time of Drake and Raleigh, explorers and soldiers, strong men raised in a hard school typified by the bear pit and the cock fight, the public floggings and executions. It was an age when England was first discovering a broad-shouldered, brawling nationalism that fuelled by the Armada victory and the growth of empire, would dominate our national character down to our own times. Into this England Campion returned as a scholar and priest to be put to the test as a man of action. Despite this contradiction in terms Campion was very much a man of his times. He came not from the old feudal aristocracy but the new burgeoning middle class. The son of a City tradesman, he won a scholarship offered by the London Grocers to Oxford where at St John's College his natural genius and scholastic brilliance marked him out for patronage and academic success. He was the darling of the University. When Queen Elizabeth and the court visited Oxford in 1566 it was Campion who was chosen to debate before her and Campion who won the royal approval and academic plaudits. Leicester, the Queen's favourite, summoned him and promised him patronage. The State needed leaders for its new Church. On the passing of the Elizabethan Religious Settlement in 1559, the whole bench of Bishops had resigned except the Bishop of Llandaff, and he refused to officiate and ordain. The rest were now in prison, retirement or exile. For the clever and ambitious there was a swift route to the top and Campion had all the necessary qualities.

But this was also an age of religious ferment and debate. England was newborn to its Protestant destiny and the wounds of Reformation had not yet healed to scars. It was a bare forty years since Elizabeth's father had set out to loot and destroy the monastic foundations that provided England with its only educational and charitable network. All over the land the abbeys stood gaunt and empty, quarries for the building of the great houses of the newly enriched. It would take another century for them to become the romantic ruins we see today. As families munch their picnics amongst the stones of a ruined abbey church, I wonder whether they ever pause to think about those who prayed, worked and lived there. In his excellent book *The Stripping of the Altars*,[1] Eamon Duffy reveals a picture of English Christian life altogether different from that offered by apologists for the dissolution of monastic life.

In the sixteenth century Englishmen were still mostly Catholic in sympathy and sub-Catholic in practice. The Reformation had been imposed from the top down and it had prompted both rebellion and riot. But the new learning of Geneva and Magdeburg was making ground. The brief and bloody reaction under Mary I with the brutal burning of Protestant dissenters had failed to halt the progress of Protestantism in England. All this was reflected in Oxford where the University was riven into factions of reactionary Catholics and radical Protestants. Campion hitched his coat to the ascendant Anglican star and received minor orders. That way lay preferment and success, but as he studied and read the Church Fathers his conscience began to nag. He took his doubts to his friend Tobie Matthew, later Archbishop of York. Matthew's reply must have shaken him: 'If I believed them as well as read them you would have good reason to ask.'

The moment of decision was upon him. Future promotion depended on Anglican ordination. He was probably already attending secret Catholic services. What did he hear God say as he bowed his head in prayer? On the one hand lay peace, status and wealth; on the other lay turmoil, sacrifice and oblivion. It was Campion's private Gethsemane. He left Oxford and travelled to the English colony at Dublin. There he threw himself into the work of the foundation of what was to become

Trinity College. But he was not allowed to rest. His patrons pursued him with letters and demands for an explanation, they were not about to let him slip through their fingers. He left Ireland and slipped back to London. He was probably present at the trial of Dr Storey, a Catholic refugee and a former Oxford tutor. He had been kidnapped from Antwerp and arraigned on a charge of high treason. He was condemned to death and hanged, drawn and quartered. Before the month was out Campion had taken ship for France.

At Douai he presented himself to Dr, later Cardinal, William Allen. Allen, another former Oxford don, presided over a new English Catholic College, established beyond the reach of persecution with the objective of training a new generation of English priests to take the place of those who had conformed or were now languishing in prison. At Douai Campion was welcomed with open arms, he was reconciled to the Church and began to live that regular Catholic life of a religious house with its round of prayer, praise and the sacraments. But still he felt drawn on. He left Douai and undertook a pilgrimage on foot to Rome, begging his bread on the way. On arrival he found the residence of the General of the Jesuits and asked to be admitted as a novice.

The Society of Jesus, known as the Jesuits, was then a mere thirty years old and had been founded by a fiery Basque nobleman, Ignatius Loyola. Ignatius, a soldier of uncertain morals and unquestioned courage, had been wounded in a border skirmish between France and Spain. The conversion experience that dominated his recuperation had prompted him to seek Christ in all things, and he developed a new 'Ignatian' spirituality that culminated in the formation of a new religious order. It was an order fit for its time, the spearhead of the Counter-Reformation and Catholic renewal.

From the beginning the Jesuits attracted men of brilliance and action. Vowed to poverty, chastity and obedience, Jesuits refused Church careers and promotion and concentrated on evangelism. Men such as Francis Xavier were opening new mission fields around the world, taking the Gospel to the Indians of Canada and the slaves of South America, to the Courts of the Emperor of China and the Great Mogul of India. In Europe Jesuit philosophers and academics dominated the religious and scientific debates. Others founded a new network of free schools, colleges and universities where children of all denominations were taught on the then revolutionary theory that pupils learned more when they enjoyed their work. Jesuit theologians were at the centre of the reforming Church Council of Trent and Jesuit confessors guarded the consciences of the Catholic Courts of Europe. The epitome of a 'preaching and teaching' order, Campion had at last found a home and was at peace.

But it was a demanding home. The training of a Jesuit novice took no account of personal status and paid no respect for congenial or safe surroundings. Campion was dispatched to Prague, an area at the heart of the Reformation debate. There he scrubbed the college floors, dug the garden and manned the kitchen with fellow novices. As he progressed through the Society he taught in the school, wrote plays for his pupils and made pastoral visits to the local community. He had been absent from England for nearly ten years and his vocation as a priest and teacher stretched before him. The Jesuits had no thought of a mission to England and all Church authorities, except Cardinal Allen, were agreed that the country was too dangerous for priests to operate in, without going like lambs to the slaughter.

That policy changed in 1579. In part this was due to Cardinal Allen's persistence in pleading the case for a mission; it was also due to the repeated urgings of the English Catholic community themselves. English Catholics had been without a bishop since 1559. While some priests from Mary's reign remained at large, they were a rapidly declining group. Old age and the rigours of a life in hiding were taking their toll. If the faith was to survive, then the vineyard must have labourers. Rules for operating undercover in England were drawn up, and the first of these was that those on the English mission should not become involved in politics or political discussion. Their first and only duty was the cure of souls.

The English mission would operate against a background of a series of 'penal' laws designed to eradicate Catholicism in a generation. This legislation, the bulk of which would remain on the statute books for the next two and a half centuries, was both comprehensive and savage and attacked every aspect of Catholic life. Emancipation finally came in 1829, when Catholics were once again permitted to stand for Parliament. Some vestiges – such as the provisions which disbar a member of the Royal family from the succession for marrying a Catholic – remain to this day. Intriguingly, only Catholics are singled out in this way in modern Britain, these disabilities do not affect any other denomination or faith.

The main target for the legislation was the Mass. For those who would not conform to Anglicanism, failure to attend the State Church brought with it massive fines amounting to £20 per person per month, more than a working man's annual income. For hearing Mass the penalty was a year's imprisonment and a £66 fine. Failure to pay fines led to confiscation of land and property. 'Harbouring' or giving hospitality to a priest was high treason. Returning as a priest ordained overseas was also high treason. High treason was punished with the barbaric ritual of hanging, drawing and quartering.

The State extracted oaths of religious conformity. Failure to swear involved fines, imprisonment and loss of estates and land. The penalty for a second refusal was death. Catholics were barred from all offices and state employment requiring oaths and from the universities where oaths were required to graduate. Children of Catholic families could be removed from their parents to be educated in Protestant families. Sending children overseas for education was a crime. A Catholic could not own weapons, a horse of a value of more than £5. And a Catholic could not go within five miles of a major town.

In 1559 the country had been almost wholly Catholic in sympathy, but by 1580 the laws were taking their toll. Fines threatened to ruin families at all levels of society. The heads of leading Catholic families around whom resistance might have gathered were either in prison or threatened with imprisonment. Those who remained at large were constantly beset by informers and 'priesthunters', men specifically employed to track down and capture priests and their hosts and who were paid from the proceeds of the fines and confiscations that resulted.

Such a penal system stretched conscience to the limit. For those who were Catholic in faith had to choose between conforming to the State Church or the loss of family, fortune and liberty. Against this background the coming of the first Jesuits was like rain to a parched land. And their coming was well heralded. The final party included, besides Persons and Campion, Ralph Sherwin and Luke Kirby. All except Persons would be called to make the final sacrifice. They gathered in Rome and spent their last night at the English College. The risks of the mission were well known. The night before they left Campion found a note pinned to his door inscribed: 'Fr E. Campion, Martyr'. As they left they were blessed by St Philip Neri with the words '*Salvete flores martryrum*' 'Hail to the flower of Martyrs'. Last year on a visit to Rome I stayed at the English College. In the balcony of the College Church are murals depicting the martyrdom suffered by the young Englishmen from the college when they returned home.

In London the missionaries found a Church devoid of leadership and beset by confusion. Attempts to find a compromise with the State had split the community. There was a desperate need for priests with many Catholics having been deprived of the sacraments for many years.

Their first action was to summon a meeting of the Catholic

laity and clergy. The secret 'Southwark Synod' reviewed all the points at issue and decided on a policy of no-compromise. Catholics were not to attend Anglican churches or receive Anglican sacraments. It was also decided that the Papal Bull excommunicating Elizabeth, and absolving Catholics of their obedience to the State in all things but faith was not applicable because it had not yet been published in England. Campion at all stages honoured the Queen's right to rule. He dissented in matters of faith, following Thomas More's famous dictum that he was 'The king's good servant, but God's first.'

One of Campion's first Masses on English soil was celebrated at the house of Lord Norreys. The room was packed with Londoners and courtiers, many of whom had not attended Mass in years. A contemporary observer records that the audience was moved to tears when Campion preached on the text: 'Tu Es Petrus ...'; 'You are Peter and upon this rock I will build my Church.'

It was in London that Campion met George Gilbert, a young man about town. Gilbert's interests had been devoted to the hunting field before a conversion experience had changed his priorities. He gathered about him a group of young Catholic gentlemen. They would escort the priests and provide local knowledge as well as funding the mission.

Persons and Campion split the country between them for their first missionary tour. Persons would ride through the West Midlands and Campion through the Home Counties. On the day they left they met at Hoxton on the outskirts of the City. There they were approached by Thomas Pounde, himself under sentence of imprisonment. Pounde argued that if they were caught, the Government would seek to prove them traitors. They should now write a statement of their purpose which could be produced in the event of capture. It was the work of a few moments but Pounde was so moved by the document that he had it immediately printed and circulated. Copies proliferated rapidly and 'Campion's Brag', as it came to be called, became the manifesto of the mission. Campion wrote it as a challenge to debate; he had come 'of free cost to preach the Gospel, to minister the Sacraments, to instruct the simple, to reform sinners, to confute errors – in brief to cry alarm spiritual against foul vice and proud ignorance . . .' And he ends:

> If these my offers be refused . . . and I having run thousands of miles to do you good, shall be rewarded with rigour, I have no more to say but to recommend your case and mine to Almighty God, the searcher of hearts, who send us His grace, and set us at accord before the day of payment, to the end we may at last be friends in heaven, when all injuries shall be forgotten.

The missionaries spent the next few months riding a wide circuit through the countryside. It is possible to piece together their route, but any exercise of this kind is always open to doubt. They travelled dressed as gentlemen. The objects for the Mass were hidden in their saddle bags. The open hospitality of the great houses of the day allowed them to stay in Protestant homes and minister to the Catholic servants. Introductions from one Catholic family to the next led them on and laid the basis for the network of houses that would shelter priests for the next century.

The fact that two Jesuits were at large in England was treated as something of a crisis by the Government. Propaganda talked of a Spanish-inspired fifth column active in the lanes and villages. Persons and Campion were now the subject of a concerted man-hunt. Compared to those who followed, they were ill-provided for. Arrest and betrayal were a constant threat. Some Catholic houses were equipped with hiding holes but these were few and far between. On one occasion when the priesthunters came into view it was the quick wits of a maidservant that saved Campion. She pushed him into a duck pond and read him a lecture as the priesthunters rode laughing by.

On another occasion Persons was forced to spend a wet and miserable night hiding in a haystack.

Campion commented:

> I cannot long escape ... The enemy have so many eyes, so many tongues, so many crafts. I am in apparel to myself very ridiculous; I often change my name also. I read letters sometimes myself that in the first front tell news that Campion is taken ... I find many neglecting their own security to have only care for my safety.

While Campion was away four of the few priests in England were tracked down and arrested. On his return to London he met Persons at Uxbridge. The capital was now too dangerous and Persons dispatched Campion into Lancashire and Yorkshire, both still heavily Catholic in sympathy. Persons also instructed him to produce a new statement of faith to follow up on the success of the 'Brag'. Meanwhile, Persons would remain in London to organise printing and meet incoming priests.

It was six months before Campion returned to London. By then a secret press had been established at East Ham. But London was too hot to hold such a venture. The servant of the stationer informed on his master and Persons' home was raided. Fr Alexander Briant was arrested nearby, hurried to the rack, and only emerged from the Tower for his trial and execution. The press was finally moved to the attics of Stonor Park near Henley after one of Persons' workmen was arrested and tortured. Campion's manuscript was ready by Easter and the final work was printed in June 1581. The 'Ten Reasons' was a further challenge to debate. It was a work of its time dealing with the controversies of the day. The Sunday after publication it was distributed in the pews of St Mary's Oxford, the University church, before the service began. The work caused a sensation and, rare for its kind, has been reprinted more than fifty times since.

Campion left London shortly afterwards. Persons and he exchanged hats as they parted, perhaps a sign at the time of a particularly solemn farewell. Campion's first call was the house of Lyford Grange in Oxfordshire. The owner, Mr Yates was in prison but his wife Margaret still ran the house as a local Catholic centre. There was even a group of Catholic nuns in residence. Campion said Mass, preached and then hurried on his way to Oxford. Shortly afterwards a group of Catholic friends arrived at Lyford. They were disappointed to have missed the famous Fr Campion and Mrs Yates was prevailed upon to dispatch a servant to plead with the priest to return. The messenger caught up with Campion at an inn outside Oxford, and the priest, ever willing to answer the call, agreed to ride back.

Mass that evening was crowded and emotional. In the dimly lit upper room Campion heard confessions, and then offered up the Eucharist. As he said the words still present in the Mass 'On the night He was betrayed He took bread . . .' Campion began his own passion, for at the back of the room was the man who would betray him. After Mass he preached on the subject of Christ weeping over Jerusalem. The text of the Gospel of the day could not have been more appropriate: 'Jerusalem, Jerusalem, thou that killest the prophets.' It was as though he had an intimation that the race was coming to an end. He had always felt that he had been singled out for sacrifice. Persons records that Campion when he was riding out of London would stop at Tyburn, the scene of so many martyrdoms, to pray 'because he said he would have his combat there'.

George Elliot was a professional priesthunter, a man who masqueraded as a Catholic and then passed the information he gathered to the State. He must have thought that he had struck gold when he discovered Campion in the house and as the party dispersed he rode post-haste to the nearest Justice of the Peace and summoned out the Watch. Later that night Lyford Grange was surrounded. As the Justices hammered on the gate, servants were dispatched to delay them while Campion and another priest were hurried into a priest hole.

The search was brutal and competent. The rooms were measured, the walls and chimneys sounded. Where the walls rang hollow the panelling and plaster were ripped out. After two days, while it was obvious that Mass had been said in the house, the Justices were on the verge of giving up. But Elliot prevailed on them to stay at the task. Finally one of the searchers spotted a chink of light in an area of unbroken panelling, and seizing a crowbar, he tore away the wood to reveal the two priests lying in a narrow space. The priests, seeing that the game was up, 'courteously surrendered themselves'.

Campion was led to London tied to a mule with a cap bearing the legend 'Campion, seditious Jesuit'. At the inn where they stopped for the night the party was woken by screams. One of the other prisoners had dreamed that he was being disembowelled by the hangman. Campion was taken to the Tower, where he disappears from view for four months. What happened within its walls has been pieced together from Government records. Campion was the Government's most important catch and their dealings with him had two aims. First, to reveal the names of those who sheltered him and second, to make him conform. In the Elizabethan police state there were no qualms about means. He was questioned closely but refused both the offer of an Anglican Church career and his freedom if he would conform. He would not reveal the names of his hosts. His gaolers placed him in the cell known as 'Little ease'. The space hollowed out of the damp Tower walls was too small to lie down or to stand up in. Campion remained there, his body wracked with cramp and cold. Then he was suddenly removed and brought before the Queen and Leicester. They questioned him closely. Was his mission treasonable? At the end they said they could find no fault with him except his Catholicism, 'Which is my greatest glory,' Campion replied. They offered him life, career and position if he would reject his faith. He again refused; then the warrant to put him to the torture was produced.

Strong men were known to break down at the sight of the rack. Campion, the gentle scholar, stretched out his arms voluntarily. He said afterwards that he was racked so severely that he thought they meant to kill him. The rack stretched every muscle to breaking point and then stretched them a little more. At every point the promise of an end to the pain was offered if only he would answer the questions; instead Campion prayed. When the pain became too intense he passed out. Asked by his gaoler how he felt after a session on the rack Campion replied, 'Not ill, because not at all.' When he later appeared at his trial he was unable to lift his right arm to take the oath.

Meanwhile the Government began to arrest Catholics on the grounds that Campion had confessed all and implicated them. There were Government-sponsored reports that he had weakened and would attend an Anglican service and repudiate Catholicism. Persons could get no news and feared the worst. And then Campion was paraded in public, not as a broken man, but to debate religion with the leading Anglican authorities. Having failed to torture him into acquiescence, the government now wished to discredit him and his case in debate. But they had mistaken their man: Campion, weak from torture, still possessed his incisive mind. Dragged from the Tower he faced a panel of learned theologians. Those who attended the debate heard again the old eloquence, the reasoned phrases that had made him the champion of Oxford debates. 'In condemning us you condemn all your own ancestors – all the ancient priests, bishops and kings – all that was once the glory of England ... For what have we taught, however you may qualify it with the odious name of treason, that they did not uniformly teach?' The Government divines were coming off worst, the debates were hurriedly stopped and Campion was scheduled with other Catholic prisoners for trial for his life on a charge of high treason.

Fifty years earlier Thomas More had stood his trial in the same cause in Westminster Hall. Now Campion and six other priests were brought to the same place packed with the London crowd. There was no attorney for the defence, the jury had been handpicked and brought in its verdict of 'guilty'. The judge pronounced sentence of death by hanging, drawing and quartering. The prisoners at the bar with one voice broke into the ancient hymn of thanksgiving 'Te Deum Laudamus', 'We praise Thee God'.

On a wet December morning Campion and two other priests were taken from the Tower and bound upside down on wicker hurdles, each hurdle behind a horse. As Campion emerged from the Tower he blessed the crowds. As the hurdles jolted their way along the muddy road down what is now Holborn and Oxford Street the procession became a Tudor road to Calvary. A man stepped out from the crowd and wiped the mud from Campion's face. As they passed beneath Newgate Arch Campion noticed a statue of the Virgin that had escaped the Calvinist hammers and saluted it with his bound hands.

Tudor executions were a public spectacle and entertainment. The crowd was densely packed around the gallows, not far from where Marble Arch stands today. A community of contemplative nuns now have their convent in the shadow of Tyburn dedicating their lives to prayer for our country. Close to the foot of the cross-bar were a group of mounted courtiers come to argue the toss to the moment when Campion was swung out into eternity. It was customary to speak to the crowd before the hangman began his work. Campion began to talk but was shouted down by the courtiers. He began to pray in Latin, the courtiers called on him to pray in English. 'I will pray to God,' said Campion, 'In a language that both He and I understand.' They called on him to pray for the Queen, then asked him which Queen he prayed for: 'Yea for Elizabeth, your Queen and my Queen unto whom I wish a long quiet reign with all prosperity.' With the noose around his neck he forgave those who had brought about this death. Then with the words 'Into Your hands, Lord I commend my spirit' on his lips, he was turned into the open air.

Campion's Legacy

It is a measure of a man's life to consider his legacy. In material terms there is little to say for Campion died vowed to poverty. The State may have assumed that they had done for him for good but the effects of his life and death continued long after the executioner had hacked his body into quarters.

At the scafford among the finely dressed young men was a young courtier, Henry Walpole. From a landed family he had conformed to Anglicanism with few qualms and joined the pursuit of honours and wealth at Court. When the hangman threw Campion's quarters into a cauldron of pitch, Walpole was standing so close that he was splashed with Campion's blood. At that instant he pledged to follow Campion and within weeks had crossed the seas to begin a new life as a Jesuit priest. He returned on the English mission and was executed at York in 1593.

There were more humble people who benefited from Campion's life. His gaoler converted and found a permanent refuge for his family and himself in a Catholic house on the Continent. There were the many who owed their baptism and faith to Campion but whose gratitude through the secrecy of the times went unrecorded. And then there was the folk memory surviving down to the last century of the disguised priest riding through the countryside summoning the people back to the faith with that irresistible eloquence and good humour.

For his fellow Catholics Campion stood at the head of the

roll-call of English martyrs. He epitomised all the fervour, the gallantry and the sacrifice of what seemed a hopeless and pointless cause. Two and a half centuries after his martyrdom when it became legal to practise the faith again, the fact that it had survived in so many places was a testimony to Campion and his friends. And his example is still before us challenging us to stand against the seemingly irresistible tide that sweeps against Christianity. We enjoy the peace and harmony between Christians that he prayed for, now we face in a gentler time the threat of apathy and secularism. With Campion we should remind ourselves that we are engaged in an ongoing struggle and take heart from his words: 'The expense is reckoned, the enterprise begun. It is of God, it cannot be withstood. Thus the faith was planted, thus shall it be restored.'

Chapter Seven

Maggie Gobran

MOTHER OF CAIRO

Truth lives on in the midst of deception.

Schiller, *On The Aesthetic Education of Man*, 1795

Egypt has the largest Christian community in the Arab world. One conservative estimate suggests that there are 9,900,000 Christians there. Most of the Christians are members of the Coptic Orthodox Church. The writer of one of the four Gospels, St Mark, is traditionally described as the founder of the Coptic Church. Coptic simply means Egyptian in the pre-Arabic language of the country.

In my travels to Egypt, I have had the privilege of meeting many devout and inspiring Christians who are working against tremendous odds to be faithful servants of God. One example is Maggie Gobran, who is one of those extraordinary women you meet from time to time. You meet them in chaotic surroundings, calmly making sense of suffering and hardship which would crush most of us. You meet them in refugee camps, in relief operations, in war zones. You find them with the sick, the handicapped and in the suffocating poverty of sprawling slums. When no one else cares, you will find women like Maggie Gobran loving the unloved. This forty-sixty-year-old woman, the daughter of an Egyptian doctor, is a remarkable person and a true sign of contradiction in our times.

It is to the poorest of Cairo's many poor people that Maggie Gobran has committed her life and, seeing her at work there, I was not surprised to hear the words 'Mother of Cairo' on the lips of those who know her work. Her philosophy was wonderfully familiar; quoting Mother Teresa of Calcutta, Maggie Gobran says, 'We can do no great things – only small things with great love.'

Youth With A Mission leader Floyd McClung calls Maggie Gobran 'the Mother Teresa of Cairo'. Expatriates living in the city have dubbed her 'St Maggie', but to thousands of children and their parents who live in the squalid shanty towns of Cairo – a city of 14 million people – Maggie is simply known as 'Mama Maggie'. 'This is all I want to be – a mother to them all,' Maggie has said. For the past four years Maggie Gobran has been taking small, practical initiatives to help allieviate the grinding poverty which faces so many families in Cairo. Her workers are trained to give advice and practical support to struggling families. Great emphasis is placed on self-help and personal enrichment. Children who have had little or no education are given training in a range of new skills. I saw for myself a workshop which she has established in a Cairo slum, equipping young trainees with a skill which will make them a living. Practical support is also given to mothers struggling to rear children in impossible circumstances. All too frequently women have been abandoned by men seeking a second wife or by a man who has travelled abroad looking for work and has then absconded. His former wife and children become trapped in the hell of slum life. In tiny rooms they sleep on floors and in makeshift beds. There without the protection of a father, the whole family becomes vulnerable to repeated attacks.

Physical and sexual abuse of children has become widespread as some men living in adjacent accommodation take advantage of the situation. Abused and defiled, one little girl with whom Maggie Gobran has been working had become introverted and withdrawn, refusing to speak to anyone. The child's suffering could not have been healed by a hand-out or by a polemical discourse about the root causes of poverty. She needed, and has been shown, a healing hand. By spending time with youngsters like this little girl, Maggie Gobran helps the children to discover what it feels like to be loved and valued. Rebuilding a family's self-esteem is a laborious and painstaking task. There are no short cuts. Sometimes the help which is given will be training in a workshop or the provision of equipment or tools. Sometimes, it will be good food and health care or time away at one of the family camps which she has established.

'My team goes and sits with the children in their homes,' Maggie says. 'They just go and sit and listen.' By doing this, the team members learn more intimately the specific needs of the children. 'Like Jesus did,' Maggie says. 'He went from place to place and stretched out His hand and touched people.'

Watching girls making their own clothes with the aid of modern looms, and young boys turning out shoes in an adjacent workshop, graphically illustrated to me how small steps can so easily be taken to give youngsters basic skills. Bigger, long-term projects, including land reclamation schemes and manufacturing co-operatives, are also planned.

I was struck by another similarity with the work undertaken by Mother Teresa. Maggie Gobran has the same great capacity to inspire people to do things which they might not normally consider doing. A doctor's daughter herself, she has secured the voluntary help of some of Cairo's top doctors in providing medical check-ups for needy families. She has also inspired young people to commit themselves to individual families; and she is bringing to the Church in Egypt, whose own members number some 2 million slum dwellers in Cairo, a sense of urgency in addressing chronic poverty.

Maggie Gobran's Vision

Maggie Gobran is a soft-spoken spiritual woman, whose manner is compassionate and deeply rooted in her own Coptic Christian spirituality. Her organisation, 'Stephen's Children', is well named. It recalls the suffering of the first Christian martyr, Stephen. The youngest daughter of a well-to-do family in Cairo's Coptic Orthodox community, Maggie says she became a 'serious Christian' in her early school years. She was inspired by a godly aunt who demonstrated the power of Christ's love to change lives.

About fifteen years ago, when Maggie and her husband were raising their own two children, a dream to reach out to the city's poorest children took shape. 'After my own children were born, I pictured myself with maybe ten needy children sitting around me,' she recalls. A vision formed in her mind, to adopt them all. It was her dream 'to give them care and love, to tell them stories from the Bible, to like them just the way they are – dirty, ugly, whatever. And then to see them grow up with love'. But she admits that her vision ended there. She never intended it to evolve into the far-reaching ministry she heads today.

Over the years Maggie became a successful professional, first on the management team of a marketing firm and later as a university professor in computer science. But her real satisfaction came in seeing her friends and students respond to Christ's love. Even then she had the vision of a circle of needy children seated around her. The vision grew stronger after a devout Christian prophesied to her, 'You will minister among both the very rich and the very poor.' At that time, like most urban Egyptians, she had little idea of what central Cairo's slums – some twenty-three districts with a combined population of 6 million – even looked like. 'Or smelled like,' she adds wryly.

She decided to experience for herself what conditions were like in the slums. Together with Christians from the Coptic Orthodox, Catholic and Protestant Churches, she joined an Easter outreach, distributing food and clothing to the poor living in Cairo's shanty towns. She recalled that in the past, churches had held meetings for the poor, handing out money to the destitute mothers. 'But this ruined the mothers' self-respect, and there was hardly any touch of love. We were creating beggars through this kind of "help",' says Maggie. 'I realised then that I needed to give love and time – not just dole out money.'

Shocked by the despair she saw among families in the slums, Maggie said, 'I could not sleep for days and nights after [that first visit],' she admits. 'Those children were simply hungry for acceptance, for love and encouragement, and for someone to just listen to them and take them and their needs seriously.' Maggie began to pray for committed young people join her in working with the poor. It was to be a holistic approach by Egyptian Christians to meet the short- and long-term needs of destitute Egyptian children and their families. Drawing her team from the Coptic Church, as well as from Catholic and Protestant communities, Maggie asked them to lay aside doctrinal differences to express Jesus's love.

The Christians who joined Maggie's ministry received specialised training to work with Cairo's outcast communities. Some university graduates joined her by investing a year of their lives in practical outreach under her guidance. She was surprised to learn that among Cairo's slum population there were some 2 million people of Coptic Christian descent, scattered in 300,000 family units among predominantly Muslim neighbourhoods.

Maggie visited the children in their one-room shacks to find out what their overwhelming needs were. The typical family unit in Cairo is comprised of seven to fourteen individuals who share kitchen and bathroom facilities with several other families. 'If they have a bed, it is for the parents,' Maggie says. 'The children sleep beside them, or under the bed. One girl told me she had to lie down in the hall to find floor space to sleep!' Growing up in such close quarters often has horrible repercussions. Many of the children have been sexually abused since they were infants, often by their own siblings.

Most of the children's parents are villagers who move to

Cairo from rural Egypt in hope of finding jobs. They eke out an existence in the Cairo slums without electricity, sewage systems, public transportation, medical care or other services familiar to most city dwellers. Maggie points out that what further aggravates the situation is the near absence of husbands or fathers. Practically speaking, they are one-parent families.

One Coptic family that she vividly remembers lived in a 'home' located in a narrow alley between two houses. The space was covered with a makeshift roof. All the children were covered with scabs, simply because they had no access to water for bathing.

A Programme of Love

Maggie says that few of the Copts living in the slums have any understanding of their Christian faith. Even if they seek out the few churches within walking distance, most are ashamed to enter a church without shoes or proper clothes to wear. Although suffering from low self-esteem, the children respond quickly to consistent love. By contrast, their parents are usually too preoccupied with surviving to change their ways and values.

When specific children have been identified as requiring help, a comprehensive support programme is initiated at every level – material need, vocational training and spiritual and psychological counselling. Practical help rarely involves direct financial aid.

One moving story of how loving support can change children's lives concerns the story of little Samira. She was severely traumatised and speechless as a result of seeing her own father murder her mother in their filthy one-room apartment. Nothing could induce Samira to speak. It took months, but Maggie and her team persisted in reaching out to Samira with love and prayer for healing in the traumatised child's life. As a result of the loving care she received, Samira is now not only talking but even singing as well. Maggie says, 'This is what happens when

God touches people and really heals their wounds. At last they feel accepted and loved just as they are.'

Over the past twelve years, 'Mama Maggie' and her team have touched the lives of more than 1,000 families with this message. Because mothering remains the heart of the ministry, Maggie's dreams for her children never end. Three years ago Stephen's Children launched on-the-job training in shoemaking, sewing and knitting in a large workshop in one of Cairo's industrial zones. The vocational training unit has already equipped dozens of children to support themselves in a useful trade. When I visited it, the place was a hive of activity.

Today she is nurturing yet another dream. On the outskirts of Cairo, a land reclamation project is taking shape, which she hopes will enable the children to grow their own fruit and vegetables. 'Think what it will mean to these children!' she exclaims. The site will be suitable for a permanent training centre, far removed from the corrupt environment of slum life. Even though financing for such projects is always difficult to find, she remains undaunted. 'This is God's work. No human being can try to do this. We have seen the money we needed provided hundreds of times . . .'

The Coptic Heritage

This woman some refer to as 'Saint Maggie' does not think of herself as a hero. But, as a Coptic believer, Maggie is aware that she is part of a rich spiritual heritage. It is a heritage which we in the West ignore to our own considerable cost. There is also an unpleasing arrogance which implies that these ancient churches are semi-Christian. Their liturgy is complex and not always easy to understand but they might be similarly bemused by a Christian Greenbelt rock festival. In a Russian Orthodox church in Novgorod, in 1995, a companion was complaining to me about having to stand for nearly three hours during the liturgy we attended. She received her reply from an elderly

Russian woman behind us who had overheard these moans: 'I cannot comprehend,' she said, 'how you can sit before our God.' These are not medieval mendicants or prehistoric throwbacks bearing chronicles of wasted time. They are a part of the universal Church which has suffered grievously and which has much to teach us.

The ancient Coptic Church became ecclesiastically isolated from the Church in Europe in AD 451 when political differences with Rome led to an irrevocable split at the Council of Chalcedon. The conflict was over theology. The Copts maintained that the natures of God and Man are united in Christ, while the majority at the Council claimed that the two natures coexisted in Him. This theological difference distinguishes the Coptic Orthodox Church and other non-Chalcedonian Churches – i.e. the Armenian Apostolic Church and the Syrian Orthodox Church – from most other Christian Churches. The Coptic Orthodox Church is characterised by a strict adherence to its ancient creeds and liturgy and strong monastic tradition. In fact, one of the most sweeping influences of this Church on Christendom is monasticism, for it is in Egypt that Christian monasticism first began.

Maggie is grateful to be a part of this legacy. 'I am the daughter of all the prayers, tears and blood offered up to God in my country over many generations,' she says. 'I love my country, my people, my church and my needy children, and I am ready to give my life for them.'

The Coptic Orthodox Church has a rich spirituality to share with the world but sadly it has been isolated for many centuries and faces widespread persecution within Egypt. During two recent visits to the region I have been appalled by the persecution and privations being experienced by believers. I have also been inspired by the rich spiritual reserves on which their ancient churches draw.

Western Christians are often incredibly lazy about trying to understand the Orthodox tradition. Some are downright ignor-

ant and offensive in dismissing its rituals and way of life.
Ironically, if it were better understood it might provide the
perfect antidote to non-Christian Eastern mysticism. For those
seeking a deep spirituality and mysticism this is the real thing.

Dr Otto Meinardus gives an excellent introduction in his
book, *Monks and Monasteries Of The Egyptian Desert*, and
writes, 'St Antony (Abba Antunius) is the prototype of Coptic
asceticism in particular and of Christian monasticism in general.
The life, attitudes, the words and works of this great hermit of
the desert have influenced, and still influence, the lives of the
desert fathers, be they anchorites or coenobitic monks.'[1]

The monks were not escapists. The ancient Egyptians
regarded the desert as the domain of the devil to which he was
banished by God. Countless monks belonged to rich and
influential families and could have lived a life of luxury instead.
Whenever persecutions or plagues raged, these desert dwellers
left their abodes and went into the cities to face torture with
their brothers in the world. In addition, the persecutors
marched into the desert and did not hesitate to kill the monks.
Those who left the world sought seclusion with God. All the
early writers describe them as 'God's Athletes' seeking to be
'alone with the Alone'. It was hardly a quiet or soft life.

Coptic monasticism passed through three stages. The first
was complete solitude. The person seeking a life of prayer,
fasting and meditation, went alone into the desert, found some
natural cave or dug one for his or her purpose and lived there
for the rest of his or her life; unknown, unsought and completely alone. The most outstanding hermit is said to be St
Paul, the first solitary monk, who lived ninety years in utter
solitude, having left the world at twenty. According to tradition,
only a week before his death, an angel disclosed his secret to
St Antony, who sought him out and heard from him his own
story. A monastery still stands in the Eastern desert which
bears his name – it is in the vicinity of the cave where he lived.

The second stage was the Antonian rule. St Antony is the

prototype of Coptic asceticism in particular and of Christian monasticism in general. By the end of the fourth century the life of this saint was read even in faraway Gaul. When St Antony went into the desert, he assumed that he would be left alone like others who had gone before him. But he was not left alone for long. Many sought him out for spiritual counsel and physical healing. Many people today could do with the wise counsel of a spiritual director, preferable to the senior 'shrink' or psychiatrist's chair. Some of Antony's contemporaries were so attracted by his magnetic personality that they desired to stay with him. He advised each to find a cell in which to live from Sunday evening to noon on Saturday. At noon on that day, they all gathered round him and they spent time together until Sunday evening. He taught them that each had to work with their hands, alternating prayer with handiwork. 'For,' he said, 'a monk must earn his living. Also if many devils beset the idle, one only besets the worker.' He also prescribed a specific garb consisting of a white robe of flax reaching halfway between the knee and ankle, with a wide leather belt tightened round their waist. The present-day black robes worn by the Coptic monks and clergy were imposed by Sultan Al-Hakim in AD 979. This rule of five and a half days in solitude, and one and a half in companionship is known as Antonian monasticism. Since Abba Antony was the first desert dweller to have disciples whom he taught and directed he is known as 'The Father of Monks'.

The third stage of Coptic monasticism was the Coenobitical or Communal life, which was inaugurated by Abba Pakhom. Born of pagan parents, he entered the army of the Emperor Constantine aged twenty. One evening, he and his companions were made to encamp outside the city of Esnah (just north of Aswan). To his astonishment, some Esnites came out to them with food and water. They washed their hands and feet for them, then offered them the food and waited on them as though they were their servants. Amazed by this kindness,

Pakhom asked why. One of his companions answered: 'They are Christians, and their Christ enjoins them to love all people.'

Pakhom thought about this answer, and reflected that, 'If this is the commandment of Christ, then I must be a Christian if I return safely from the war.' On his return, he went to Esnah where he found, in the nearby desert caves, an aged ascetic called Palamon with whom he lived for three years. At the end of this period the saintly man advised him to find a cave in which to live alone. He began to believe that there must have been many who desired to give themselves wholly to God, but could not endure solitude. He began to pray about this and in answer to his prayers an angel guided him to build a monastery in which to gather those seeking to live in prayer and devotion but who were unable to live alone. He built the first monastery for men in Tabenissi in the upper reaches of the Nile. A few months later his sister Mary came to look for him. Charmed by his mode of life, she asked him to build a monastery for women and some of his monks built it for her nearby.

St Pakhom's monasteries did not attract only Egyptians – men and women from different countries came to live with them. Some stayed for the rest of their lives while others returned home after some years to start monastic life according to the Pakhomian Rule. In Egypt, the Pakhomian Rule remained the only order of monasticism, whereas in the West numerous orders evolved, yet they all sprouted from the same source. Hence, St Pakhom is called 'Father of the Coenobites'.

Coptic monasticism is characterised by its asceticism, mysticism and sacerdotalism. Although Egyptian monasticism and asceticism are usually regarded as synonymous, this assumption is not always correct, since not all monks are necessarily ascetes in the strict sense of the term. Asceticism and mysticism are different. The distinction is clearly pointed out by a monk of the Eastern Church who states: 'There is the same difference as between rowing a boat and sailing it; the oar is the ascetic effort, the sail is the mystical passivity which is unfurled to catch the divine wind.' This means that the ascetic life is a life of 'acquired' virtues, depending upon fasting, patient endurance, vigils, abstinence, weeping and mourning, voluntary poverty, humility, love and hospitality.

It is difficult to define an exact ascetic pattern among the monks of Egypt. All of them, however, held that the gratification of the senses was sinful, and that the desires of the flesh were to be subdued by fasting, abstinence, vigils, prayer and contemplation. Asceticism in Coptic monasticism is expressed in two forms: the solitary or anchoritic and communal or coenobitic type. Though the great hermits of the Wadi' Natroun and the Wadi' Arabah began their ascetic life as solitaries, they made their followers enter the cenobium first in order to be trained in the practice of asceticism. St Anthony forbade the young and inexperienced to enter the desert without passing through a period of probation. Thus, in order to live the solitary life, the monk first had to prove his worth in the communal life, and only after a period of probation was he permitted to undertake the solitary life.

Pope Shenouda the Third is the present Patriarch of the Coptic Orthodox Church. I met him in Cairo and subsequently in London when he spoke at the Anglican church of St Pancras. Pope Shenouda describes five stages or grades through which the solitary must pass before he reaches the stage of absolute isolation from the world. They are as follows:

1. As a member of the coenobitic community. 2. As a beginner in the solitary life within the monastery itself. The beginner observes complete silence, performing his work quietly, while remaining in his cell. He thereby develops a feeling of alienation from the community, so that he becomes 'a stranger' among his brethren. 3. He perseveres in this solitude for several weeks. At this stage, the monk still lives in the monastery, but leaves his cell only once a week on Sunday to attend the celebration of

the Divine Liturgy. 4. Transfer from the monastery to the cave, so as to be removed from all people. 5. The final stage is that of the itinerant anchorite, who lives in caves, unknown to anyone save God. Should, by chance, a solitary pay a temporary visit to his fellow monks or for some other reason be forced to leave his cave, he must on his return go through the earlier stages of preparation again before he can resume his solitary life.

Persecution of Christians

This, then, is the spiritually rich Egyptian Church of which Maggie Gobran is a member but it is also a Church bloodied by continuous persecutions. It was to Egypt that the Holy Family fled as refugees, escaping the fanaticism and infanticide of Herod. Legend has it that they lived in the Old City of Cairo, where Maggie continues the work of the contemporary Church.

Egypt's Christians regularly have to put up with fanaticism and persecution, with attacks from the Islamic extremists on the one hand and government persecution and indifference on the other. There are many Egyptian Muslims who have lived, for centuries, in a spirit of co-existence alongside their Coptic neighbours. This harmony has been threatened by an upsurge of Iranian-style extremism and by indifference from the authorities when minor officials behave in an unacceptable manner. One example of persecution is the treatment of converts from Islam to Christianity. For example, a twenty-six-year-old convert, Hanaan Assofti, was arrested by Egyptian State Security Officers on 10th October 1992 at Cairo International Airport. She was attempting to leave the country and to seek asylum and join her fiancé in Europe. Police told her father that she had intended to leave for Europe, where Christians would employ her as a prostitute. The woman's parents were advised that she should not be permitted to leave home without an escort for a period of one year. She has been regularly beaten by family members who are trying to convert her back to Islam. She has been forced to attend the Islamic Institute, where she has been told she will die for her conversion. At the time of writing her situation is still the same, despite numerous representations to the Egyptian authorities to ensure she is allowed to leave the country as she chooses. Many British Muslims who have campaigned alongside me on human rights issues would deplore this denial of human rights as strongly as I do. As both the 1994 Cairo Conference and 1995 Beijing Conference demonstrated, there are significant human rights questions – such as the sanctity of human life – about which a Christian–Muslim consensus can be created. Such co-operation is endangered when co-existence in either a predominantly Christian or Muslim country is threatened by belligerence and intolerance by the majority. This can manifest itself in life-threatening ways but also in petty niggling things.

A particular problem Egyptian Christians face is that of church building and maintenance. After my last visit to Egypt I launched a Jubilee Campaign report.[2] I helped establish the campaign in Parliament in the mid-1980s and have been its Parliamentary Sponsor. It has the active support of more than 100 MPs. In this we detailed the legal foundation for the Egyptian state's control of church property: the Ottoman Hamayouni Decree of 1856, which was amplified by the interior Ministry in 1934. The Hamayouni Decree remains a valid part of Egypt's civil law. It requires Christian congregations to submit petitions for any form of building, repair or renovation of church buildings to President Hosni Mubarak, the head of state. Any such work depends on his personal approval. Great bureaucratic hurdles must be overcome to build a church or even replace a pane of glass or to repair a toilet. The idea that the President must personally sanction repairs to a water closest is patently absurd. The church must satisfy the Ministry of the Interior, on behalf of the President, that the building is not less than 100 metres from a mosque or is not in a predominantly

Muslim neighbourhood, that local businesses and residents do not object and that there is no other place for local Christians to worship. By means of the decree the State officials can and routinely do obstruct church life by refusing or delaying permission for the building and repair of churches. Militant Muslims have been known to set up makeshift mosques near the site of planned churches or beside churches in need of repair, thereby giving the Government a legal pretext for preventing construction or repair.

To make matters worse, Egypt's Christians are under increasing pressure from extremists to convert to Islam. One common incentive being offered to Christians is the promise of financial rewards. Reliable sources indicate that the extremists are receiving funding for this 'evangelistic work' from countries like Saudi Arabia. Many of those born into poor Christian families are especially vulnerable to such pressure to convert as they usually know little about their own faith and are often illiterate. The Egyptian Church's attempts to strengthen the faith of these vulnerable impoverished Copts are seriously undermined by the Egyptian Government's refusal to replace the unjust laws on church building and maintenance with fair laws applying to both churches and mosques.

With an estimated 5,000 Copts pressured into converting to Islam each year, how many Christians will be left in Egypt in the medium to long term? Will the government of Egypt continue to look the other way while the decimation of the Coptic community continues?

I have seen with my own eyes the devastating results to which the indifference of the government and that of the international community can lead. In the autumn of 1994 I went to the restricted zone in the south-east of Turkey with the Jubilee Campaign and witnessed the remains of what was once a thriving ancient Christian community. It has many of the same characteristics and scars of Maggie Gobran's Coptic Church. Their story is a chilling warning of what may happen to the Copts. I published details in a further Jubilee Campaign report which I launched at a meeting in Parliament.[3]

The Assyrians (people whose traditional language is Syriac, a dialect of Aramaic, the language which Jesus spoke) inhabit the region of Tur Abdin, a mountainous area of south-eastern Turkey, near to the Syrian and Iraqi borders. Many Assyrians belong to the Syrian Orthodox Church. They were among the first to accept Christianity, probably as early as the first century. Since that time, the Christians in that region have frequently found themselves caught at the centre of numerous wars and political struggles. Around eighty years ago there were over 200,000 Assyrians in Tur Abdin but now the figure is nearer 2,000. Many left during and after the First World War, migrating to Europe, Australia and America. Since the commencement of hostilities between the Kurdistan Workers Party (PKK) and the Turkish Government, many more have preferred to leave rather than be embroiled in the conflict. The Assyrians are caught between the Kurdish rebels and government forces and are often accused by one side of helping the other. The destruction of Christian villages continues unabated. Bote, Zaz, Kerburan, Arnas, Keferbe, Mansurye and Kovankaya have all been emptied of Christians and, in many cases, their property has been divided among the Muslims.

Many churches have been converted into mosques including the Catholic Chaldean Church at Bote, the St Behnem Syrian Orthodox Church in Cizre and the St Esyo Syrian Orthodox Church in Mansurye. In 1994, an application was also made to convert the church in Goliye into a mosque.

One Christian contact told me when I was in Tur Abdin that the Turkish Government is indifferent to the plight of the Christian villages. There are mixed Christian and Muslim villages where the Christians have been pushed out. The source added that the Turkish Government should care for the villages and not let them be destroyed. As in Egypt, he believed that the government does nothing to help the Christians to stay.

The ancient homeland of the Assyrians has steadily been cleared of its Christian presence yet the international community and the Church have more or less been silent. If the cause of the Christians in that region had consistently been supported earlier, the decimation of their community might not have occurred.

Likewise, in Iran, Christians face terrible persecution from the fundamentalist government of that country. In December 1989, Rev. Hossein Soodmand, of the Assemblies of God, was hung by the regime simply because he had once been a Muslim and had converted to Christianity. He left a blind wife and four children. In 1994, three evangelical Christian leaders were assassinated in Iran. They were Bishop Haik Hovsepian-Mehr, Reverend Mehdi Dibaj and Reverend Tateos Michaelian. There is evidence that these killings were carried out by a death squad acting on the orders of the Iranian Government. Mehdi Dibaj's life was one long process of martyrdom. He was imprisoned by the regime for nine years, his only 'crime' being that of converting from Islam to Christianity. For two years he was held in solitary confinement in a tiny unlit cell, systematically tortured and subjected to a number of 'mock' executions to make him recant his Christian faith. In 1994, in *The Times* Bernard Levin wrote compellingly about the plight and fate of Mehdi Dibaj.

Pressure groups such as the Jubilee Campaign exist to raise awareness about the plight of persecuted Christians worldwide and to campaign for their rights. One Christian from a persecuted community in the Middle East told a member of the Jubilee Campaign, 'Your organisation should have existed 100 years ago.' I think he is right. Although we cannot turn back the clock, we can at least try to learn from the past and help those parts of the Church facing persecution.

Nowadays, Christianity is often perceived as a Western religion. This view is inaccurate and does little justice to the Christian communities such as the Coptic and Assyrian Christians that have existed in the Middle East since the time of the Early Church. We should not forget that many of the letters in the Bible to the Early Church were to churches in the Middle East, in parts of the world which are today predominantly Muslim. With the rise of Islamic extremism, many churches in the Muslim world are facing increasing persecution, as fanatics attempt to erase all traces of non-Islamic religions. The methods of the Crusaders are simply unacceptable whoever uses them.

While it is important not to show bigotry against Islam and Muslim people, we must also recognise that more extreme forms of Islam are being used to justify the persecution of others simply because of their religious beliefs. This is a growing problem. So what is the response of Christians in other parts of the world? I believe that Christians have to first recognise that there is a problem and seek to be informed about the issue. This information can be supplied by groups such as the Jubilee Campaign.[4] The next step would be to pray and campaign by, for example, writing to Members of Parliament, asking the MP to raise the matter with the ambassador of the country involved. The Jubilee Campaign gives helpful guidelines for those willing to take such action. There is a real danger that unless the Church in the non-Islamic world mobilises itself on this issue, we will eventually see the extinction of the Christian communities in the Muslim world. The populous Coptic Church of Egypt is one of the principal targets.

In countries like Egypt women like Maggie Gobran continue to bravely hold a candle for their faith. She reminds me of the New Testament women who were there with Christ at Calvary until the very end. After all the promises of loyalty and boasts of personal steadfastness had been made, it is disquieting to recall that the men – with the exception of John – cut and ran. Maggie Gobran and women like her in these ancient churches will quietly continue in their faithfulness, making sense of situations that others have abandoned.

Chapter Eight

Lin Xiangao

STILL PAYING A TERRIBLE PRICE

> And who-so wants to know where that Treuth dwells,
> I will direct you wel right to his place.
>
> William Langland, *Piers Ploughman*

The Chinese house church leader, Lin Xiangao, has been resisting the authorities ever since he was first arrested in 1950, when he said, 'If I have to choose between God and the rulers, I follow God.' I have included him in this collection because his brief story allows me to say something about the vast suffering of the Church in China, and the collaboration of the British Government in human rights abuses in China where infanticide is state-funded and women are forcibly sterilised.

Prisoner of Conscience

Lin Xiangao was born into a Christian family in Macau in 1924. 'Xian' means to offer and 'Gao' means the Lamb of God. His surname is also pronounced Lamb; Samuel Lam is his English name. His family greatly influenced him in spiritual matters from an early age as his father, Paul Lam was the pastor of a Baptist church. In 1955 Lin, who was at the time pastoring a church of 300, was branded an 'anti-revolutionist' and was imprisoned for two years. He later returned to his church but in 1958 was arrested again, this time for twenty years. As part of state-his punishment, he had to do hard labour, five years on a farm in Guangdong, followed by fifteen years in a coal mine. The conditions in the coal mine were extremely hazardous and there were several casualties, but Lin survived.

After sixteen years in prison, the Chinese authorites ordered him to criticise Christ and Christianity and he was told it would benefit him to do so. But Lin thought, 'What benefit? Perhaps I could be released immediately. But if I criticised Christ to come out four years early, my sixteen years in jail were all in vain.' He refused to do it. In his testimony, Lin says, 'I learnt a lesson from Peter. Peter boasted and fell. I was weaker than Peter, so I prayed and asked God to keep my faith, and God heard my prayer. In twenty years, I hadn't denied the Lord once. The Lord kept my faith.'

Lin was released from prison in 1978 and returned to Guangzhou (Canton) where he was welcomed by his children and grandchildren, but his wife had sadly died two years earlier. He began to teach English and the first one to believe in Christ was a young girl. Soon four people were meeting to worship God and these were baptised in 1980; since then, over 1,000 people have been baptised and despite the persecution, the church has grown. Today it has more than 1200 members.

Lin Xiangao has consistently resisted government pressure to register his church with the state-controlled religious organisation, the Three Self Patriotic Movement (TSPM) on the grounds that it is 'a tool to destroy Christianity'. He says, 'If I registered, it would become a political church and I couldn't preach the Bible freely.' His story eloquently and graphically contradicts the apologists for the Beijing Government who claim that religious liberties are enjoyed today in China.

Around midnight on Thursday 22nd February 1990 when 100 believers were worshipping in his church, officers of the Public Security Bureau (PSB) entered the building and challenged Lin to sign the official paper, registering his church with the TSPM. What followed is all too typical. Lin refused and was taken away by the PSB and interrogated with twelve others. Everything in his church was confiscated – Bibles, Christian literature, money, video equipment, a television, tape recording equipment and tapes. He was released after twenty-three hours of detention, ordered to stop religious activities and put under very close police surveillance. Despite all the harassment, he immediately began prayer meetings, and less than two months later held his first full-scale preaching service.

In November 1990, despite reported threats about his execution, it was business as usual at Lin's home. Talk of his execution did not slow down his campaign to restore his church activities to what they were prior to his arrest and the forced closure of his church. Lin said, 'I'm alive – at least for today.'

Since then, the questioning and the harassment have continued at regular intervals. Police posted a notice on his door forbidding 'illegal religious meetings' – someone tore it down.

In March 1992, the Guangzhou Public Security Bureau and the Religious Affairs Bureau (RAB) stepped up their coercion of Lin. He was interviewed by PSB and RAB officials on six separate occasions between 17th March and 10th April. On 24th March, his church was raided by PSB officers who were apparently searching for foreign-printed Bibles and Christian literature.

In the midst of his suffering, Pastor Lin remains calm and looks to God in faith. He has not capitulated to intimidation even though the closure of the Damazhan house church is still possible. Lin is a very public figure, but what happens to him is happening to many other house church pastors in China.

In an interview in 1992 Lin was asked what he remembered most from his time in prison. His reply was, 'Here you see ten fingers. The Lord protected them! I worked in a coal mine for fifteen years, and I estimate that I coupled up 2 million coal trucks in that time. It was back-breaking – rather, finger-breaking – work. The trucks would rush together; I had to join them. It is the grace of God I remember most.'

When asked what he missed most, his reply was reminiscent

of what priests sent by the Soviets to Siberia used to tell me. 'No Bible!' He paused, as if the very memory of the absence of a Bible caused him pain, then he continued, 'But the Lord had been preparing me, by training me to learn the Psalms and Epistles by heart, so I was able to recite the Scriptures to myself.'

His time in prison was not the only occasion that Lin felt under God's protection. From childhood he has believed, and related the many times God has spared his life. In his testimony he writes:

We lived in a damp place in a mountainous area. At about five years of age, I had a severe case of diphtheria. A doctor was called to give me a check up. He told my father that it was a very serious kind of bronchitis and I needed to go to hospital immediately. At that time there was a Baptist hospital in my area. An American doctor by the name of Dr Hartley, an ENT specialist began to treat me. There was little or no change in my condition.

In those days medicine was not comparable to what we have today. The doctors put me in a room and told my father that they may have to perform a tracheotomy to enable me to breathe. However, the doctors warned that I only had a 10 per cent chance of survival. My father said, 'If my son has only a 10 per cent chance of survival, I want him to die at home.' He took me home and asked all the people who believed in God to pray from night until day break. The next day Dr Hartley came to the house expecting me to be dead. He walked up the stairs very quietly and gently called my name. My father helped me up, and Dr Hartley cried out, 'Miracle! Miracle!' He was also a Christian. God had healed me.

Religious Persecution in China

Thankfully, there are many more Christians like Lin, who have
shown great courage in the face of persecution. In their joint
report, which I helped launch in Parliament in 1995, 'Religious
Persecution in the People's Republic of China',[1] produced by
the Jubilee Campaign and June 4th China Support, they record
Christianity's long history in China although until recent times,
it has largely been confined to immigrant groups. Christianity
has spread through China in four separate waves.

The first wave was Nestorian missionaries who arrived from
the Middle East in Xian (then the capital) in AD 635. Nestori-
anism never took root in China, partly because of syncretism
with Buddhism and the vast distances separating the church
from its home base. The Nestorian tablet in Xian remains the
chief evidence of this community.

Second, Franciscan friars were sent to China by the Pope,
arriving in 1294. By 1305 there were about 6,000 converts.
However, China was then ruled by the Mongols, and the
church seems to have been more successful among foreigners
living in China than among the Chinese themselves. In 1368
the native Ming dynasty drove the Mongol rulers from China
and the church soon disappeared in the tumult.

The third wave was more successful, although only among
the ruling elite. Jesuits, of whom the most famous was Matteo
Ricci, established themselves in Peking in 1601 at the court of
the Qing emperors. The Jesuits won several high officials to the
faith, and even members of the imperial family. Some 200,000
converts were made and churches set up in many parts of
China. However, these successes were reversed when the Pope
decreed in 1645 and again in 1704 and 1742 that ancestor
worship was idolatrous. The emperors retaliated, expelling
foreign priests and closing most churches. Only a remnant
community survived.

The fourth wave was the modern missionary movement

which began in earnest after 1842 when the Opium War opened China to foreign trade and foreign missionaries, both Protestant and Catholic. Robert Morrison had previously translated the Bible into Chinese. In 1865 Hudson Taylor founded the China Inland Mission which became the largest Protestant society, penetrating the remotest provinces. A large number of mission societies established schools, universities, hospitals and clinics. On the eve of the Communist victory in 1949 there were about 1 million Protestants and 3 million Roman Catholics in China.

Christianity, in the eyes of the Chinese Communist Party (CCP), was tainted through its associations with Western imperialism and gunboat diplomacy. Ideologically, the CCP is atheistic, and its policies towards religion in the 1950s appear to have been modelled on Stalinism, as this was the period when China was closely allied with the USSR. Premier Zhou Enlai met the Protestant leaders in 1950 and encouraged them to distance the Chinese Church from Western imperialism. Thereafter, pressures were increasingly brought to bear on the small Chinese Church. In 1950 during the Korean War all economic aid from the West to the Church was cut off and by 1952 most missionaries had been expelled. The CCP strongly pressed the churches to follow the concept of 'Three Self' (self-governing, self-supporting and self-propagating) which had been developed earlier by Protestant missionaries and Chinese church leaders.

However, 'Three Self' as advocated by the CCP and its supporters within the churches merely replaced dominance by Western missions with dominance by the CCP. Accusation meetings were held at CCP instigation at which church leaders who did not obey CCP policies were denounced and imprisoned. By the mid-1950s all denominational organisations had been dissolved. In 1958 most churches were closed under the pretence of unification under the 'Three Self' banner. Simultaneously, the Roman Catholic Church was attacked for its continued loyalty to Rome. The Catholic Patriotic Association (CPA) was formed and bishops were ordained without papal permission. Loyal Catholics went underground, and many bishops were imprisoned for over two decades for their refusal to accept a Communist-controlled church. However, as the Puebla Institute point out, the distinction between the CPA and Roman Catholicism is not clear cut. In September 1991, it was revealed that Pope John Paul II had recognised as many as twenty CPA-appointed bishops. In 1995 tentative links and attempts at rapprochement continued.

Along with their Catholic brethren, Protestants, particularly evangelicals, suffered for their beliefs. Besides Lin Xiangao, other well-known Christian leaders who suffered for their faith were Wang Mingdao, who was in a labour camp for twenty-two years, and Ni Tuosheng (better known in the West as Watchman Nee) who died shortly after his release from labour camp in 1972.

Scars from the 1950s remain: some Christians joined the TSPM or CPA willingly or under duress; some openly renounced their faith and joined the CCP. Others, at great personal cost, refused all compromise and were imprisoned, and the divisions today between TSPM/CPA registered churches and house church/'underground' Catholic unregistered congregations have their roots in this period. In addition, many Christians believe that underground worship is safer even though it is illegal: putting their names on membership lists kept by the official church might expose them to persecution in the future.

There were two dominant ideological viewpoints on religion within the CCP. The first took a relatively 'soft' line, believing as the Soviet Union's leaders had done, that religion would eventually die out in a socialist society, and in the meantime should be tolerated, controlled and used in line with CCP policies. The second took a 'hard' line, believing religion should be suppressed. It was the latter view which was implemented in the 1950s and triumphed during the Cultural Revolution (1966–1976).

On the eve of the Cultural Revolution foreign visitors to China reported that most church buildings had been closed (over 200 in Shanghai down to twenty; sixty-four in Beijing down to four) and congregations were elderly and dwindling. The few remaining pastors preached CCP dogma with a thin religious veneer. When I first went to Shanghai in the 1980s, I visited several churches which had been converted into living accommodation or into factories or warehouses and believers were turfed out or jailed.

The Cultural Revolution appeared to destroy the Chinese Church. Apart from the buildings which were closed or desecrated, all Bibles and Christian literature were burnt or confiscated by the Red Guards. Christian priests, pastors and lay-people were dragged through the streets and forced to attend 'struggle meetings'. Many were imprisoned. The institutional Church was totally destroyed and for thirteen years (1966–1979) there were no churches in China where Chinese could openly worship. It seemed that the 'fourth wave' of missionary endeavour begun in the nineteeen century had perished like its predecessors. But, as Edmund Campion would have said, 'The enterprise had begun, it was of God, it cannot be withstood.'

Only fifteen years later the Church is experiencing a revival. Much of the revival is centred on unregistered – and therefore illegal – house churches. Some conservative estimates put the number of Christians in China today at about 36 million. In the 1950s some Christians withdrew from the TSPM and CPA churches to meet for worship in the home. There is now evidence that some of these meetings continued even at the height of the Cultural Revolution. By the early 1970s these home-meetings were secretly proliferating. Evangelism was largely by contact with relatives and neighbours, but gradually the Church became bolder, using funerals as opportunities for public displays of faith and holding training sessions for young people. This was very much a grass-roots movement and was often led by women, as many male priests and pastors were still in labour camps. It is important to realise that the 'house church' movement in China pre-dated the restoration of the official TSPM/CPA church structures in 1979/80. The re-introduction of these structures was in part an admission by the CCP of the existence of independent Christian churches and an attempt to bring them under State supervision.

The success of some of the independent churches in attracting members is shown by the clampdown in the early 1980s on such groups as the 'Shouters'. Many of the people imprisoned at this time received sentences of between ten and fifteen years' imprisonment and therefore have not yet been released. But because they were overwhelmingly farmers from remote rural areas with no contacts outside China their plight was not widely known until recently.

The 1989 events in Tiananmen Square precipitated an increased repression of all activity which the Chinese State perceived as a threat. This included religious practice. The tone was set by 'Document No 6', issued by the CCP Central Committee in February 1991 which called for the elimination of all 'illegal' religious groups. Legislation on the religious activities of foreign nationals in China and on the venues for worship was passed in January 1994.

Up to now, conditions for Christians have varied greatly from province to province. The flourishing city churches in places like Shanghai and Beijing are not typical of the country as a whole. In some areas, things have changed little from the Cultural Revolution; in others, there is great freedom to evangelise, depending on the attitude of the local cadres who are given the responsibility of interpreting and implementing the general guidelines laid down in the legislation. Some observers fear that the 1994 decrees will be used by the central authorities to carry out a systematic repression of Christians.

The Jubilee Campaign has drawn to the attention of MPs and reports that, based on the available CPA and TSPM documentation, and on numerous interviews conducted with Christians in China over the last twelve years, repression can usually be traced to one or more of the following reasons:

Refusal to join the 'patriotic' religious organisation (TSPM or CPA) for reasons of conscience; this is construed as a political act by the authorities.

Evangelistic activities such as itinerant preaching.

Holding 'illegal' unregistered house church meetings.

Underground printing and distribution of religious literature.

Reception and distribution of religious literature from overseas.

Contact with overseas religious organisations, especially the Vatican, Protestant missions etc.

Praying for or healing the sick, deemed to be 'feudal superstition'.

Listening to, and corresponding with, overseas Christian radio broadcasting stations.

Holding clandestine theological seminaries or Bible training classes.

Baptising, evangelising or influencing children and young people under the age of eighteen.

Repression takes many forms, such as long periods of imprisonment in labour camps; large-scale round-ups of Christians in a certain area; frequent detention of individuals for questioning; restriction of an individual to a town or village; removal of elderly clergy to so-called 'old-people's homes'; destruction of church buildings; confiscation of property; and censorship of religious publications. Torture, although forbidden in Chinese law, has led to the death of several religious believers since 1992.

One example of this is the case of the Roman Catholic bishop, Fan Xueyan. He was arrested in 1982 and sentenced to ten years' 'Convicted Labour Reform' for ordaining priests. He disappeared in September 1990 along with many other religious figures. He remained missing until his death in April 1992. His body was delivered to his family on 16th April 1992 without any explanation. The body was emaciated and there were signs of apparent beatings. Photographs taken show signs of both legs being dislocated below the knee and large marks on his forehead and one cheek. No official statement was made. Mourners were prevented from attending his burial, some having their transport confiscated and high fines imposed.

The horrific trials which many Chinese Christians have had to endure for their faith have led to the development of a spirituality based on perseverance in suffering. One of the great Chinese house church leaders, the late Wang Ming Tao, spent more than twenty years in prison for refusing to join the TSPM and knew first-hand what suffering for faith is all about. Brother David, in his book, *Walking The Hard Road: Wang Ming Tao* records Wang Ming Tao's words:

> Human nature loves ease and comfort. But God demands of us high virtue and perfect good deeds. He knows easy circumstances are not as conducive to our progress as suffering is; and he sees farther than our human eyes can look. God wants us to endure temporary and light affliction so that we may be sanctified and perfect, fit for the Master's use.
>
> Fire is often used in the Bible to symbolize suffering, and very fitting it is. Gold and silver don't come from the mine pure and complete. Once mined, they come as ore mixed with many impurities. They are neither beautiful to look at nor useful. But what do you do with the ore? Throw it away?
>
> Of course not. The ore is not discarded because it is not

pure and fine. People put it into the fire. They refine it once, twice and even many, many times. The harsher the refining process, the purer and finer the metal becomes. Only then can it be made into precious utensils and objects of the highest value and usefulness.

Believers are just like gold and silver in God's sight. God wants to make each of us into precious vessels; to purify our hearts and minds.

Our Lord doesn't discard us. In the crucible of affliction we can burn away the impurities. How painful and unbearable the process may often be! In the course of this suffering, God causes us to confess and reject our personal sins. That way we learn to achieve the virtue God expects of us. Gradually we become perfect.[2]

In the face of persecution, many of China's Christians have not had the luxury of picking and choosing which bits of Christianity they wish to take seriously, as many of us do in the West. Most of China's Christians have had to make a clear decision on where they stand and be prepared to suffer for their beliefs. There is little room for half-baked Christianity. These writings and the experiences which they represent make our own problems as Christians in the West seem small by comparison. In *Walking The Hard Road*, Brother David asks Wang Ming Tao, 'Uncle, do you have any precious lessons to share with the Christians in free countries?'

He describes Wang Ming Tao's response as follows, 'I can still see him, framed in the simple doorway, his nearly-blind eyes focused on my face. He nodded, beginning to close the door as he answered me. "Tell them," he replied, a gentle smile at his lips, "to walk the hard road."'

Many Christians worldwide are 'walking the hard road' for God and not just in China. It is probably the case that more Christians have been persecuted and killed for their faith in this century than during the time of the Roman Empire.

China's Family Planning Policies

Until the fall of Communism in the Soviet bloc, Communist ideology was generally seen as the number one enemy of Christians. This implies that with the momentous changes in the Soviet Union and Eastern Europe in the late 1980s, the persecution of Christians should have sharply decreased. Sadly, this is not the case. The Jubilee Campaign has documented numerous recent cases of persecution of Christians throughout the world, especially in the remaining Communist states and in many parts of the Islamic world. This includes China, Vietnam, North Korea, Egypt, Pakistan, Saudi Arabia, Turkey, Iran and Sudan. The story of Lin Xiangao simply serves to remind us of the ordeal faced by millions in China. In a debate in Parliament, in June 1995, I took the opportunity to highlight the latest atrocities being meted out by the Chinese authorities. Christians are being especially targeted under China's one-child policy and our Government is a collaborator. As women and children suffer how ironic that the United Nations should choose Beijing as the place to hold its conference on women's rights. Needless to say, none of the 35,000 who gathered as delegates were Chinese women who have suffered unspeakably. How have we aided and abetted their repression?

In 1994, the British Government gave £8.5 million to the United Nations Family Planning Association (UNFPA), and £7.5 million to the International Planned Parenthood Federation (IPPF). This, in turn, was given to the Chinese Population Association. Their methods are now well documented. British taxpayers have been underwriting forced abortion, forced sterilisation, the forcible fitting of inter-uterine contraceptive devices (IUDs) and even infanticide for more than twenty years. Successive ministers have defended one of the greatest scandals in the use of overseas aid that I have ever come across. They have used a succession of arguments to justify the £100 million of British taxpayers' money spent on undergirding this policy over the past decade.

The first of those arguments was expressed by Baroness Chalker. Funding such programmes, she says, enables us to influence them. There is, however, no supporting evidence to show that funding leads to influence over policies. This is the same argument put forward by the Archbishop of Canterbury about the position of China's Church after he returned from his recent visit to China. We should seek to influence rather than criticise, although he criticised those who smuggle Bibles into China and endorsed the state-established churches. The second argument which the Government deploys is that there is insufficient evidence – even though, naturally, the Government did not approve of coercion. The next argument was the rural aberration one. The Government argued that such policies might be pursued, but they were only the work of a few over-zealous officials in some backwoods area of China.

The Government, of course, say that they are 'deeply concerned'. However, they are not concerned enough to do anything to stop the systematic abuse of women and children. The greatest deceit of all is to trot out the platitude that we are all opposed to the principle of coercion, while continuing to fund the perpetrators of these crimes against humanity. The shocking thing is that it took something as horrific as the broadcast of Channel Four's *The Dying Rooms* in June 1995, to shake us out of our complacency. This excellent programme exposed the killing of little girls and the infanticide which flows from the State's one-child policy.

At the height of the mass sterilisation campaign in the 1970s the UNFPA gave China the first-ever UN population award for its success in curbing population. The UNFPA provided training for central government officials responsible for the policy. It provided computer systems that monitor the effectiveness of the programmes in reaching their targets. It funded the building of two facilities that have made China self-sufficient in IUD

production. Some 41 per cent of Chinese women now have
IUDs, which, once inserted – often against their will – they can
do little about. X-ray machines are used to ensure that women
have not removed them.

The UNFPA is a United Nations agency. The UN purports
to guarantee the 'right to freely found a family and decide on
the number and spacing of the children'. Yet, in direct contradiction of that, the Communist Chinese Minister for family
planning, Qian Zinzhong, has said: 'The size of the family is far
too important to be left to the couple. Births are a matter of
state planning.'

China's one-child policy uniquely marks it out as a country
where it is illegal to have a brother or a sister; where little girls
are eliminated in favour of their brothers and where eugenics
laws like those so favoured by the eugenicists who founded the
IPPF now permit the killing of disabled children.

In October 1994 China passed a law on maternal and infant
health care that came into force in June 1995. It allows the
government to force newly married couples to be sterilised and
unborn babies to be aborted, where there is disability, illness
or 'relevant mental disorders'. Poor people from ethnic minorities and disabled people have always been the target of racists
and eugenicists everywhere. The simple test is whether we
would permit such procedures here and, if not, what in the
world are we doing funding them in China?

The IPPF, with its historic links with eugenicists such as
Huxley, Stopes, Sangster and Galton should never be used as
an instrument for utilising British funds. Marie Stopes refused
to speak to her daughter again after she married a man who
wore glasses – he was judged to be of inferior stock. Marie
Stopes International continues to fund British MPs to go on
overseas trips and who then act as apologists for the IPPF. It's
all very cosy.

In 1995 reports from Feng Jia Zhuang and Long Tian Gou,
two Catholic areas of China, reveal a combination of religious

repression and political coercion. Using their slogan, 'It is better to have more graves than one more child', the local authorities repeatedly raid people's homes, confiscate the family's property, round up the people and beat those who escape into nearby fields. Forced abortions have been performed on women in their last weeks of pregnancy. Several women have been forcibly sterilised against their will. Monstrous fines – bigger than an annual average income – are imposed on couples who do not comply. One villager had his legs so badly broken that he nearly died. When concerned relatives enquired about him they were arrested, abused and forced to pay a huge fine. Another villager unsuccessfully tried to sell his two children in an effort to have his wife freed from gaol.

People are subjected to terrible torture. Men and women have been hung upside down; some have been exposed to the elements during extreme weather conditions for sustained periods. Some people have had their tongues burnt with electric batons to prevent them from invoking the help of God. Through our funding, we are collaborating in those crimes against the ordinary people of China.

The systematic killing of little girls is now beginning to reveal itself in the population shift in China and in slave trade in women. At least 114 boys are now born in China for every 100 girls. The plight of adult women is equally harrowing. The Human Rights Law Review details instances of women being taken from bed late at night and brought to 24-hour sterilisation clinics. It records examples of women being inserted with IUDs without their knowledge or consent immediately after giving birth and newborn babies being killed while still partly in the womb. Local officials who violate women's rights are promoted for their ruthless cold-blooded efficiency.

China's population policy has been approved by the executive director of the UNFPA, Nafis Sadiq, who said: 'China has every reason to feel proud and pleased with its remarkable achievements in its family planning policy and control of its population growth over the past ten years. Now China could offer its experiences and special experts to other countries.' When I put this to Baroness Chalker she did not believe he had ever said it. I pointed out that the quotation had been included in briefing material sent to me by her own department.

Britain should have no part in the programmes. We should use our overseas budget to help those 800 million people who are racked by starvation or despair and who live below any rational definition of human decency. We should not allow resources to be used for such evil practices. The British Government have become fanatical in their population policies. Their programmes should attack poverty not people. They should recall the words of William Wilberforce who said nearly 200 years ago that we should 'Disclaim that dangerous sophistry that out of doing evil some good may come.'

I hope that it will not be long before we stop collaboration in the funding of forced abortions, forced sterilisation and oppression of women's rights in China.

But I also hope it will not be long before the British Churches wake up from their day-dream. They should remember the Cultural Revolution and the abysmal failure to condemn. They should ponder deeply on the plight of their co-religionists who in 1997 will be handed over to the Communist authorities when they resume control of Hong Kong. In 1981 in Parliament I condemned the Nationality Act for its failure to address the potential plight of Hong Kong Chinese. If we had offered the right of abode in Commonwealth countries to all Hong Kong residents, as I argued, China would have been more interested in upholding human rights in Hong Kong as a way of preventing an exodus.

The Chinese Church suffered terribly for ten years, even more so than now, during that 'long dark night' of the Cultural Revolution. What were the international community and the Church in the free world doing about it? What have we done now to speak out against the systematic and shocking abuse of

Christians and others victimised by coercive family planning? What will happen to the hundreds of thousands of Christians in Hong Kong in 1997?

It is not only governments who are often indifferent to the plight of the persecuted. The Church can be strangely silent as well. All too often Christians overlook the importance of caring about other believers who are suffering for their faith. They may get worked up over very commendable human rights issues, but overlook the suffering of their fellow believers. St Paul, speaking about the Church as the Body of Christ, writes in 1 Corinthians 12:25–7, that 'there should be no division in the body, but that its parts should have equal concern for each other. If one part suffers, every part suffers with it; if one part is honoured, every part rejoices with it. Now you are the body of Christ, and each one of you is a part of it.'

When Christians suffer, Christ suffers too, because we are all part of His body. When we try to help the suffering Church, we are helping to alleviate Christ's pain. We are acknowledging our role as part of Christ's body and the universal fellowship of Christians in Him. This fellowship transcends cultures, political boundaries and, yes, even denominations. In Galatians 6:9–10, St Paul writes, 'Let us not become weary in doing good, for at the proper time we will reap a harvest if we do not give up. Therefore, as we have opportunity, let us do good to all people, *especially* to those who belong to the family of believers' (my emphasis added).

I began this chapter by saying that Lin Xiangao is a sign of contradiction, representative of the numerous Christians who have in recent times faced persecution because of their faith. His life stands as a stark reminder of the uncomfortable position of millions. The question for each of us is what are we going to do to support men and women like him.

Chapter Nine

C. S. Lewis

BATTLING WITH WORDS AND IDEAS

You will find that the truth is often unpopular and the contest between agreeable fancy and disagreeable fact is unequal.

Adlai Stevenson, 1958

C. S. Lewis cared nothing for fashionable ideas and little for public opinion. Throughout his life, through his prolific writing, and in the literary and academic world in which he worked, he eschewed popular positions opting instead for eternal truths. He said: 'Thirst is made for water, inquiry for truth.' Through wartime broadcasts, children's books, poetry, Christian apologetics, and literary criticism, Lewis pursued the inquiry for truth by challenging the ideas of the time and refused to be sucked into the new orthodoxies of secularism.

Along with G. K. Chesterton and J. R. R. Tolkien he is one of the most influential writers of the twentieth century. Not wishing to recognise this, the secular educational and literary establishment, to this day, rarely include Lewis's works in the curriculum. Yet sales of his books continue to be phenomenal and, as with Chesterton, his following in the United States has never been greater. Though dead for thirty years, through the power of his pen Lewis continues to contradict contemporary folly. Nor does he cease to inspire. *Mere Christianity*[1] remains, for me, the most concise and compelling case for the Christian faith which I have ever read. I have included him in this collection because he can also teach us how to face grief and death.

The Relevance of Lewis's Work

Like most people, I discovered Lewis as a child, stumbling by accident on the Narnian chronicles in our local library. The secret land which was reached through the wardrobe thrilled and excited me, just as I have now seen it captivate my own children. First as a teacher, now as a parent, re-reading those books aloud has reminded me what a fine storyteller Lewis is; but, every time I hear the familiar tales, I also realise that like a Russian doll there is another story and a deeper meaning still to be revealed.

In Turkey, in 1994, I visited the small Christian community. At their publishing centre I was intrigued to see that the first children's novel which they had translated into Turkish was *The Lion, The Witch And The Wardrobe*.[2] It was particularly appropriate because, as they explained, Aslan is the Turkish word for lion. Aslan's death at the hands of the witch and her allies is a sacrifice to save the previously treacherous Edmund. Yet it ends with Aslan's ultimate triumph. There was a 'deeper magic'.

Lewis's principal characters, Peter, Susan, Edmund and Lucy, all have the strengths and weaknesses which are familiar to every child. In *Prince Caspian*[3] it is once more to Lucy, the youngest child, that Aslan reveals himself. Once more, the others refuse to believe her and choose to go their own way. Her sister tells her that she has been dreaming, accuses her of talking nonsense and behaving badly. Here are all the usual emotions of superiority mixed with envy. I am older or cleverer. Why would he reveal himself to her anyway? If I can't see it why should I believe?

Here also is the plague of modern life, scepticism. Susan had previously met Aslan but she still could not bring herself to believe. In the final work of the Narnian chronicles, *The Last Battle*,[4] she is the one who is absent from the reunion in the new Narnia, because despite her experiences and inner knowledge, intellect had reduced her to non-belief.

In *Prince Caspian* Lucy summons up the strength to defy the others and to be guided by her own belief in Aslan and to act in his and her own strength. In a tremulous voice she says to the other children: 'And I do hope that you will all come with me. Because – because I'll have to go with him whether anyone else does or not.'

Lewis is reminding us that truth is not the prerogative of the strong. Two of the great saints, St Francis of Assisi and St Thérèse of Lisieux – the little flower – knew that it was by becoming smaller that there was true spiritual growth. In choosing Lucy, Aslan is confounding the powerful and the strong.

In his earlier works of science fiction, *Voyage To Venus*,[5] *Out of The Silent Planet*[6] and *That Hideous Strength*[7] some of the themes familiar to Narnian devotees begin to emerge. Lewis has no hesitation in addressing the great moral and ethical issues which had plunged the world into a second global conflict through the vehicle of popular fiction. This was the way to influence the masses. The conflict between good and evil and the ever-present seductive pressures of the devil are further popularised in his *The Screwtape Letters*.[8] This was Lewis's way of ensuring that the devil doesn't have all the good tunes. At different turns, amusing, gripping, chilling and provocative, his fiction has stood the test of time remarkably well.

Mark Studdock, the central figure in *That Hideous Strength*, faces all the dilemmas that an up-and-coming bright young academic faces today. He must have been a familiar figure in the Common Rooms frequented by Lewis. The National Institute of Coordinated Experiments are pouring money into Bracton College. Lord Feverstone, their director, is a fellow of the College supported by the Progressive Element who are ranged against the Die-Hards. Studdock chooses to ingratiate himself with the ascendency. As the Institute gradually takes over the entire College Studdock asks its director what was planned: 'Quite simple and obvious things, at first – sterilisation of the unfit, liquidation of backward races, selective breeding.' Ultimately they will create 'a new type of man: and it's people like you who've got to begin to make him'. This appeal to Studdock's intellectual vanity succeeds and he becomes more and more deeply enmeshed. If the force of argument fails there is always the Institute's evil Miss Hardcastle, her secret police and their sadistic methods to fall back upon.

Lewis also uses the opportunity to explore the sterile relationship of Mark Studdock and his wife, Jane. She begins to have spiritual insights and is led by the approachable and supportive Dimbles to Dr Ransom, who is pitted against the Institute. Ransom tells her that 'your trouble has been what the old poets called *Daungier*. We call it Pride.' There follows an examination of the feminine and masculine and a rejoicing in the differences.

Studdock's mistake was his desperate desire to belong, to be included and a part of the new ascendency. His journey of self-discovery, the easy assimilation of the weak into totalitarian organisations, the fashioning of the lie into an entire system, and the personal capitulation to ambition are the core of this book. So too is the anger that Mark and Jane both feel when they discover how badly they had been prepared for their battles. The de-Christianisation of society, and the uselessness of their secular education and upbringing, left them with little wisdom and no real knowledge. They cry out with frustration when they realise just how much they have lost.

Lewis, during his Oxford and Cambridge University days, relished his battles with his own 'Progressive Element'. He passionately believed in the old alliance of *eruditio et religio*; that good scholarship without faith is as dry as dust. Lewis held that religion provides the necessary direction for living out the restless yearning for academic discovery. He would have agreed with St Augustine that our hearts are restless until they rest in God.

In the twentieth century there has been an almost complete break between Christian discipleship and scholarship. This is something Lewis resisted throughout his life. Yet, almost every university and college was originally founded under Christian inspiration.

What has become sacred today in university life is the inviolability of the department. Inquiry is shaped by the specialised needs of individual disciplines as discrete departments pursue their own objectives with no over-arching vision. When religion is not viewed as an extra-curriculum embarrassment or an mildly eccentric hobby, it is met with the hostility afforded to an accursed taboo.

Lewis would have had no time for the false humility and feeble silence of so many believers in academia today. Terrier-like he would have been growling at the false ideologies of secular liberalism and nihilism. The divorce of the *eruditio et religio* has left its mark on how we write and teach history, how we analyse economic data, how we debate with cynical ideologues, or counter the latest politically correct fad in the English Department. It irredeemably alters the way we perceive the person and the dignity we afford him.

A person needs a deep and stable centre around which he or she can unify various personal experiences. If we are to avoid becoming mechanical men and women this unity must exist. Without it, life is like a shattered mirror, incapable of reflecting the total man.

G. K. Chesterton and Lewis both perceived the dangers of the systematic secularisation of our world. Chesterton foresaw 'the coming peril', describing it as 'vast and vague . . . of which capitalism and collectivism are only economic by-products'.[9] Lewis prophetically wrote about the coming of eugenics, of the abuse of power, the presence of evil, and the corruption of man.

Even as he broadcast to the nation during the Second World War, encouraging and strengthening his listeners, he did not delude them into believing that victory over Nazism was enough. He knew that liberal freedom can become the mere power of choice and that in its exercise we may become less free. The more fundamental choice is one which chooses for others, not self; that real freedom is the possession of life and that love is the giving of self and the giving of life. Like a gifted painter he would sketch the lights and the shadows and encourage us to choose one over the other. But who was C. S. Lewis?

Christian Influences

Beyond the rumbustious exterior of this intellectual heavy-weight was a personality which could be unassuming, genial and sensitive. From his birth in Belfast, to his rise to fame in the 1940s, and in his marriage to Joy Gresham, and his struggle during her premature death, there is revealed a man of great quality.

Lewis's mother, Flora, died of cancer in 1908, when he was just nine years old. Within two weeks he was sent to school in England, to Wynyard House in Watford. His older brother, Warren, or Warnie, had already been there for three years and hated it. The headmaster, the Reverend Robert Capron, had subjected him to regular beatings. This was hardly the ideal environment in which to come to terms with the loss of his mother. His father had become emotionally crippled and Lewis's experience was to profoundly affect his life, and particularly his relationships with women. For years he simply buried his grief.

By the age of eleven the young Lewis was already a prodigious reader. Moved from Wynyard House, and under the more enlightened gaze of his father's former tutor, William Kirkpatrick, he quickly developed. Kirkpatrick initially considered Lewis to be ideally suited to a career as a lawyer believing he had 'every gift, a goodly presence, a clear resonant voice, an unfailing source of clear and adequate expression'.[10] He also noted that 'it is the maturity of his literary judgements which is so unusual and surprising'.

In 1917 Lewis went to University College, Oxford. The college was largely bereft of young men – they were nearly all fighting in the trenches of Flanders. As an Irishman, Lewis was not obliged to enlist for service but he did so anyway. He went for military training in mid-June. Whilst it would be ridiculous to suggest that Lewis actually enjoyed serving in the First World War, he found the camaraderie of his men (he served as an officer) extremely refreshing and grew fond of many of them. During bounts of sickness, he took full advantage of the opportunities to read various authors including G. K. Chesterton who was to become an increasing influence in Lewis's thinking. Slaughter was taking place all around him and Lewis himself was very nearly killed at Mount Bernenchon during the battle of Arras on 15th April 1918. He was standing with a close friend, Sergeant Ayres, when a shell exploded. Ayres was killed, while Lewis suffered shrapnel wounds to the face, leg and under the arm. He momentarily stopped breathing and thought he had died. It was the kind of wound that every soldier desired, not serious but bad enough to be removed from the field and returned home to hospital. It was not until January 1919 that he was back in Oxford and began in earnest his academic career as an undergraduate. In 1925 his first professional appointment came as an English tutor at Magdalen College. Lewis was twenty-seven and was responsible for lecturing once a week, helping in the administration of the college as a Fellow of Magdalen, as well as fulfilling his duties as a college tutor.

At the same time, another academic, J. R. R. Tolkien arrived at the English Faculty. Lewis first met him at a faculty meeting at Merton College in May 1926 and could not help being charmed by this 'smooth, pale, fluent little chap'. Tolkien was to play a vital role in the eventual conversion of Lewis to Christianity. Albeit unwittingly, Lewis was beginning to surround himself with sympathetic Christian men, including Nevill Coghill, a colleague in the English Faculty, Tolkien, and Owen Barfield who had been an undergraduate with Lewis and was by now working as a solicitor in London. In addition, Lewis continued to read Chesterton and eventually realised that he was drawing nearer to belief. He was also challenged by one of his undergraduate students, Richard Griffiths who, after a summer vacation in the Cotswolds with some friends, had become a Christian. Lewis eventually attended his ordination as a monk at Prinknash Abbey when he took the name Bede Griffiths. Lewis dedicated *A Pilgrim's Regress*[11] to Griffiths and they remained life-long friends and correspondents.

One day a defining moment came when Lewis was travelling on a bus and suddenly became aware that he was living inside a shell, and it was his choice as to whether he remained inside the shell or came out and became what God intended. Lewis writes in *Surprised by Joy*[12] of the time somewhat later in the summer of 1929 when in his rooms at Magdalen he 'gave in and admitted that God was God, and knelt and prayed; perhaps that night, the most dejected and reluctant convert in all England.'

It was, however, to be a further two years before Lewis finally came to believe in the divinity of Christ. It was in an equally remarkably ordinary fashion (if anyone's conversion to faith in God can be termed ordinary) that Lewis found himself cornered.

He and his brother Warnie were travelling by motorbike and sidecar to Whipsnade Zoo for a day trip with the other members of their household, Mrs Moore, her daughter Maureen, and the family dog, Mr Papworth. The others were making their way to the zoo by car. All Lewis says about the experience in his autobiography, *Surprised by Joy*[12] is that 'when we set out I did not believe that Jesus Christ is the Son of God and when we reached the zoo I did'. A conversation he had with Tolkien and another Christian friend, Hugo Dyson, at Magdalen nine days prior to the visit to the zoo had played a significant part in Lewis's decision.

As his friendship with Tolkien grew, Lewis began a regular gathering that called itself the Inklings. An undergraduate had originally coined the name for another group and it had broken up in 1933. Both Lewis and Tolkien had attended some of those earlier gatherings, and it was they who decided to reinvent the club. It was not a formal club with minutes or apologies and the like but a literary gathering where an 'inner circle' of friends were invited to come and share their ideas, read aloud their work and generally enjoy the presence of each other's company. They met at Oxford's Eagle and Child – 'the bird and baby' – where Warren Lewis said the atmosphere would grow riotous, he and his brother enjoying every minute.

What was really happening, of course, was that Lewis, Tolkien and the others of similar religious belief, were supporting each other in the midst of hostile reaction to their work, their philosophy and interpretation of literature. They unashamedly existed to contradict those who doubted the existence of God. This circle of friends was set up to challenge the powerful circle which dominated Magdalen and university politics.

Even within this group, however, there were to be tensions. Lewis's more radical writings strained his relationship with Tolkien in particular. Although Tolkien was a devout Catholic and Lewis a Protestant, which gave rise to occasional theological differences, they remained great friends for many years. Tolkien said that it was only through his friend's constant demand for more material that ensured that his most famous work, *The Lord of the Rings* was ever finished at all. (Tolkien was the kind of careful writer who literally took years to complete anything, if, indeed, it ever was finished.)

The Inklings brought together Lewis's three favourite activities: writing, reading and being with his friends. His wonderfully hospitable life tellingly contradicts the sackcloth and ashes brigade who equate belief with a dirge-like existence.

For the second time in his life, a world war was to destroy the happy pattern of his existence, but he blossomed during those years. *The Screwtape Letters* were published by a High Church weekly called *The Guardian* in weekly instalments from May to November 1941. Ashley Sampson, who had commissioned *The Problem of Pain*,[13] persuaded his publisher to make an offer for the publication of *Screwtape* in book form. The first print run of 2000 in February 1942 was sold immediately. There were a further two reprints in March, and the book has been in print ever since, selling over a million copies. *Screwtape* made Lewis a household name.

Meanwhile, Lewis had accepted an invitation from the RAF chaplains to travel the country and give talks to the men in various RAF stations. While most public speakers were harping on about political differences between right and left, Lewis accepted and began to conduct talks on elementary themes such as 'Why we think there is a Right and a Wrong'. He would, like all great communicators, adapt his language to get across his message.

In February 1941 Lewis was approached by the Director of Religious Broadcasting at the BBC and asked if he would consider giving a series of talks under the general title of 'The Christian Faith as I see it – by a Layman'. Once again, Lewis accepted the opportunity to explore new avenues of communication and began broadcasting in the late summer of that year every Wednesday between 7.45 and 8.00 p.m.

Lewis's broadcasts went out as a series of three and were published virtually as spoken over the air. They were *Broadcast Talks*,[14] *Christian Behaviour*[15] and *Beyond Personality*.[16]

Though restricted by the time he was permitted on the air – a mere fifteen minutes – it was obvious that Lewis was a master of describing the Christian faith in plain and simple terms, in an articulate and arresting fashion that could give new understanding to the believer as well as an interesting insight to the non-believer. In many respects he was Britain's first broadcast evangelist.

By the time Lewis began receiving letters from Joy Gresham in early 1950, he was already a famous literary figure on both sides of the Atlantic. Perhaps it was because Lewis knew how to express emotion on the page but not face to face that he invested so much time in his correspondence with his devoted readers. He would answer their pleas for help on a variety of issues ranging from their sexuality or marriage problems to their troubles with prayer and God. Lewis clearly cared for those who sought his advice and was often willing to meet those who were bold enough to ask.

Even as his fame spread he never grew proud or arrogant. He always had time for people with a need; although he never claimed to be a 'pastoral' figure. This willingness to respond and to take time for total strangers was to open up the next chapter of the book.

Joy in his Life

Joy Gresham was thirty-five years old when she started writing to Lewis. She shared Lewis's love of literature. At Hunter College, New York City, she had won the Bernard Cohen Short Story Prize. An early desire to write screenplays for Hollywood led her into marriage with Bill Gresham who sold his first novel to a studio for $60,000. It brought instant wealth but not much else to their relationship. Bill Gresham was an alcoholic and a hopeless adulterer. Shortly after the birth of their second son, Douglas, Joy learned of yet another affair. She could take no more. In the midst of her despair, she encountered God. In her biography she writes: 'All my defences – the walls of arrogance and cocksureness and self-love behind which I hid from God – went down momentarily – and God came in.'[17] Initially her husband accepted her conversion. He assumed it was merely another of Joy's phases. After a few months he realised it was permanent and that he would never himself become a Christian. By September 1952 their marriage was over, and Joy Gresham travelled to England. What happened next has been brilliantly captured in the film *Shadowlands*, the stage version of which, by William Nicholson, left London audiences in tears.

Upon their first meeting in the Eastgate Hotel just opposite Magdalen, Lewis was instantly charmed by Joy's American forthrightness. Others, especially Lewis's colleagues – whom she was to meet soon after – found this rather offensive. Very early on he found in Joy a woman with whom he could be himself. There was no threat. Lewis found Joy intoxicating, laughing at almost everything she said. Much as he wanted to be 'an ordinary man' few accepted him as such. Here was a woman with no 'airs and graces' and who instantly relaxed in his company, and allowed him to be himself at last. As they grew to know each other, she saw that Lewis had surrounded himself with people who could not hurt him in the same way that he had been hurt as a child. It was Joy Gresham who enabled Lewis to become both the boy he had never been as well as the man he was ultimately designed to become.

In early 1956 the Home Office refused Joy a permit to remain in England. The only way she would be able to secure a permanent future in her adopted country would be to marry a citizen of the United Kingdom. As a technical device, a marriage took place between Gresham and Lewis, enabling her to remain in Britain.

These rather farcical circumstances caused Lewis to look long and hard at the woman that had so captivated him. There is no question that he held her in high esteem and had not wanted her to leave, but that is altogether different from a life-long commitment to another person. Subsequent events soon forced him to face up to his real feelings and emotions. On 19th October he received a call, informing him that Joy's rheumatic pains had been investigated and that she had a broken left thigh bone. She also had a lump on her breast. He went to see her and found her in high spirits. The biopsy which followed revealed the worst news imaginable. Her tumour was malignant. Survival was unlikely.

Faced with the probability of losing the woman he truly loved Lewis now found himself in the position of needing the help and blessing of the Church. He immediately ran up against church law and tradition concerning divorce and remarriage. After much unsuccessful petitioning, seeking permission to marry, Lewis turned to a friend, Peter Bide. Lewis knew Bide from Oxford, where he had come to read English Literature just before the Second World War. He had subsequently become a Christian. After ordination he had developed a healing ministry. Lewis asked him to intercede for Joy and to lay hands on her. He also asked him if he could, in any way, facilitate their marriage. Given the exceptional circumstances Bide agreed that the wedding could proceed. On 21st March 1957 they were married in Joy's ward at the Churchill Hospital in Oxford. Warnie accompanied his brother. The only other witness was the ward sister. They made their sacramental vows before God and an announcement appeared in *The Times* the following day.

The doctors at the Churchill Hospital had given up all hope of Joy recovering from cancer. She returned to Lewis's home in Oxford, The Kilns, expecting to die quite quickly. Unpredictably, she began to recover. When her friend from college, Bel Kaufman came to visit her in August 1957, she was looking radiant, despite not being able to walk. She recalled that Lewis was extremely happy, enjoying the recovery of his wife. He later wrote: 'Years ago, when I wrote about medieval love poetry and described its strange half make-believe "religion of Love" I was blind enough to treat this as an almost entirely literary phenomenon. I know better now.'[18] It really did appear that there had been a miracle, Joy was recovering – slowly but surely. As A. N. Wilson notes in his biography of Lewis:

> In the happiness of his love for Joy, pathetically fragile as he knew her physical condition still to be, he was boy-like, exuberant. 'Do you know,' he said to Coghill and Peter Bayley, as they were crossing a quadrangle at Merton, 'I am experiencing what I thought would never be mine. I never thought I would have in my sixties the happiness that passed me by in my twenties.'[19]

A year after their wedding day when Joy had been on her death bed she was walking with a stick. The doctors told her that the cancer had been arrested and the cancerous spots in her bones had disappeared. Intriguingly Lewis was simultaneously suffering from osteoporosis, a bone disease that, whilst not fatal in itself, brings with it excruciating pain. He was forced to wear a surgical belt and sleep on a board for several months during 1956.

In January 1959 Lewis wrote:

> I have stood by the bedside of a woman whose thigh bone was eaten through with cancer and who had thriving colonies of the disease in many other bones as well. It took three people to move her in bed. The doctors predicted a few months of life: the nurses (who often know better) a few weeks. A good man laid his hands on her and prayed. A year later the patient was walking (uphill, too, through rough woodland) and the man who took the last X-ray photographs was saying 'These bones are as solid as rock'. It's miraculous.[20]

The recovery, however, proved to be a respite. In the film *Shadowlands*, where Lewis is brilliantly portrayed by Anthony Hopkins with Debra Winger as Joy, there is a scene towards the end where they have gone away for their 'honeymoon'. They have just made it to a barn to escape the rain when Joy forces Lewis to listen and face the reality of their situation. 'The happiness now,' Joy reminds him, 'is part of the pain later . . . that's the deal.'[21]

The sheer happiness of the little over three years of marriage they shared together was a period which Lewis regarded as the happiest of his entire life. Yet it was paradoxically also the most painful. In his heart-rending book *A Grief Observed*[22] Lewis memorably questions why God allowed such suffering to take place. Why did such pain have to be inflicted upon someone as committed as he was? Why did his beloved wife have to endure the horror of cancer? You could spend an eternity asking these questions, and no doubt we will. But for Lewis came the realisation that through 'the megaphone of pain, God speaks to an unlistening world'.

Belief and faith are not an inoculation against pain but they do help us to bear it. Throughout it all Lewis must have been ever mindful of the story of Job and of the suffering of Christ Himself. The obscene and harrowing pain of the cross is the only thing which makes sense of pain. The cross quells the war and heals the pain in our hearts. Lewis knew what God could not possibly be, and from there began to retrace his steps to the Creator who must be.

On 14th July at around two in the morning, Joy Lewis finally died. It had been a fight to the very end. I say very end rather than bitter end because she had come to terms with death and had helped Lewis to prepare for the inevitable. Just before she died, she had said that she was 'at peace with God' and was ready to depart.

Death and Faith

The Victorians talked openly about death but were embarrassed by sex. We are just the opposite. Death has become a frightening subject in a technocratic age which thinks it has conquered everything. That is why Lewis's *A Grief Observed* is such a powerful book. His opening words capture the raw emotion of death: 'No one ever told me that grief felt so like fear. I am not afraid but the sensation is like being afraid. The same fluttering in the stomach, the same restlessness, the yawning. I keep on swallowing.'

He continues: 'I almost prefer the moments of agony. These are at least clean and honest. But the bath of self-pity, the wallow, the loathsome sticky-sweet pleasure of indulging it – that disgusts me.' Here, Lewis is trying to find a way through the pain of loss.

He is astonishingly honest about himself, about his wife's thoughts and about his perception of where God is in the midst of his crisis: 'Part of every misery, so to speak, the misery's shadow or reflection: the fact that you don't merely suffer but have to keep on thinking about the fact that you suffer. I not only live each endless day in grief, but live each day thinking about living each day in grief.' Notwithstanding all the pain, Lewis admits that he does not want to regress into the unreality of his previous life. For most of us the temptation would simply be to blame God.

Nor did he believe that his brief marriage had been a waste or a mistake:

The most precious gift that marriage gave me was this constant impact of something very close and intimate yet at the same time unmistakably other, resistant – in a word, real. Is all that work to be undone? Is what I shall still call H [H = Helen, Joy's Christian name] to sink back horribly into being not much more than one of my old bachelor pipe-dreams?

Oh my dear, my dear, come back for one moment and drive that miserable phantom away. Oh God, God, why did you take such trouble to force this creature out of its shell if it is now doomed to crawl back – to be sucked back – into it?

A Grief Observed is simply the collection of jottings that Lewis made during the immediate period after Joy's death. Unlike most of his other books it was not subjected to the usual procedure of editing and rewrites. It is pure unadulterated emotion with wonderful use of analogy in the midst of true pain and heartfelt anguish. In one passage, he has just had to face more despairing thoughts:

Why do I make room in my mind for such filth and nonsense? Do I hope that if feeling disguises itself as thought I shall feel less? Aren't all these notes the senseless writhings of a man who won't accept the fact that there is nothing we can do with suffering except to suffer it? Who still thinks there is some device (if only he could find it) which will make pain not to be pain? It doesn't really matter whether you grip the arms of the dentist's chair or let your hands lie in your lap. The drill drills on.

Yet even in the midst of the grief there was hope:

I have gradually been coming to feel that the door is no longer shut and bolted. Was it my own frantic need that slammed it in my face? The time when there is nothing at all in your soul except a cry for help must be just the time when God can't give it: you are like the drowning man who can't be helped because he clutches and grabs.

Perhaps your own reiterated cries deafen you to the voice you hoped to hear.

Then there is the Lewis who is beginning to more deeply understand something of the ways of God.

God has not been trying an experiment on my faith or love in order to find out their quality. He knew it already. It was I who didn't. In this trial He makes us occupy the dock, the witness box, and the bench all at once. He always knew that my temple was a house of cards. His only way of making me realise the fact was to knock it down . . .

Grief is like a long valley, a winding valley where any bend may reveal a totally new landscape. As I've already noted, not every bend does. Sometimes, the surprise is the opposite one; you are presented with exactly the same sort of country you thought you had left behind miles ago. That is when you wonder whether the valley is a circular trench. But it isn't. There are partial recurrences, but the sequence doesn't repeat.

Often, Lewis would find himself talking directly to God about the questions which bothered him most about the mystery of death, suffering and grief. 'When I lay these questions before God I get no answer. But a rather special sort of "No answer". It is not the locked door. It is more like a silent, certainly not uncompassionate gaze. As though He shook His head not in refusal but waiving the question. Like, "Peace, child; you don't understand."'

And finally right at the end of *A Grief Observed* C. S. Lewis concludes that, 'We cannot understand. The best is perhaps what we understand least.'

Although Lewis may have felt a deep sense of frustration that he could not fully explain the nature and necessity of pain and suffering, he probably did not appreciate how much his experience would help others. In facing the issue of terminal cancer, *A Grief Observed*, and the late David Watson's *Fear No Evil*[23] remain, for me, the two most helpful books I have read.

We used to talk about 'a good death'. Lewis reminds us how to prepare for one. His personal testimony is not a theoretical paper on the theological questions that surround pain; it is his own excruciating and harrowing ordeal and the hope which lies beyond that experience which arrest the reader. It is also an account which contradicts the purveyors of euthanasia, the latest anti-life ideology. Killing the patient is no substitute for giving the patient a good death, surrounded by love and care. Surely this is what Joy Gresham experienced. Death is the ultimate experience which we all know we must face eventually. Lewis does us all a favour in sharing with us the intimate details of how he and Joy faced a particularly painful parting.

In the space of this short chapter, of necessity much has been left unsaid. The nature and quality of Lewis's friendships, the personal problems which he and his brother both experienced, and his career disappointments and frustrations, all contribute to the complexity of this extraordinary man. The warts and all are particularly comforting because Lewis didn't let them get in the way. He could never have been accused of being too perfect; which is why his legacy of great writing continues to encourage and inspire us all.

Chapter Ten

Jackie Pullinger

SLAYING DRAGONS

Love does not delight in evil but rejoices with the truth.

1 Corinthians 13:6

I have included Jackie Pullinger in this collection because after seeing her work first-hand I was genuinely struck by her qualities and by the improbability of her mission to the drug addicts of Hong Kong. This is an opportune moment to also reflect on the nature of drug addiction in Britain. Just as Jackie Pullinger contradicts those who say there is no hope or cure for an addict, her story acts as a warning to those who want easier access to drugs.

Drugs and Society

In her powerful account of her life in Hong Kong (*Chasing the Dragon*),[1] Jackie Pullinger offers a radical and hopeful alternative to the despair of drug addiction.

Fashionable political opinion is now increasingly wedded to the idea of the easier, legal, and more widespread availability of drugs. For young people especially, who are the chief targets of the pushers, it is increasingly difficult to steer clear of experimenting with drugs. Being a sign of contradiction at school, at the youth club, at a rave or at a party becomes a relentless battle.

Even those who refuse can unwittingly be caught up by the

drugs culture. Last year a young woman in Cheshire died after Ecstasy was put into her orange juice. She had never used drugs and did not even drink alcohol. Others she was out with were determined to suck her into their life style. Even having them as acquaintances can prove to be a fatal mistake.

Drugs in Britain today are one of the most powerful pressures for crime. Hardly a community has been left untouched by their effects. Hundreds of thousands of British families have had first-hand experience of their corrosive and debilitating effects. Enforcement agencies devote neverending numbers of personnel and resources to combat dealers. International agencies try to root out the producers. Counsellors and clinics try to sort out the casualties.

Politicians argue about whether to change the law, about whether drugs should be decriminalised. Parents see their children change unrecognisably and there seem to be no real solutions available to them – simply different options.

During the 1980s I saw, at first hand, the destructive effect of drugs on family and community life in Liverpool. After a baby was born a heroin addict someone called it Crack City. But its story was being replicated all over Britain; and it soon became apparent that drug abuse was no respecter of class or wealth. Advocating easier availability of drugs is to offer young people a diet of broken glass.

I followed the issue in Parliament, where I serve as the Vice Chairman of the All Party Drugs Misuse Group. I also took the opportunity, during a visit to the Far East to see how drug abuse is tackled in the city which had been at the heart of China's opium trade: Hong Kong.

I flew out to one of the Colony's small islands which the Hong Kong Government uses for the almost exclusive treatment of addicts. There I saw doctors working with addicts going 'cold turkey', trying to beat their addiction. The staff told me that the level of recidivism was phenomenally high. They fully expected to see the young men they cleaned up back again within weeks. They were not offering cures.

The conditions on that island were all that you could have wished for: sanitary, hygienic, clean. This pristine cleanliness and competent, caring staff – and all the chemical and alternative drugs-based 'cures' you could care for – were extremely impressive. But none of it worked. All that they were doing was to put a poultice on the problem.

The contrast to the working environment of Jackie Pullinger, whom I visited the following day, could not have been greater. Here was a former local Home Counties beauty queen who felt called to come and live in the Far East, scrambling about in the squalor of the notorious Walled City. The hope and long-term healing which she was bringing into the lives of some of the toughest and most acute cases of addiction should give even the greatest cynic pause for thought.

This chapter is about two things: drugs and Jackie Pullinger. It is written to give encouragement to people who find it hard to say no, who find it difficult to resist the temptation to go along with the crowd. It is also another account of a remarkable person who has contradicted prevailing attitudes through her practical actions as well as her beliefs.

Application of Jackie Pullinger's work in the British setting might offer a more profound solution to the victims of our rampant drugs culture than yet another blind alley, dead-end option. Turning an illegal activity into a legal one is irrelevant to the debate about the desirability of becoming a drug addict in the first place. Who wants to see generations of people turned into zombies, pathetically craving for substances which dehumanise them? Perhaps the answer is broadly those who are already prisoners.

By following the impulse of her heart, rather than doing what society would have expected of a young woman from her background, Jackie Pullinger has become a respected member of the Hong Kong community. Her story offers a radically different approach to drugs abuse, but, obviously, it also has much wider application.

In The Walled City

After her arrival in Hong Kong the inevitable theatre for her work was the Walled City. For historic reasons this pocket-handkerchief piece of territory has never come under Hong Kong jurisdiction but had remained a Chinese enclave; it was effectively a fiefdom of Triad bosses where anarchy allowed the narcotics business to prosper beyond the laws of the Colony. It was an unbelievably squalid, lawless place. I remember it as putrid and festering.

When its walls were finally demolished in May 1994 it was like the walls collapsing at Jericho . . . God had said to Joshua, 'See, I have delivered Jericho into your hands along with its king and its fighting men.' He gave the Walled City to Jackie Pullinger, who must have felt the same elation as Joshua. Many of the city's lowest citizens had been delivered into her hands.

Anyone who has ever visited the notoriously narrow streets and alleyways of the Walled City knows what a truly terrifying experience it is. For a young woman to have done this on a daily basis, in the hope that somehow she would be able to help those who had no choice but to struggle to survive in a hell-like den of drugs, prostitution and pornography, is a remarkable feat in itself. The way to understanding her success rests on her absolute commitment to the people she felt drawn to work with. Her commitment remained strong despite the inevitable legion of obstacles, including initial disappointment, frustration and the absence of immediate fruit. Jackie Pullinger's steadfastness enabled her to win through. When the men of the Walled City came to realise that Jackie Pullinger, or Poon Siu Jeh, as she become known, was totally different from the other evangelists they had seen come and go she began to win their respect. In *Chasing the Dragon* she describes how scepticism and opposition had to be overcome. Jackie recalls a conversation with one of the drug addicts, Ah Ping:

Ah Ping could really talk when he got warmed up and today he was going to say what most of them really felt. I respected his honesty, for few Chinese ever tell Westerners what they really feel about them. 'You Westerners,' he continued, 'you come here and tell us about Jesus. You can stay for a year or two, and your conscience will feel good, and then you can go away. Your Jesus will call you to other work back home. It's true some of you raise a lot of money on behalf of us underprivileged people. But you'll still be living in your nice houses with your refrigerators and servants and we'll still be living here. What you are doing really has nothing to do with us. You'll go home anyhow, sooner or later.'

This kind of conversation took place many times; it was an indictment of those evangelists who flew into Hong Kong, sang sweet songs about the love of Jesus on stage and on Hong Kong television, then jumped back into their planes and flew away again.

'Fine,' said Ah Ping to me savagely one day, 'fine for them, fine for us too. We wouldn't mind believing in Jesus too if we could get into a plane and fly away around the world like them. They can sing about love very nicely, but what do they know about us? They don't touch us – they know nothing.'

Many people who experience ephemeral Christianity, or for that matter, do-good organisations that are here today and gone tomorrow, will feel some sympathy for Pullinger's interrogator. Drug addicts are often especially cynical about the way they are used by people who show them no long-term commitment.

Actions always speak immeasurably louder than words and

it was the action Jackie Pullinger took that finally convinced the doubters that she had every intention of staying and seeing change in the lives of those she cared for. That and the power of the Holy Spirit. The Willans, an American couple working in Hong Kong are responsible for that change being realised. Jean Willan encouraged Jackie to use her gift of praying in tongues and although Jackie initially felt embarrassed doing so, she agreed.

I would have done anything not to be praying out loud in a strange language in front of strange Americans, but just as I thought I would die of self-consciousness God said to me, 'Are you willing to be a fool for my sake?'

I gave in. 'All right, Lord – this doesn't make sense to me but since You invented it, it must be a good gift, so I'll go ahead in obedience and You teach me how to pray.'

After we finished praying Jean said she understood what I had said, God had given her the interpretation. She translated. But it was beautiful; my heart was yearning for the Lord and calling as from the depths of a valley stream to the mountain tops for Him. I loved Him and worshipped Him and longed for Him to use me. It was in language so much more explicit and glorious than any I could have formulated. I decided that if God helped me to pray like that when I was praying in tongues, then I would never despise this gift again. I accepted that He was helping me to pray perfectly.

Every day – as I had promised the Willans – I prayed in the language of the Spirit. Fifteen minutes by the clock. I still felt it to be an exercise. Before praying in the Spirit I said, 'Lord – I don't know how to pray, or whom to pray for. Will You pray through me – and will You lead me to the people who want You?' Then I would begin my fifteen minute stint.

After about six weeks I noticed something remarkable.

Those I talked to about Christ believed. I could not understand it at first and wondered how my Chinese had so suddenly improved, or if I had stumbled on a splendid new evangelistic technique. But I was saying the same things as before. It was some time before I realised what had changed. This time I was talking about Jesus to people who wanted to hear. I had let God have a hand in my prayers and it produced a direct result. Instead of my deciding what I wanted to do for God and asking His blessing I was asking Him to do His will through me as I prayed in the language He gave me.

Now I found that person after person wanted to receive Jesus. I could not be proud – I could only wonder that God let me be a small part of His work. And so the emotion came. It never came while I prayed, but when I saw the results of these prayers I was literally delighted.

There is quite a contrast between this intoxication of the spirit and the spiritual vacuum which is often filled by drugs. What Jackie Pullinger had also discovered was the crucial importance of prayer. Ghandi – a non-Christian – once took two years off from his hectic political struggle to fast and pray, saying 'my greatest fight is with the demons inside me. My next fight is with the demons inside my people, and only after that comes my fight with the British.' In fighting drug abuse and the underworld Pullinger saw that there was a spiritual battle and that if she simply relied on her own strength, she would fail. In the UK we increasingly rely on ourselves to fix all our national ills. Like Gandhi we have to start with the demons within.

Britain's Drug Problems

A great deal has been written about Britain's drugs problems. The political issue of the moment concerns legalisation or decriminalisation of cannabis. Whilst there is still strong government hostility towards drugs, there is a growing and worrying collection of voices who appear to have given up on trying to curb the availability of drugs. This is a disastrous message to convey to the nation's youth. It is especially irresponsible in the light of all the medical evidence heavily stacked against those who say that cannabis is less harmful than either alcohol or tobacco.

A good, clear and comprehensive argument needs to be effectively communicated about the risks of drugs. The present debate confuses people, but especially those most at risk in the playgrounds and streets of Britain. The debate which rages on in media newsrooms and political conferences does them no favours. The human consequences could be nothing short of disastrous.

Although it would be unrealistic to attempt to usher in a totally 'Pullingeresque' style of tackling the current drug problem in the UK, we clearly need to embrace the philosophy at the heart of her work. Like her we should recognise that perhaps the main reason – if not the only reason – why so many young people fall headfirst into a life of drug dependency is because there is little else on offer. In a country which doesn't even have a statutory youth service we should not be wholly surprised by the numbers of disaffected and alienated young people. What chance have they got if the future is a choice of selling crack or working part-time at McDonald's? Society desperately needs to give time and effort to those who are desperately in need of both. Young people who grow up in areas where long-term unemployment is no longer exceptional face a massive and inevitably overwhelming task of living a drug-free, moral life-style. The last thing they need is the politically correct claptrap which says: 'We know you feel helpless, we also know there is no hope for you; therefore we can only help you by decriminalising the use of the nation's most popular drug and hope that this will enable you to live a crime-free life since we have given up on you living a drug-free life.'

The issue then is not so much whether to criminalise or decriminalise, but is more a question of desirability. Is it desirable to have thousands of mainly young people dependent on destructive and corrosive substances? Is it desirable to create a dependency culture, an addicted society? The whole social context in which we live today, in contemporary society, is an addictive one. Materialism, consumerism, drugs, alcohol, money; all feed on one another. Possession and consumption are all part and parcel of the manipulative structures of contemporary society. Playing games with words such as criminalisation and decriminalisation simply disguises the reality of that.

Let's be clear about what drug addiction means to broken communities and disfigured neighbourhoods. Streets awash with drugs – in London, Liverpool, Glasgow or Manchester – bring violence in their train. The 'Mr Big' who organise and profit from the drugs war systematically up the ante. Rival organisations take to the streets to claim their share of the market. Crime escalates, guns become the norm, shootings and deaths follow.

Perhaps most despicable of all is the use of young people, often children, acting like a grocer's delivery boy taking drugs into streets or blocks where the dealers will not be seen themselves. Once lured into this profitable business, young people develop a taste, and start living a life commensurate with the substantial income they generate. It makes for a more lucrative way of living than unemployment or low-wage, dead-end jobs.

This trend apes the drug economies of great American cities and by aping their response to this phenomenon we will be equally unsuccessful in combating it. In America, well-meaning programmes have been established everywhere with a view to treating the symptoms of drug addiction. We have the same sort of things here in the UK. They do not get to the root of the problem. Dysfunctional society must be remade with the culture values of modern society repudiated. When we create the desire for affluence – incessantly hyped up by television advertising – but then close off any legitimate means of satisfying that desire, we shake together a dangerous cocktail of combustible properties where communities implode and young men seek illicit ways of accessing wealth.

When we talk about the evidence against the decriminalisation of cannabis, we are not referring to some outdated and well-worn, simplified set of statistics. No, we are talking about genuine, hard-hitting facts. Susan Kaplin, research officer for the British branch of the US-based Drug Watch International, points to 10,000 medical studies documenting the harmful effects of cannabis. 'It adversely affects the respiratory, cardio-vascular and immune systems. There are more than 420 chemicals in cannabis, and many of these are toxic. The amounts of cancer-causing chemicals in cannabis smoke are 50 to 70 per cent greater than those in tobacco smoke.'[2] The hackneyed argument that cannabis use is less harmful than tobacco should be relegated to the dungeons along with other discredited notions such as 'the earth is flat' and 'asbestos is harmless'. It is also faintly bizarre that just as governments all over the world are spending millions of pounds to dissuade people from smoking, legislators should simultaneously consider legalising the use of drugs.

The libertarian argues that the actions of one individual do not have to adversely affect the rest of society. But how do you measure this? If one person's eventual dependency – physical or emotional – upon a drug such as cannabis, leads them to neglect an employer, a spouse, a relative or friend, then the use of drugs has adversely affected the rest of society. When the actions of one individual are multiplied by all the others who believe their actions are not harming anybody else, the impact on society will be phenomenal. This leads us to the crucial point in the debate. It is not so much the actions of those who use illicit drugs that is the primary concern here. Rather, it is the message that we as a nation want to convey to the general population and to our youth in particular. We will do them no service if we cave in and decide that the use of cannabis or other drugs is no different from buying chocolate from the local newsagent.

Some people have also erroneously argued that the money raised from the legal sale of drugs could finance treatment and education programmes. Tim Rathbone MP, Chairman of the All-Party Parliamentary Drugs Misuse Group correctly disagrees: 'How could a parent or teacher tell a teenager, "The government has made heroin legal but you mustn't try it."?' The same argument applies to all drugs. Without decriminalisation there are phenomenal levels of drug reliance in Britain.

We already have too many drugs, legal and illegal, freely in circulation. Thirty years ago benzodiazephines (tranquilliser/sleeping pills) were introduced as a replacement for barbiturates, which were highly toxic. Valium followed Librium, both were promoted with films showing wild and ferocious cats turning into kitten-like animals once the pills were administered. Doctors prescribed these legal drugs as a cure for all evils. Bereavement, marital problems, tension, stress, headaches, backaches: you name it, Valium would solve it.

Then in the 1970s, first in the USA and later in this country, people increasingly found themselves addicted to benzodiazephines. If they did stop taking them they often found they suffered from an illness which was worse than their initial illness.

By the 1980s many of the patients whose suffering was not caused by overuse, misuse, abuse or illegal procurement, but by prescribed tablets recommended by doctors, had begun legal actions against the drug companies. In Parliament, recently, ministers confirmed to me that thousands of these cases are still to be heard.

The long-term effects of these drugs on many individuals and families have been horrific. Benzodiazephines have proved to be Britain's biggest drugs disaster. These legal drugs have turned people into zombies, split up homes, destroyed careers and cost jobs. They have created a servile state in which users are kept in a pacified form of bondage. Hundreds of people have been driven to suicide or have tried to kill themselves because of benzodiazephines. Whole estate and tower blocks have been tranquillised into ill-health.

In the Mersey Region alone 130,000 men and women are dependent on benzodiazephines, yet there are no officially dedicated facilities in the area to help people. They are lumped together with heroin addicts and junkies – and yet they have done nothing more than follow the instructions of their GPs.

In addition to these already legal and grossly over-prescribed drugs, there are the quick-trip killers peddled by illegal drug pushers. Two years ago, Brian Moss was rushed to Liverpool's Walton Hospital. His mother found her twenty-year-old son writhing on the floor in convulsions. Sweat was pouring off him in buckets and his body felt as if it was on fire. 'He kept convulsing, then he fell unconscious, and foam started coming out of his mouth, mixed with blood,' his mother said. Brian died on the way to hospital. He had taken the so-called 'fun' drug, Ecstasy, that has already claimed at least fifteen lives in Britain and damaged hundreds of others. It is now taken by an estimated 500,000 young people out for a good time at night-clubs and 'raves'.

Increasingly, Ecstasy is being mixed during manufacture with other drugs such as LSD, heroin, or even ketamine (a veterinary anaesthetic), so that unwitting youngsters build up a dependency. One Glasgow dealer admitted: 'Half the time I don't know what I'm selling. I do know that I wouldn't touch it myself.' That, of course, doesn't stop him from taking the money which youngsters part with to feed their addiction.

Whether they are 'soft' or 'hard' drugs they are all a part of the same process which turns a free personality into a slave, with all the inevitable loss of dignity and self-respect.

It has become fashionable to argue that because something is widely used that, by itself, makes it right. Surely the example of those who have become dependent on legally prescribed drugs is warning enough against this folly? We would do far better to cultivate an anti-drugs culture in Britain, one which values a lack of dependence on mind-bending substances. We would also do far better to put more money into the pockets of farmers who have become reliant on growing opium and pay them instead to grow food crops. And some of the money to do that could come from the sequestration of the assets of the drug pushers and from the irresponsible drug companies which have grown fat on the misery which they have created. So 'mass surrender' on the intellectual front is no way forward.

Jackie Pullinger's Work

It is in this context that Jackie Pullinger's work might help us to put together a detailed and radical proposal. It is the heart of Jackie Pullinger's work which is the key. We must embrace those who have been afflicted by a sense of despair and utter hopelessness. Words like empathy, compassion and encouragement should replace condemnation, ignorance and the pitting of them against us. One of the most attractive aspects of Jackie Pullinger's character is her uncompromising faith in God. He took her to Hong Kong in the first place. Time and time again, she finds herself realising that inner change is the only real solution and that she has to live in faith. One particular story illustrates this. She took some boys from the youth club she ran in the Walled City to the nearby hills for a barbecue. A senior leader of the boys joined them and was busily devouring all the food that Jackie had bought with her own money. Even the other boys were donating their rations to him as they sat there mesmerised by his every word. Concerned that this might be a takeover bid for the attention of the boys, Jackie took him aside for a talk.

He was amused at this request from a mere girl and made a great show of rising from his haunches and lumbering towards me amidst cat-calls and whistles. But when we were out of ear-shot he dropped the macho attitude and listened quite seriously when I told him that the whole reason for the club was that I wanted them [the boys] to know the love of Jesus.

His reply was an indictment and a confirmation. 'I know,' he said, 'we've been watching you. Many missionaries come to Hong Kong to help us poor people. They put us in sociological boxes and analyse us. Then they take our pictures to shock the Westerners by our living conditions. Some men get famous because they've been here. But inside the Walled City we usually get rid of them within six months. We find ways to discourage them until they have no heart to continue – had you been a man we would have had you beaten long ago. We couldn't care less if you have big buildings or small ones. You can be offering free rice, free schools, judo classes or needlework to us. It doesn't matter if you have a daily programme or hymn singing once a week. These things don't touch us because the people who run them have nothing to do with us. What we want to know is if you are concerned with us. Now that you have been here for four years we have decided that maybe you mean what you say.'

I did not sing in front of him but my heart was bursting, there on a hump in the Chinese mountains.

Young people are the same the world over. All they need and want is to know that they are not simply outcasts of society because they do not fit into a pre-set mould. The problem with the mould is that those who make it always have their own agenda for what a perfect young person on the threshold of adult life should be. We fail to take sufficient account of the influences that invariably have shaped their attitudes and perspective of the world. We also make the mistake of assuming that all people grow up with fundamental moral values and an inherent knowledge of what is morally right and wrong. It is simply not the case any more. Young people need guidance and access to sound teaching. Then they can understand what they are doing to themselves and others.

So apart from winning the respect of the hardest of drug dealers over a period of years not months, what else can we learn from Jackie Pullinger's efforts? Her methods are unique in that they are wholly reliant upon the power of God and yet at the same time very practical in the instances where extra effort and persistence are required. For example, there are several accounts of young men who, after initially displaying a desire to be freed from their addiction, go back on their decision when faced with the very real pain of withdrawal. Countless times she was called in the middle of the night to rescue a young man who had once again either fallen foul of the law or, worse, fallen into the hands of a rival gang and as a result, lay bleeding in the street. Other times, Jackie would hire a solicitor to represent one of her boys in court. She had discovered previously that though the boys of the Walled City did of course, commit many crimes, they were often picked up for things they had not done. They would invariably plead guilty to appease the police who simply wanted ten-minute hearings in front of a magistrates' court and then to be done with the matter. She began to plead with the boys to tell the truth regardless of whether they were guilty or not. And once again, after great persistence and effort, there were rewards. She recalls one time when she was in the street, listening to two brothers talking about her.

'833179. Remember that number next time you are arrested. It doesn't matter what time of day or night you call, Miss Poon will come. It doesn't matter whether you've done the crime you're arrested for or not, she'll come. The only thing you must do is to tell the truth. You see, she's a Christian.' As I walked home I knew that, 'Your labour in the Lord is not in vain.' Here I was privileged enough to see the fruits of some of those labours. Some of the vilest criminals in Hong Kong now knew that Jesus' name was truth.

Jackie spent endless hours in court supporting her boys, irrespective of their guilt, enduring the mockery that came her way simply because she was willing to be associated with the 'lowest of the low'. She recalls the case of Johnny. At the time, he was the epitome of the hopeless drug addict.

On the way to the police station, I thought about Johnny who was one of the most repulsive-looking drug addicts I knew. He was small and desperately thin, more a skeleton than a man. 'If that one can be saved – anyone can,' I had thought when I first saw him. He was a carpenter earning quite a good wage but using the entire lot to smoke heroin. He was a Triad too but useless to his gang.

It later transpired that Johnny had already signed a 'confession' before Jackie arrived at the station. She did, however, get a chance to pray for him. He agreed that in principle it would be right to tell the truth though he felt unable to do so given the circumstances. Eventually, the case came to trial and Johnny was still saying he would plead guilty even though he had not committed the crime. When he stood up in court, however, he later told Jackie that he suddenly had an overwhelming conviction that he had to tell the truth though he did not want to at all. What might have been a simple case lasting a few moments became a major battle lasting over a week. Johnny's solicitor, whom Jackie had hired at the cost of a whole month's living expenses, cross-examined the police evidence. Eventually the magistrate accepted the prosecution's case and found Johnny guilty. He was sent to prison and from there to a drug rehabilitation centre. Opposition to Jackie's further involvement came from a probation officer but she continued nonetheless. On appeal, the Chief Justice overruled his conviction, and Johnny was free. However he went back to drugs and was soon caught up in the same vicious circle. But he never forgot that experience in court. After about two years, he finally became a Christian and went to a Christian drug rehabilitation centre. After graduating from there, he became a male nurse in a TB sanatorium, working on an addicts' ward.

The other major breakthrough which came from Johnny's case was the attitude of the police to boys who were in Jackie's care. Whenever they stopped anyone in the street, they would enquire, 'Are you from that place? Are you from that woman's club?' When they replied yes, they would not be detained and the reason was simple. The police knew that if they picked up one of Jackie's boys under false pretences, she would fight tooth and nail for them and rather than a ten-minute hearing, they would incur the expense and fuss of a week's trial.

Then there are the cases of boys who came to Jackie's meetings inside the Walled City. Some of these are nothing short of miraculous. During my own visit to the Walled City I met young men who told me that having prayed to Jesus for healing they had been delivered from their addiction to heroin right there and then. Others would stay for several days until the withdrawal was complete. The rule laid down by Jackie and her friends was always the same: 'If you want to be set free from your addiction without suffering the normal excruciating pains of "cold turkey" then you must pray in the Spirit.' Addicts who had not yet made a commitment to Christ would understandably have a problem with this but they couldn't help but be impressed by the miracle which they saw for themselves in their friends who were healed from heroin and set free to begin a new life. Jackie learned though, that just because a young man had been transformed physically, it did not mean he would be ready for a 'normal' life of work. In any event, a healing experience has to be sustained. I would dearly like to know what happened subsequently to some of the people Jesus healed in the New Testament stories. Was their whole life healed? Did they build on the miracle or did they quickly revert? Often, Jackie Pullinger's former addicts would live with her for weeks and even months before they ventured out on their own in search of work and new opportunities. Again, this illustrates the principle of care and discipleship that is necessary to ensure any lasting success. She was aware also that she was nearly always dealing with severely disturbed youths who had not known even the suggestion of real parental love or care. It was only as they saw the love of God through the actions of Jackie and her friends that they could begin to accept that perhaps Jesus could be real for them too. Many, if not most, of the boys who came to Jackie first experienced the power of God for themselves as they surrendered themselves to Him; and only later as they were able to adjust to the miracle of a new life could they begin to understand the theological aspects of who Jesus is. The Gospel as preached by Jackie Pullinger is a very simple one indeed: Jesus loves you so much that He died so that you can be free from drugs and death, and in turn live a new life for Him. That the servant He had sent cared enough to help them was worth more than a thousand words.

One of the best examples of God's transforming power occurred in a young man called Tony. He was persuaded by Jackie to come with her instead of launching into a suicidal gang raid. She took him back to her flat where several other boys were living at the time. This is his testimony as told in *Chasing the Dragon*:

They prayed for me and I accepted Jesus as my Lord and I received the baptism of the Spirit. At first I felt very cold but when I was filled with the Spirit a surprising thing happened – I felt my heart burning within me and my whole body grew warm and I wept. I had not cried since I was a child. I sat shamelessly weeping in front of everyone and I knew that I had truly been 'born-again'.

They took me to Stephen's Third House to come off heroin. I had tried many times to come off drugs. The pain had always been greater than I could bear. The first time I went to prison I had to come off 'cold turkey' and it was so terrible that I broke out of prison into barbed wire and bear the scars to this day. From that day on I always had heroin hidden on my person so that I was never caught without it. But this time it was different. My brothers in Jesus prayed for me and I also prayed in tongues and the pain disappeared. Two months later, I went to live with Mr and Mrs Willans who run the houses. My own parents cannot be traced but Mr and Mrs Willans are now my parents.

I have witnessed God moving in many areas of my life since that time. I not only went with my new mother and father to China, but in 1976 I visited America and England with them and joined them in speaking in a number of churches and on radio and television. What an amazing thing for me, a former Red Pole fighter in the 14K Triad Society, an ex-convict and heroin addict, to be given a special waiver to visit the United States of America. And the Home Secretary himself cleared my travel to England when everyone said it was impossible.

I have since been trained in a first class hairdressing school to be a hair stylist. I work in a leading salon in Hong Kong and live with my parents in a nice apartment. It is truly astonishing and shows that my Lord Jesus is very powerful. But the greatest thing He has done for me is to

change my heart and now I no longer follow sin because I
follow Him.

Tony's story is unusual but he is far from alone in testifying to
the power of God at work in his life. This surely presents us
with the real solution to the problem of drugs in our society
today.

The stories and principles applied in Jackie Pullinger's work
will be embarrassing to some. But as we contemplate communities littered with drugs and their casualties, remember that
many of the boys she has treated and continues to treat today
began their experimentation with drugs via the so-called 'soft
drugs' route of cannabis and amphetamines. If we can be
encouraged rather than embarrassed by her experiences with
heroin addicts in Hong Kong then surely we can see an
application in the UK. The treatment of the whole person, not
simply the symptoms, is the real point.

A Change of Approach

For those who are policy-makers, there is a similar need to
change their approach. Punitive sentences against the organis-
ers of the drugs trade, counselling and help for addicts, and
disincentives to opium farmers, will all play their part. In
addition, I would like to see the confiscated assets of drugs
pushers reinvested in the communities which they have
exploited. Brand new facilities for young people should bear
the inscription: 'These facilities were provided through the
seizure of confiscated assets of drugs pushers'.

The message should be clear: not only does crime not pay
but the communities which have been abused ultimately obtain
practical help and justice. In turn this should also encourage
the people of drugs-ridden communities to provide information
and assistance to law enforcers.

Even more fundamentally, the policy-makers must understand the sheer ugliness of the world occupied by the drugs fraternity and the customers. Dostoyevsky put the words 'beauty will save the world' into the mouth of Prince Mishkin. Everyone laughed at the Prince. But beauty, whether it is the beauty of integrity, purity and truth, or the physical beauty of the environment, is what makes life worth living. For the Christian this beauty is at its zenith in the person of Christ. During the Transfiguration on Mount Tabor, that beauty was so overwhelming that the disciples fell on their faces. They couldn't stand the beauty that was to save the world.

Were there no hope of this beauty, God would appear like a vandal rather than an artist. The repulsiveness of eternal decay, the darkness of Sheol, the hideousness of death – if there was no Resurrection – would be to be condemned to a life of perpetual ugliness devoid of beauty. Christ ensures that there is no ugliness in any of us that cannot be refashioned. So Dostoyevsky's foolish Prince was right. Divine beauty saves the world.

For the addict, wallowing in a world of infinite ugliness, there is a desperate need for every kind of beauty. Self-respect and an appreciation that they are unique and valued individuals are what they need most to know.

From the exterior ugliness of hypodermic syringes, tin foil, and quick fixes we must create a sense of interior beauty and orderliness; of being valued and appreciated. The precious pearl only is formed in the oyster shell when sand enters it. There can be no pearl without suffering. Policy-makers should not pretend that there will be solutions to the drugs epidemic without fundamental personal changes which also involve pain.

Chapter Eleven

Ellen Wilkie

REPUDIATING PERFECTION TESTS ON LIFE

The truth is cruel, but it can be loved, and it makes free those
who have loved it.

George Santayana, *Little Essays* (1920)

I met Ellen Wilkie for the first time on 13th October 1987, less
than two years before she died. Most of us could not hope to
pack into our entire lives what Ellen achieved in her short thirty-
one years; an honours degree in Classics from Bristol University;
a published poet, prison worker, author, actress, radio and
television presenter, journalist and musician; the list only covers
some of things she achieved. The packed church in Bristol,
where people from many walks of life had gathered for her
funeral, was the best testimony of all to the varied and rich life
which she had.

Ellen struggled all her life with Duchenne muscular dystrophy,
a very rare muscle-wasting disease. Not only did she have to
battle to overcome the barriers placed in her way by able-bodied
society, but even amongst disabled persons she was at a disad-
vantage. Whilst paraplegics, for example, can develop very
strong arms enabling them to do almost everything for themselves except walk, Ellen's disability was lack of strength generally, and there was little hope that she would ever get any
physically stronger.

The chance of having this condition was one in a million, but
in many ways Ellen was very much the exception rather than the
rule. What makes her life such an inspiration is summed up by

the words she used in her autobiography[1] in commenting on an invitation received shortly before she died. When asked to return to address a school assembly about her achievements she said, 'It would make a boring assembly. Anybody could do what I've done.' Whether anyone could in fact do what she did is debatable. The point is that anyone *might* do what she did. Her life and approach to life should be an inspiration to us all.

Who Are the Disabled?

When Ellen was in her second year of life, her parents were told that she would be in a wheelchair by the time she was ten and would probably not survive her teens. We might ask ourselves what we would do if we were told that our life was to be cut by two-thirds. We might rush to patch up broken relationships, run around in a frenzy of activity, go on a holiday or give all our money to the poor. It would certainly focus our minds, and might even be quite liberating. Each moment of life would become that much more special. Ellen believed that our time is a gift from God; that our mission is to reflect God in every moment of our lives. Ellen certainly tried to carry out her mission and lived each day to the full.

Apart from the drugs and medical tests Ellen's childhood in Bristol was much like any other's. An experimental treatment from the age of six was probably what caused Ellen to survive her teens, although it meant that she had to endure three injections a week until her early twenties. Aged three, a muscle biopsy which removed a piece of muscle from the back of her leg left her with a shortened tendon and meant that she had to walk on tiptoe for the rest of her life. Despite these hardships, Ellen still did all the things that other children do. She had to perform her household chores, she danced, swam, fought with her brothers, slid down the stairs on mattresses, and argued with her mother over the length of her hair. Even when she couldn't walk properly she carried on her dancing. We might expect that her disability would set her apart from other children, but in fact she felt more alienated from her friends because her Brethren parents wouldn't allow a television in the house, than by her disability. 'It seems that children often respond in a far less judgemental way to disability, for they have not yet developed any prejudices,' Ellen observed in her autobiography, as she recalled how she would wave in response to her grandfather's uncontrolled movements, not realising that he had Parkinson's disease.

It was not until the sixth form that Ellen had to face the full consequences of the prejudice that most disabled people experience. Quite suddenly, Ellen's school announced that they wanted her to go to a special college for the 'handicapped' so that she could 'learn to cope' with her disability. Ellen always felt that special schools by no means helped people without disability to relate to the disabled. Their academic standards and opportunities were seldom as high as in an ordinary school. Although she had gained seven O levels, at a special school she would not be able to do the A levels she wanted, and her attention would be divided between learning academically, and learning to 'cope' with her disability. The very limited range of academic subjects focused on courses such as book-keeping and typewriting.

There was no reasonable argument why Ellen should suddenly leave for a 'special' school. One of the reasons cited was that she sometimes needed help getting up and down flights of stairs and along corridors between classrooms. Usually, the other pupils would help her – she only weighed three stone – but now the school was saying that the pupils could no longer do that, despite her friends' willingness to do so and even the evidence given by a gynaecologist that the exercise would probably do her friends good!

In what would be typical behaviour for the rest of her life, Ellen was not going to move schools without a fight. She assertively turned up at the school on the first day of her A-level year and refused to leave. Her mother had to accompany her around the school. At the subsequent emergency meeting of the school Governors, a paediatrician said firmly that every person with muscular dystrophy should be in an institution. The prejudice seemed to spread like wildfire around the school. All the teachers that had previously been quite happy at Ellen's presence suddenly had doubts. Her English teacher considered that reading literature which described things that Ellen could not possibly hope to do in her life would be too upsetting for her. Ellen defiantly continued to attend the school week after week, until a petition signed by 251 parents finally brought enough pressure to persuade the Governors to let her stay.

It was the attitudes of other people that had handicapped Ellen, not her disability. This was to be the first of many similar situations that Ellen encountered in her life:

> When I looked up the word 'handicapped' in the dictionary, I found that it meant 'something imposed on you which hampers', and that is what I discovered – that other people were imposing, and have imposed at various times in my life, their own handicapping prejudices on me, putting me down into a disadvantaged position. It is this attitude, more than narrow doorways and split-level corridors, which makes life difficult for disabled people. For the first time in my life I was made to feel that having muscular dystrophy would prevent me from having a normal life, if other people got their way.

Happily this fact is beginning to be more widely acknowledged. Baroness Lockwood said recently,

> It is now increasingly accepted and recognised that disability is not so much a medical problem for the individual but rather it concerns the relationship between someone with a disability and his or her environment. By viewing

disability as a social issue in that way we are able to focus on the real problem, which is the way that society structures its institutions and environment.[2]

This environment includes people's attitudes. One campaigner for the rights of the disabled has often started her talks by asking the question 'Who thinks they have a disability?' In an average sample of people, few are likely to raise their hands. This has more to do with the way that disability is viewed than the actual reality. If, as the campaigner goes on to show, 'disability' is defined as any physical, mental, emotional or spiritual impairment to our being wholly perfect human beings, there is no one who does not in fact have a disability.[3] None of us are perfect. We are all disabled to a certain degree, in one way or another. It is therefore wrong to section off one group in society and label them as less than whole human beings. In the words of Shakespeare; 'In nature there's no blemish but the mind; None can be call'd deform'd but the unkind.'

Despite a 'two E's' offer from Bristol University to study Classics, and the battles of her A-level years, Ellen obtained two 'A's' and one 'B' in her exams. Bristol University was, however, to present further problems for Ellen. The mock Gothic-Victorian structure of the University, and Ellen's physical condition meant that a wheelchair was necessary for getting around. Unable to use the main entrance with all the steps, she used a side-door to the building in which her lectures were held because it only had one step. Despite this, she still relied on a student to place a moveable wooden ramp in front of the entrance to get in.

Disabled people are alienated from taking an active part in our society, by the environment that has been created, although given the right (or wrong) environment, everyone might be handicapped. It is interesting to note incidentally that Dr Who's greatest foe, the Daleks, were not so omnipotent after all. They could always be defeated by their environment. Since they were on wheels, all Dr Who really needed to do to get away from them was to run upstairs! Unfortunately people seem unable to see past a disability to the person. The 'disabled' are seen as a homogenous group, as if 'disabled' is the only characteristic that they have. It is by this one characteristic that they are accorded worth both socially and economically. This is perhaps why we do not offer more provision for the disabled.

Over the last few years, several Private Members' Bills have been brought before Parliament regarding the civil rights of, and measures to prevent discrimination against, disabled people. The big argument against such legislation has continually been that the cost would be too great. In 1993, Nicholas Scott, then Minister for Disabled People and Social Security spoke on the day that the debate on the Second Reading of Baroness Lockwood's Civil Rights (Disabled Persons) Bill was due, giving the government's reasons for not supporting it. It had been objected to by the Conservative Member for Berkshire East, the virulently pro-abortion Andrew MacKay, and so had proceeded no further. 'Undoubtly, expense for the government and other providers would be implicit in the passage of the Civil Rights (Disabled Persons) Bill and we need to deal with such issues.' Again later he said: 'The Civil Rights (Disabled Persons) Bill . . . is wide-ranging and would imply considerable costs for employers, suppliers and the Government.'[4] He did not go as far as Lord Reay who, in arguing for destructive experiments on human embryos, said that this would allow 'the culling of the handicapped'.

In 1995, the government has bowed to pressure and now acknowledges the need for a comprehensive legal framework. Disability groups still feel that the government's position falls far short of the sort of legislation they desire, whilst the Institute of Directors (IOD) continues to express concern over the cost to business. According to the Institute of Directors Press Release, the Disability Bill is a 'Blank Cheque'.

Alarm bells must surely start ringing when the overriding

measure of a group's worth is economic terms. We should at least look back at past experience. This was what drew Ellen to study Classics. On her arrival at University, Ellen was immediately struck by the introductory talk given by her Head of Department. 'If people were going to start saying it was pointless to study aspects of the past, then ... what was the point of doing Shakespeare, English Literature, or even discussing what happened last year? We learn from the past and that's why we study it.' But the past reveals that attitudes to the disabled are not all that different from today.

Attitudes to Disability

As far back as 1720, the social theorist Bernard Mandeville attempted to show in his 'Fable of the Bees' that progress and prosperity were only possible if nature were to take its course, men's natural desires were given full reign, and that the promotion of values such as abstinence and self-restraint were destructive of public welfare. 'It is sentiment that is echoed in contemporary laissez-faire thinking.'[5] Milton Friedman, the great influence behind the New Right is in some important respects a modern Mandevillian. The reasoning behind such thought is demonstrated in Darwin's theory of natural selection – the survival of the fittest, where the outcome of nature, whatever it may be, is seen as the desired result.

At the turn of the century, two developments of 'Social Darwinism' were the Eugenics Movement and an organised attempt to slow down all social legislation which might help the less able members of society. The first issue of the *Eugenics Review* (April 1909) emphasised that the social legislation of the day was 'penalising the fit for the sake of the unfit'. One of the Eugenics Laboratory lecturers complained that 'practically all social legislation has been based on the (false) assumption that better environment means race progress'[6] (*Endangered lives: Public Health in Victorian Britain*).

As the middle-class birth rate began to fall in the late nineteenth century due to the increasing use of contraception, and the lower-class birth rate remained high, there were fears that the quality of the population would be undermined. Nature was given a helping hand. In the 1920s one of the results was the 'Sterilisation of the Mentally Handicapped Movement'. A Department Committee on Voluntary Sterilisation recommended as late as 1934 that sterilisation should be more readily available. In the words of one historian, 'Eugenicists prescribed the severest medicine for an ailing nation: that the feeble be sterilised so as not to breed more congenital defectives, when the reproduction rate of the healthy and intelligent was becoming more modest.'[7]

This situation may seem far removed from the present day. But look at modern China for examples of how similar thinking is being used today. I have written elsewhere (see Chapter 8: Lin Xiangao) about the effect of their one-child policy on women and on human rights. But the approach adopted towards disability is downright fascist.

In Britain the former BBC social services correspondent, Polly Toynbee, criticised the birth in Manchester of Siamese twins who should, she says, have been screened out and aborted.

The new Chinese Maternal and Infant Health Care Law, effective from 1 June 1995, stipulates obligatory pre-natal tests and requires doctors to advise a couple to abort if they detect a hereditary disease or an abnormality. In law, a healthy woman still has the option to refuse an abortion. The reality may be less liberal. Although the final decision on abortion lies with the mother, critics of the law are worried that 'advice' can often turn into forceful persuasion.

It is not just the unborn disabled in China who will suffer under the Maternal and Infant Health Care Law. People suffering from mental illness or a contagious disease are also regarded as 'medically unsuitable for reproduction'. They are not allowed to marry until they have agreed to 'permanent measures' of contraception, and in practice this usually means sterilisation. The law has been criticised as 'a diluted version of a Eugenics law' which aims to stop 'inferior' births, and compared to Nazi-style eugenics.[8] According to Frank Dikotter of London University's School of Oriental and African Studies, ideas of selective breeding go back to the 1920s and 1930s and have simply been shown not to work ... you can't engineer a population to get rid of so-called deleterious features.'[9] It is alarming though to compare our situation in this country with that of China. The situation in China may not be as far removed from ours as we might like to think.

As in China, in this country it is financial considerations that dominate the arguments. The Chinese Politburo sees the new law as a logical economic decision. Part of the justification for the new law given by The New China News Agency was that the country had '10 million disabled persons who could have been prevented'.[10] Labour MP Brian Wilson has pointed out that with regard to babies with Down's Syndrome in this country, a financial calculation is also made. It costs £38,000 to avoid one Down's baby whilst the lifetime costs of caring for one Down's child have been estimated at £120,000. The difference between £38,000 and £120,000 plays a significant part in determining whether children live or die. This leads Mr Wilson to ask, 'Why do we stop at Down's Syndrome?'[11] There are plenty of other conditions which cost more to support than they would to eliminate. Avoiding handicap certainly makes accountancy sense but, as Dominic Lawson, the editor of the *Sunday Telegraph* and himself the father of a disabled child has passionately charged: it does not make ethical or moral sense.

In this country in 1993 there were just 311 Down's Syndrome babies born in England and Wales compared to 505 in 1984. 'Ninety per cent of Down's pregnancies where "risk" has been defined, meet a similar end as a by-product of the drive to identify in order to prevent.' Some 2,000 women each year opt for a termination following diagnosis of a fetal abnormality.[12] Almost all antenatal clinics offer routine screen tests for fetal abnormality. Methods include ultrasound, Chorionic Villus sampling where a small piece of tissue surrounding the developing baby is examined for chromosomal abnormalities, amniocentesis which involves examining a sample of the amniotic fluid that surrounds the baby in the womb, and blood tests. Paradoxically reports have recently appeared of tests being withdrawn after the tests themselves caused disabilities; amniocentesis leads to spontaneous abortion in at least 3 per cent of cases. The tests allow seventy different disabling conditions to be examined. These include maternal serum screen tests for Down's Syndrome and fetal anomaly scans to detect structural deformities. The tests are the first part of a search and destroy mission. Their hunter-killer tests also enable doctors to put enormous pressure on parents. Those who refuse to comply are often told they are 'irresponsible'.

Where does all this leave Down's Syndrome children who are inconsiderate enough to have slipped through the net and avoided the perfection tests? In justifying the new law, the argument of the Communist Government was that 'it would be better for society if such children were not born'.[13] The state involves itself in the private lives of individuals 'for the good of society and the country'. Clare Rayner, a well-known media-styled counsel for the youth of our country used just such an argument recently. Parents of Down's children, she pointed out 'will not be paying the full price of their choice'. When the parents die, 'we all share that burden'. It was, therefore, irresponsible to bring a disabled child into the world. This attitude is reflected in our law which allows a disabled baby to be aborted up to birth. It is not surprising to find that in China, the new law goes arm-in-arm with the terrible treatment of disabled children after they are born as well. Most disabled children are either abandoned or left in state institutions in appalling conditions. The situation in this country may not be so extreme. We must, however, ask ourselves what prospect there is of giving disabled people the kind of provision which offers a real chance of fulfilling their potential when this is the attitude of society and when the whole thrust of social policy, as in China, is to ensure that this generation of the disabled is the last? In a letter to the editor of the *Guardian*, Philippa and Tim Woods put it well when they said 'Society must knock on the head the idea of the perfect child'.[14]

This idea of 'perfection' in China has led to discrimination against not just disabled people, but against females before they are born. Ironically it is the same technology, said by many to extend women's choice that has been employed to screen out female babies in China, and so been used as a tool of oppression against women. Because of a nearly universal preference for boys, millions of Chinese have used ultrasound tests to screen for males and to abort females.

'If I joined any pro-life group it would be Feminists Against Eugenic Practices, because that is very much the angle I find congenial' said Ellen Wilkie, in her autobiography. For so long, feminism has been associated with a pro-abortion stance. The myth that feminists are all of one mind needs to be exposed. They may all have the common aim of alleviating the oppression of women but differ on their reasons for women's oppression. Marxist feminist, Radical feminist, Libertarian feminist, Black feminist ... the list goes on. Some will put the locus of oppression with women's bodies, others with a class struggle.

The emphasis also changes over time. The first wave of feminists opposed contraception. 'Of all the Women's issues, birth control had the least public support among feminists.'[15] Many feminists expressed hostility towards the birth control movement. In the 1990s a new and long overdue debate is currently re-opening about natural family planning, which the World Health Organisation says is more effective than artificial methods and avoids the dangers to women's health associated with the pill. Other feminists advance another argument: that the separation of the sexual act from reproduction meant more sex for women, and men could go elsewhere for their gratification, with fewer consequences. Dr Elizabeth Blackwell, for example, known for her advanced views on women's sexuality and the need for sex education, said that she was opposed to all such 'artifices to indulge a husband's sensuality while counteracting Nature' (quoted in Himmelfarb). While feminists will work for the liberation or equality of women, they will differ in the means to achieve it. This is precisely Ellen's point; 'It would not harm any pro-abortion feminist to look at the opposing opinions within their movement.'[16] This is just what Jane Roe and Naomi Wolf have done in the US.

Ellen would not join a pro-life movement in order to avoid categorisation, the prejudice and sterotypes that are placed upon you if you are 'pro-life', or indeed, a 'feminist'. But she was pro-life in both her defence of the unborn and in the way she lived her life. In an interview she once said, 'I did not see how anyone could be part of the disability movement and advocate abortion on the grounds of disability.'[17]

Choice

Ellen also had a line about the slogan: 'pro-choice'. She believed that women should be in full possession of all the facts. It has become clear over the last few years the extent to which midwives and obstetricians do not always provide adequate and accurate information about antenatal tests. In one study,[18] only one in five women undergoing routine antenatal consultations was told about the possibility of having a false positive result in a serum screening test, although almost all were told about the test itself. The conclusion of the study was that health professionals 'were failing to give women a choice in the decision whether to be tested for fetal abnormality with all its implications'.[19]

Choice is the key word here. 'Choice without balanced

information is a meaningless concept, and there is no doubt that the whole medical growth industry in so-called "triple tests" is geared towards the assumption that identification of "risk" will be followed by termination.'[20] There have been many cases where women have been wrongly advised to have abortions, for example when they are diagnosed with toxoplasmosis, an infection which affects 600 babies a year and can lead to blindness and epilepsy. The Toxoplasmosis Trust has said that they know from women who have contacted them that doctors have advised them to terminate their pregnancy on the assumption the fetus will be severely damaged.

Additionally, there is no way of knowing how severely handicapped the baby will be, although technology promises to make it more and more possible. In other cases such as toxoplasmosis, treatment during pregnancy can be highly successful and termination is 'rarely warranted'.[21] Mothers who terminate and later find out that treatment could have been possible are not surprisingly devastated.

Ellen was also 'pro-choice' for the disabled baby. Abortion gives the disabled no chance to have a crack at the world. New technology now even makes the possibility of treatment in the womb a reality not to mention breakthrough in the treatment of handicap after birth. Ellen was given injections of Laevadosin, which significantly stopped the disability from worsening. Recent research suggests that the cells of people with Down's Syndrome are sensitive to a chemical which may eventually lead to the development of a medication to diminish the effects of the syndrome or to neutralise them altogether.[22] To abort is to deny the child any chance of overcoming disability. Parents' claims that 'the choice was ours alone, not the doctor's, the hospital's, or society's' are fatally flawed in that the disabled are given no voice.[23]

We have to question our 'civilised' society, if we act in a similar way to the Roman Empire who left their unwanted babies 'exposed' to die. In the Netherlands there have been documented cases where death has taken place after birth. Dr H. Prins gave two lethal injections to a severely handicapped three-day-old girl in the Netherlands in 1993, was found guilty of murder, but the court decided not to impose any penalty. The case was not one of euthanasia because the child was too young to express a will. In 1992, Dr C. Versluys, chairman of a group of experts on neonatal medicine, reported that each year the lives of about ten babies are deliberately terminated by doctors, and about 200 die because of a decision to withhold treatment. In this country, Professor Peter Dunn of Bristol and Dr Malcom Chiswick of Manchester admit that they 'allow to die' on average one disabled baby a month.[24]

Ellen's Full Life

Ellen Wilkie wrote the following poem:

Therapeutic Termination

We are the ones
who were to you
nothing to lose
we are the ones
who gave our lives
for your freedom to choose
we are the ones
who forgot all rights
we are the ones
deprived of a chance to fight
we are the ones
who never became your sons
we are the ones
who were silently slaughtered
before we became daughters
we are the ones

cut out in the prime
(but where do you draw the line?)
                              of life

though voiceless
you will hear us
though powerless
we will triumph

outside time
in another place
we join the ranks
for confrontation face to face

we are the ones
who stand before you
and demand
a life before death

Ellen Wilkie's poetry is an angry rebuttal of those who would have wished her never to have been born. As she once said to me 'No-one can say what a disabled person will be capable of.' But in addition to anger Ellen also had a sense of realism. She knew that the disabled can become a group apart from society, unwanted, unvalued. It was in the sixth form and on into university that Ellen really began to feel the effects herself. She was at an age when her friends were becoming increasingly independent, whilst she was becoming increasingly dependent. Her friends seem to develop into adults as she developed more into a child – or so it seemed. There was no private life, nothing that wasn't invaded by a physical reliance on other people. Her friends talked of pop concerts, discos and pubs with boyfriends, but she could do none of these things spontaneously on her own.

Her mother recalls vividly how Ellen came to her one day in

floods of tears because she wanted to take friends out but could never offer to do so since any evening out always entailed lifting her in and out of a car, pushing her in a wheelchair. As she got older, she recognised that she had as much right to a full life as everyone else. In her second year of university Ellen decided to embark on a career in the media and arts.

Her attempts involved endless letter writing, frequent rejections and occasional progress. Her desperate desire was to act, but since she did not see how she could do it on stage at first, she tried for the next best thing – radio drama. Her first break came when a friend of her mother tried to get her an opportunity to do five short talks about herself on BBC Radio Bristol. Not having an Equity card she could not get acting work, but someone suggested that she write to the BBC Radio 4 programme *Does He Take Sugar?* They wrote back to say that they were doing a programme on drama for disabled people, and asked if she would come and talk about her aspirations. Through that she got the opportunity to do some further voice-overs for a play with disabled actors.

Ellen left university with a 2.2, and immediately registered with two agencies to try and get work, but with little success. It was at this point that loneliness began to set in. All the friends she had known at school and university had now left Bristol. In typical 'Ellen' style, out of this depression, however, came an unexpected bud that was to blossom and bear fruit in a surprising way. Ellen began to write poetry which was later to become a central part of her life and constitute her first publications.

Early in 1981, the International Year of Disabled People, Ellen set off to start her acting career for real, with the theatre company 'Theatre of the Disabled' for whom she had done the voice-overs. They went on a tour of fringe theatres, festivals, town halls and even prisons around the UK, the highlight being a show at the Dominion Theatre for the Royal Command Performance before Prince and Princess Michael of Kent, where, at the party afterwards, Harry Secombe spilt his drink all over her whilst kissing her goodbye.

During a performance at Edinburgh Prison, Ellen made friends with an inmate called John. He gave her the unexpected gift of a painting that he had painted himself, and the result was that they struck up a relationship by letter. In her autobiography Ellen reflects how their respective 'disabilities' were a great equaliser. She was in a wheelchair, he was in a prison. The difference was that his prison was a trap and her wheelchair gave her freedom. As a consequence, Ellen later did a prison-visiting course and in 1988 conducted a series of poetry workshops in Pentonville and Holloway.

Exhausted at the end of the tour, Ellen was forced to turn down the opportunity of working with the Graeae theatre company, a professional company of actors with disabilities that had established a very good reputation for itself. On returning from holiday, she heard that the company were now looking for a replacement for one of their actors and she got the job. It was during this time that Ellen became politicised, that is in disabled politics rather than party politics. On reflection she was sure that this was because for the first time in her life she was living away from home and having to fight her own battles. She could now identify with the struggle that many disabled people were undergoing.

Her work with Graeae was to take her as far as India, where the show impressed the then Indian Prime Minister Mrs Indira Gandhi so much that she cancelled her appointments in order to stay for the whole show. Ellen left Graeae in the autumn of 1984 and got a job with the Half Moon Young People's Theatre, a company of able-bodied actors. After that she founded the Double Exposure Theatre Company with several other actors and also joined the Clean Break Theatre Company which was made up of able-bodied ex-prisoners. She then got a phone call offering her a job as presenter of *Same Difference*, a Channel Four magazine programme related to disability. The timing was great since the touring and rehearsing involved in the acting were beginning to drain her in every way. Her television appearances were not confined to disability-related issues either. Her work for Television South and the BBC was not disability-related and as a result of an article written in the *Independent* about her, the BBC programme *Five to Eleven* booked her to read some of her poetry. During my parliamentary battles against eugenics and abortion tours she became a formidable ally and encourager – although she always bridled at the disgraceful lack of access for wheelchairs in many parts of Westminster. The highlight of her career was landing a major support role in the film *Raspberry Ripple* (Cockney rhyming slang for 'cripple'), which starred Faye Dunaway, which was filmed in the summer of 1986. Ellen Wilkie died on 7th August 1989.

Two mysteries are highlighted by Ellen's life. First, the divine sovereignty of God. It is God's choice to create or to take life. Second, human dignity. Human life begins at conception and a human has dignity at whatever stage of development or in whatever physical state, whether disabled or not. Both these principles were very evident in Ellen's life. There is the mystery that God created Ellen the way He did. In her autobiography she records how as a nine-year-old she asked her mother; 'Mummy, was it because of something you took when you were expecting me that I am like I am?' Her mother replied, 'No, it's nothing I took. I know that God gave you to us as you are.' This did not stop Ellen struggling with this mystery.

Sometimes I would see my reflection in the mirror and think 'Why? Why? Why? Why me? Why did God make my body like this?' I began to think a bit more about how rare my particular disability was, how it affected me and none of my brothers. I had a strong feeling that, because it was such a totally freak occurrence, it was as if God were saying to me, 'Look, there's a purpose in all this, I've allowed it to happen to you for a special reason.' It is a hard thing to explain because it is such a personal experience.'[25]

What is clear is that Ellen had the same right to life as any other person. It was not her ability or disability that determined her value: 'I longed to tell people that what was most important about me was not what was wrong with me, or how I had coped with it, but that, inside, my feelings were exactly like everyone else's. I might look different on the outside but I still had the same emotions and traumas as any other girl.'[26]

Ellen was the first to point out that as a woman with a disability she would never be able to rest on her laurels, she always had to strive, even to stay where she was. As with any disabled person in our society, she would always be 'running to stand still'. Bono of U2 also says 'Right in the middle of a contradiction; that's the place to be'.[27] Ellen Wilkie was never frightened to contradict and in the thick of the battle is where she would always be.

Chapter Twelve

Pope John Paul II

TELLING IT LIKE IT IS

Nowdays flattery wins friends, truth hatred.

Terence, *The Woman of Andros* (166 BC)

The great doctor of the Church, St Thomas Aquinas, was the theologian who has most influenced Pope John Paul II. Rome's Angelicum is where the teachings of Aquinas continue to flower today. A stone's throw away you can stand in Trajan's Market. It was here that Pope Gregory met a group of Anglo-Saxon children who were being sold into slavery. The plight of the children led the Pope to say 'non Angli, sed Angeli' (not Angles but angels). The evangelisation of the English began in that market place, for the children prompted Gregory to send Augustine of Canterbury to convert the heathen English.

Today the successors of Gregory and Augustine face a new kind of barbarism. Pope John Paul II has recognised in the culture of death and its anti-life mentality not only a new barbarism but a moment of opportunity for evangelisation. There never was a time when a child, once conceived, was less likely to be born; and once in the world, children are brutalised, exploited and abused.

Every day in Britain seventy-five children join the other 46,000 on registers of children at risk. In his repeated calls to protect the children – both born and unborn – John Paul knows he is striking modern society at its jugular vein. The urgency of his message, made visible in his exhausting exacting schedule of visits to the world's one billion Catholics, is the mark of a man

who believes the world is courting disaster if it fails to heed his
message.

The Pontificate of John Paul II

Of the dozen or so encyclicals published during the pontificate
of John Paul II, the defining letter of the leader of the Catholic
Church to his flock of more than a billion souls is undoubtedly
Evangelium Vitae[1] (The Gospel of Life).

When it was published in the spring of 1995 I was in Rome
and by a happy coincidence had the opportunity to meet the
Pope on the day after publication. We gave him some Irish
salmon – fish for Peter – and some English Stilton, Lenten
cheese.

The previous day, in London, Channel Four had invited me
to appear on their lunchtime programme to discuss the encyclical. In a slightly banal encounter I was asked whether it was
wise to have published a statement which was bound to upset
commentators and which flew in the face of public opinion. It
was not, I mildly suggested, the Pope's primary duty to consider
the effect on commentators or public opinion. This line of
questioning says quite a lot about Western attitudes and the
inappropriateness of applying the same yardstick by which we
measure political opinion to religious belief. When the Church
attempts to run its affairs by the techniques of a general
management committee, by opinion polling, or by pretending
that it can be a democracy, it does itself no service. Words like
authority and obedience may not be very fashionable but –
along with conscience – they are part of the Christian life. I
follow Peter because he follows Christ and although the Church
has made some devastating errors in its history, and all of us
must reserve our conscience and the ultimate right to dissent, I
do not believe in convenience theology which I can make up to
suit myself as I go along. The teaching authority of the Church
should be clear, rooted in orthodoxy and Scripture, and not

regarded as something which may be routinely disregarded by those who claim membership of the Church.

That morning in Rome reminded me of the awesome responsibility which falls upon the Pope. When our small group entered his private chapel for the celebration of his early morning Mass, he was kneeling at his prie-dieu before the altar. Much of his life has been spent in prayer. Among the burdens of office he has not forgotten that it is from prayer that he draws his strength. It reminded me also of the feeble excuses I make to myself about a busy life not permitting sufficient time for personal prayer. As a child I was taught the simple home-spun truth that a family which prays together, stays together. With the pressures on contemporary family life I am old-fashioned enough to think that the recitation of that mantra might be more effective than some of the other advice on offer to beleaguered and pressurised families.

I am also conscious of how easy it is to suffer spiritual burn-out. Prayer is the antidote to that emptiness which we all experience from time to time. Man – perhaps especially people in my profession – places an extraordinary reliance on his own ability to solve everything on his own. Occasionally some devastating event smashes the thin veneer of our cultured self-reliance. Inevitably we are no longer ready for it. We may have filled Filofaxes and full filing cabinets but do we have fulfilled lives? The spiritual vacuum leaves us ill-prepared for the disasters which ambush us at every turn of the road.

A Pope whose first priority is prayer and who faces problems by first calling people to prayer is instructing people in the way of true happiness. I have heard both St Augustine and St Ignatius credited with the remark that we must pray as if the entire outcome depends on God and work as if the entire outcome depends on us. Certainly whoever said it, Pope John Paul has been a living example of a man who accomplishes both.

Not being a product of Western materialism he inevitably

has none of our preoccupations with the values which such a society has spawned. Equally, he has lived under the tyranny of Nazism and Communism. He comes from a nation whose identity and culture were ruthlessly repressed. He has studied questions of theology and ethics deeply and he has personally dealt with all the questions which any good pastor confronts as priest or bishop.

What mark out his pontificate are his unswerving and uncompromising defence of life, his defence of the poor, his commitment to evangelism, his courage and the spirit of forgiveness which he showed in the aftermath of the attempt on his life, his adroitness in confronting Communism and his unwillingness to weakly accept relativism or the values of Western society.

The media have labelled him a reactionary and have preoccupied themselves with drawing up lists of potential successors whom they describe as progressive. But by what standards do they make these judgements and assessments? Is a man who condones or excuses the killing of an unborn child really such a progressive? Do the Pope's declarations on the respect which must be shown to women make him a reactionary? Labels sit uncomfortably on a man who simultaneously asserts the rights of workers and condemns the stifling and destructive culture which permits such crudeness and barbarity.

In all this he is surely standing in the steps of his Master. It has always struck me as significant that in the Bible the story of the rich man and the poor man is followed by Christ's call to faithfulness in marriage. This is neither a 'moral majority' gospel or a gospel of social justice. It is simply the Gospel in all its challenging completeness and fullness.

People say it is unrealistic to call people to such high ideals but we are in desperate need of ideals. That we all fall short is not only glaringly obvious, it is completely irrelevant. In expecting a softer approach pundits completely misunderstand their man and his job.

From an English standpoint disappointment is often expressed about the way in which ecumenical progress between Anglicans and Catholics has faltered during this pontificate. This is in stark contrast to the massive improvement in Jewish–Catholic relations and improved relations with Lutherans and Protestant denominations. Yet, in many ways Anglican–Catholic relations should have been among the easiest to move forward. The fault lines are now increasingly drawn between orthodox and liberal believers rather than between Protestant and Catholic or Jew and Catholic. I have more to say about this later. Personal relations between individual Christians and local churches in Britain are generally now conducted in a good spirit but it was inevitable that as the Church of England decided to go it alone on women's ordination and when some of its bishops spoke out in favour of destructive experiments on human embryos, or accepted cohabitation in place of marriage, any chance of further ecumenical progress was ruled out. Reunion of the Roman Catholic Church and the Church of England now seems impossible. However, it is also true that the Pope's background was never going to make Anglican–Catholic relations a priority. Coming from the east – with the traditional rivalries of the Orthodox and Catholic traditions but commonly held beliefs and doctine – it was never going to be a surprise that his main ecumenical objective would be Catholic–Orthodox reconciliation.

Catholics and the Eastern Orthodox Church

His 1995 meeting with the Ecumenical Patriarch, Bartholemew, was one of the most important meetings of his pontificate. In his encyclical, *Ut Unum Sint*[2] (That They May Be One), the Pope movingly expresses his desire that Christians from the western Catholic and eastern Orthodox traditions be reunited. He showed a profound understanding that progress in deepening Catholic–Orthodox relations offers the best possible antidote to modern secularism. Such progress would also address the poisonous conflicts historically generated through the clash of these ancient churches.

In Patriarch Bartholemew the Pope found a man who, like himself, has not simply read about suffering or studied papers describing the intolerance meted out to religious minorities. He has experienced these things himself. He also comes from a country which has been experiencing the rise of Iranian-style Islamic fundamentalism.

My first meeting with the Patriarch was eight years ago when he was the Metropolitan, dealing with diocesan affairs in Istanbul. I met him again in 1994 and was impressed with the ease with which he discussed a whole range of international questions.

Orthodoxy is organised in national churches – such as the Greek, Russian and Serbian Orthodox churches – but all Orthodox Christians look towards the ancient Byzantine city of Constantinople and to the Ecumenical Patriarch. In theory, Turkish law allows for minority religious worship, in practice Orthodoxy faces asphyxiation. The law states that the Patriarch – whom they refuse to acknowledge as 'Ecumenical', because this gives him an international role – must be a Turkish citizen. However, the historic conflict between Greece and Turkey, Christians and Muslims, has led to the evacuation of almost all Greek Orthodox believers from the country. The Patriarch's flock now only numbers 3,000 people. To draw priests and sufficient bishops to comprise the Synod which has to elect the Patriarch, from those 3,000 souls is no easy task. To have produced yet again from within that tiny elect a man of Bartholemew's calibre is truly remarkable.

To make the Orthodox Church's survival even more difficult, the Turkish authorities have closed the seminary, the theological school of Halki, on the small island of Heybeli. The building, which I visited, is kept in a state of readiness for the day they hope students will be permitted to return. One

Orthodox priest, Father Isiaas – an Englishman who spent eighteen years on Mount Athos, Orthodoxy's holy of holies – cares for the deserted island seminary, standing like a sentinel at the very gates of Christendom. The Turkish authorities have harassed the Orthodox schools and the day-to-day running of the Church. That the Church has survived at all, in the shadow of the beautiful basilica of Hagia Sophia, seized and converted into a mosque by Mehmet the Conqueror, is miraculous. Like the Pope, Patriarch Bartholemew knows all about endurance and survival.

Both religious leaders realise that the essence of the Christian message is love. That love is made a mockery of every time that conflicting brands of nationalism profess Christian convictions, legitimacy or justification. The barbarism and atrocities committed in the name of Orthodox Christianity against Bosnian Muslims and which have echoes in the tribalism which has disfigured Northern Ireland, reflect ancient hatreds which masquerade under the banner of religion.

In the context of the Balkans and the former Soviet Union, as well as in the materialistic West, reconciliation could be the key to undoing so much of the evil which confronts us. In his Apostolic Letter, *Tertio Millenio Adveniente*,[3] the Pope set the scene for their meeting by recalling 'all those times in history when we departed from the spirit of Christ and His Gospel and, instead of offering to the world the witness of life inspired by the values of faith, indulged in ways of thinking and acting which were truly forms of counterwitness and scandal'. He added that 'Acknowledging the weaknesses of the past ... helps us to face today's temptations and challenges and prepares us to meet them.' If the two leaders and their faithful followers are able to put flesh on those words their meeting will genuinely have been of historic proportions.

Catholics and Protestants

Antagonism between Orthodox and Catholics is mirrored by historic hostilities between Protestant denominations and Catholics. Between 1528 and 1767 the Hutterian Church, for instance, suffered relentless and sometimes violent persecution at the hands of the Catholic Church. More than 2,000 Hutterites died as a direct result of these persecutions and tens of thousands suffered as family members were imprisoned or executed. Homes were burned, property was confiscated, and whole settlements were uprooted. The objective was the elimination of the Hutterian Church and of all Anabaptists – who had been vilified as heretical. Their persecution did not end in the eighteenth century as a result of any change of heart by the Church authorities but because the Hutterites fled the Austro-Hungarian empire and mainly emigrated to Russia. This is a shocking period of Church history.

Ironically, radical Anabaptism has today reached much the same ground as much of the Catholic Church. The late Malcolm Muggeridge, who became a Catholic and one of the leading contemporary exponents of Christianity, lived close to the Hutterian Bruderhof in his Sussex village of Robertsbridge. They held each other in great esteem. I was privileged to visit the Bruderhof myself and felt inspired by the sharing in common and the simplicity of their lives. The same spirit is to be found in the new English Catholic lay communities of the Upper Room and the Open Door, and the Italian lay community of St Igidio, and which was founded with the Pope's personal encouragement. All are truly a sign of contradiction in the affluence of the stockbroker belt, and the pell-mell of City life.

The Bruderhof Movement regularly publish *The Plough*, which they dedicate to all who work for a personal transformation in Christ and for a radical turning away from the materialism, militarism, racism, and impurity of this world and towards the coming of God's kingdom. It reads like one of Pope John Paul's encyclicals. Nor do I think it is mere coincidence that so many of their articles are given over to the spirituality and thinking of Catholics such as Jean Vanier – the founder of the radical L'Arche communities where the able-bodied and disabled people share their lives together – Thomas Merton, Henri Nouwen and Basil Pennington.

The philosophy of the Bruderhof was expounded by Eber-hard Arnold in 1925 in *Why We Live In Community*.[4] Arnold passionately believed that fullness of life can only be found in community and that this in turn comes at the cost of complete self-sacrifice. A community animated by the Holy Spirit inevi-tably has Christ at its heart. For Catholics, with their traditional embrace of community and repudiation of individualism, there is nothing here with which they could quarrel. Down the ages the religious communities of Benedict, Bernard, Francis and countless others have enriched the life of the Church and the world around them. Writing about the Bruderhofs, Thomas Merton, one of the leading Catholic writers of this century, found himself in complete harmony with Arnold's concept of community. He said: 'The ultimate thing is that we build community not on our love but on God's love.' Pope John Paul's encyclicals re-emphasise these themes and recognise that in a world where the gulf between the haves and have nots seems ever more unbridgeable we must persistently re-empha-sise the ideals of the early Christian community.

In 1995 Bruderhof Elder, Johann Christoph Arnold and Cardinal John O'Connor, Archbishop of New York, met to foster reconciliation and a new understanding of each other's traditions. Arnold said that this meeting had been made possible by Pope John Paul's Apostolic Letter, *Tertio Millenio Adveniente*. He said that the honesty and humility of this letter, together with the Pope's book, *Crossing The Threshold of Hope*,[5] and encyclicals such as the *Gospel of Life* had made possible this remarkable and previously unthinkable encounter.

In June 1995 Christoph Arnold went to Rome where he met
Cardinal Joseph Ratzinger – former bishop of Munich – where
sixteenth- and seventeenth-century Anabaptists were martyred.
The Cardinal moved many by his eloquent and poignant
response:

> What is truly moving in these stories is the depth of faith
> of these men, their being deeply anchored in our Lord
> Jesus Christ, and their joy in this fact, a joy that is stronger
> than death. We are distressed, of course, by the fact that
> the church was so closely linked with the powers of this
> world that it could deliver other Christians to the
> executioner because of their beliefs. This should be a deep
> challenge to us, how much we all need to repent again and
> again, and how much the church must renounce worldly
> principles and standards in order to accept the truth as the
> only standard, to look to Christ; not to torture others but
> to go the way of witnessing, a way that will always lead to
> martyrdom in one form or other. I believe it is important
> for us not to adopt worldly standards, but rather to be
> ready to face the world's opposition and to learn that
> Christ's truth is expressed above all in love and forgive-
> ness, which are truth's most trustworthy signs. I believe
> that this is the point at which we all have to begin learning
> anew, the only point through which Christ can truly lead
> us together.

Unambiguously, Pope John Paul wrote in *Tertio Millenio
Adveniente* that:

> The sins of the past still burden us ... It is necessary to
> make amends for them, and earnestly to beseech Christ's
> forgiveness ... One painful chapter of history to which
> the church must return with a spirit of repentance is that
> of the acquiescence given, especially in certain centuries,

to intolerance and even the use of violence in the service of truth . . .

The consideration of mitigating factors does not exonerate the church from the obligation to express profound regret for the weakness of so many of her sons and daughters who sullied her face, preventing her from mirroring the image of her crucified Lord . . .

This honesty and willingness to repent for past failings have been a hallmark of John Paul's years as Pope and help to explain why in certain respects the relationships between Christians of different traditions have been deepened. All the more sad that Anglican–Catholic relations have been derailed.

Catholics and Anglicans

In 1982 I represented my Party at Canterbury Cathedral when Archbishop Runcie and Pope John Paul knelt together in prayer. The following day I was also present as the Pope and the Liverpool Church leaders walked together between our two Cathedrals along Hope Street. The Polish Pope was visibly moved by these simple acts of witness and unity, and by his first real encounter with Anglicanism.

Being married to an Anglican and as the son of a mixed-marriage between an Anglican and Catholic there is no point in my trying to disguise my own passionate hope that these two traditions might have been re-united. There are eight ordained Anglican clergy on my wife's side of the family and both Lizzie's father and grandfather celebrated fifty years in the priesthood. The churchmanship of Lizzie's relatives reflects the various traditions of Anglicanism, from evangelical to Anglo-Catholic. Through them I have encountered rich spirituality. Hence my own disappointment that the promise of 1982 has not blossomed.

The Venerable George Austin, Archdeacon of York,

addressing the reasons for this, says that the most recent developments within the Church of England could lead to the development of a pan-Protestant unity which would 'take the Church of England further from Catholic practice than it has been in the past four hundred years'.[6] Synod well understood that the decision to take unilateral action to ordain women would destroy the possibility of Catholic–Anglican reconciliation. Cardinal Basil Hume seemed to acknowledge this when he said that the decision inevitably presaged the realignment of Christianity in England. The disappearance of Catholicism from the Anglican tradition would in due course lead to realigned Protestants and Catholics living alongside one another in simple respect for each other's diversity. Perhaps that is right but George Austin points to a longer-term problem: the clash between Orthodoxy and liberalism.

Pope John Paul upholds Scripture and Church tradition and firmly states that even if he wanted to he could not tamper with either. As Anglicanism now looks towards Methodism, for instance, it will have to consider further the question of theological liberalism. Under pressure from post-Christian feminists, the Methodist Conference in 1992 accepted a report which took it well away from orthodox Scripture and tradition and from its rich Wesleyan roots: 'God the Father may also be spoken of as Mother, and the Son is no less an exemplar of feminine virtues as masculine ones.'

This sort of religious hermaphrodism will be about as popular with the Vatican as the statements of bishops questioning the Virgin Birth or clergymen who are permitted to stay in office while denying both eternal life and the objective existence of God. Writing in an Apostolic Letter published in 1994 the Pope left no-one in any doubt about the priesting of women: 'I declare that the Church has no authority whatsoever to confer priestly ordinations on women and that this judgement is to be held by all the Church's faithful.' In saying this he was reaffirming the earlier teaching of Pope Paul VI.

I can also imagine what Pope John Paul would make of the seminary professor who has dismissed Christianity as a 'necro-philial religion centred around a dead man'. The same teacher says Christ must be replaced by Christa 'who can represent for women what the Church has crucified with a vengeance, and what we must now raise up in our lives: the erotic as power and the love of God as embodied by erotically empowered women'. The new fault lines in Christianity are increasingly between religious liberalism and orthodoxy and there is little doubt on which side of the divide you will find John Paul II.

As he pleaded that we might be one, in *Ut Unum Sint*, Pope John Paul made it clear that false unity is worthless: 'All form of reductionism or facile agreement must be absolutely avoided,' he said. 'A being together which betrayed the truth would be opposed to both the nature of God who offers his communion and the need for truth found in the depths of every human heart.'

I agree with George Austin when he pleads for a new ecumenism which 'brings together those of all churches who love and hold fast to the unalterable and essential truths of Scripture and Tradition'. That will provide the secular world with its best point of reference: something which theological liberalism will never do.

Pope John Paul's Position

Of course the Catholic Church itself has not been immune to rationalism and relativism. Pope John Paul was criticised for the firmness which he showed in withdrawing the right to teach from the former Dominican, Matthew Fox. Yet anyone who reads his pantheistic creation theology must surely conclude that this has more in common with New Age than Christianity. If the Pope had failed to act he would have been signalling a false tolerance and allowing others to have been led astray.

Thinking back to my own college days I am well aware how

destructive false teaching can be. In the immediate aftermath of the Second Vatican Council there was a great sense of change, but not all of it was good. Among the students studying divinity with me there was a colossal attrition rate as faith was thrown into utter confusion. I am not surprised that only a handful of those who began their studies emerged with their faith intact. Even some of the lecturers ended up leaving the Church. In parenthesis I might add that the religious syllabus subsequently produced for Catholic schools by that same college was an equally unmitigated disaster. Known by the title 'Weaving The Web' it might better have been entitled 'Weaving the Web of Confusion'. Even now, Church officials, while saying that the syllabus is being superseded, are extremely reluctant to admit that its reductionism did any damage. By contrast, the Pope is absolutely clear about what Catholic education should seek to achieve: 'In reflecting on the value of Catholic schools and the importance of Catholic teachers and educators, it is necessary to stress the central point of Catholic education itself. Catholic education is, above all, a question of communicating Christ, of helping to form Christ in the lives of others.'

The Pope's position has always been to place himself alongside Scripture and tradition. But he has also declared himself a Catholic of the Second Vatican Council – with its emphasis on renewal of openness – without surrendering to every passing whim and fancy. Reconciling these tensions has been a considerable achievement. One of his favourite expressions is to encourage us to 'be not afraid'. Certainly he himself has shown no fear in challenging the spirit of our times.

Addressing the reductionism which says it is merely a matter of choice to end the life of an unborn child, the Pope says: 'If a person's right to life is violated at the moment in which they are first conceived in their mother's womb, an indirect blow is struck also at the whole of the moral order which serves to ensure the inviolable rights of man. Among those goods, life occupies the first place.'[7]

Scripture teaches us that we are each made in the image of God, each of inestimable worth, each held in the palm of the hand of God, even before we have uttered our first cry. It is this Scripture which the Pope says is non-negotiable: 'We must not tamper with God's word. We must strive to apply the Good News to the ever-changing conditions of the world but, courageously and at all costs, we must resist the temptation to alter its content or re-interpret it in order to make it fit the spirit of the present age.'

In equally strong terms he rejects the notion that Jesus was a politically committed figure involved in some sort of class struggle: 'This idea of Christ as a political figure, a revolutionary, as the subversive man from Nazareth, does not tally with the Church's catechesis.'

Certainly each day of his life in Galilee Jesus would have seen the effects of Roman oppression, the roadside crucifixions, the humiliations, the persecution. Yet it was Barabbas, not Jesus, who became the political revolutionary hero. Perhaps to remind us of the vagaries of public opinion the Gospel poignantly records how the mob went on to choose Barabbas and to reject Jesus when offered the choice by Pilate. Barabbas had of course carefully cultivated the commentators and pundits. No doubt many of those who comprised this mob had also cheered Jesus and laid palms before Him as He entered Jerusalem. Public acclaim can be very fickle. If Christ had been a political figure He would have courted public opinion. Instead, He chose the way of the cross. Reflecting on the nature of modern political ideologies the Pope says that 'man is set against man, class against class, in useless conflicts'. Paradoxically, our technological progress and mastery are greater than our wisdom about our restless and troubled selves. Our political struggles do not get to the heart of man and his troubles, and the Pope points us to the solutions beyond politics.

Today the cross is carried by the poor and the exploited, those who are tyrannised and by those who have become prisoners of materialism and hedonism. To them Pope John Paul has this to say: 'Whenever the strong exploit the weak; whenever the rich take advantage of the poor; whenever great powers seek to dominate and impose ideologies, there the work of making peace is undone; there the cathedral of peace is again destroyed.' Elsewhere he tells us not to become the slave of things, the slave of economic systems, the slave of production, or the slave of our own products.

John Paul's Story

John Paul is also clear about the crucial role which parents and families must play in the fostering of a good society. In his 1995 letter to the world's women he praises women for their genius. While he upholds the particular gifts of mothers he does not neglect to pay tribute to those women who have given themselves to a consecrated life or to the world of work. He reminds us that we are all equal before God and he asks forgiveness for the Church for the times it has failed to recognise that equality.

Tad Szulc in his excellent biography of the Pope[8] recalls that the death of John Paul's own mother inevitably had a profound effect upon him, and may have affected his view of women. It fostered his special affection and devotion to the Virgin.

It was on 13th April 1929, when the young Karol Wojtyla was almost nine years old, that his mother died aged forty-five. It then fell to his father to bring him up; a father who would himself die when Karol was only twenty-one years old.

Although their home was never oppressively religious, father and mother knew that the principal responsibility for handing on the faith lay with them. His strong prayer life stems from this period of his life. His father remonstrated with the young boy for not praying 'adequately' to the Holy Spirit. 'My father taught me a special prayer, and it was an important spiritual lesson,' he remembers. More than fifty years later this special prayer was to lead to the Pope's encyclical on the Holy Spirit. Prayer was also the comfort his father offered after the young boy's mother died, taking him to pray at the sanctuary of Kalwaria Zebrzydowska.

In their grief, the widower and his son became firm friends. They shared the domestic chores, spent a lot of time together, played together and studied together.

It was also his father who began to instil a love of Polish culture and history which would shape so many of Karol's ideals and attitudes. But he was not a xenophobe and he also inculcated in Karol a tender love and respect for other people and their way of life – especially the small Jewish community which lived in their town of Wadowice. This was not always the pattern in pre-war Poland where virulent anti-Semitism was rife.

Among the greatest of John Paul's lasting achievements the historians will surely judge the staggering improvement in Catholic–Jewish relations among the finest. This tolerance – and his passionate love of his country, so evident in the young Karol's poetry and early writings – was all learnt from his father.

In a charming little book, *Letter To A Jewish Friend*,[9] Gian Franco Svidercoschi records the lifelong friendship between the Pope and Jerzy (Jurek) Kluger, the son of a leading town lawyer in Wadowice. Almost all his boyhood Jewish friends were slaughtered during the Holocaust with the exception of Jurek, although most of his family died in the camps. After the Second World War Kluger settled in Italy and during the Second Vatican Council he realised that the Archbishop of Krakow was his childhood friend, Lolek, the affectionate name by which Karol Wojtyla was known.

Having telephoned him, the Archbishop immediately responded by inviting Kruger to see him. Later, as Pope, he asked for a commemorative plaque to be placed on the site of the Wadowice synagogue, destroyed by the Nazis. In his letter to Jerzy Kluger, from which Svidercoschi's book takes its title, the Pope movingly recalls the Wadowice of their youth:

> Many of those who perished, your co-religionists and our fellow countrymen, were our colleagues in our Elementary School and, later, in the High School where we were educated, the town to which both you and I are bound together by our memories of childhood and youth. I remember very clearly the Wadowice Synagogue, which was near our High School. I have in front of my eyes the numerous worshippers who during their Holidays passed on their way to pray there.

One of those worshippers would have been Regina Reisenfeld, whose family were the Wojtylas' neighbours. Her parents, fearing the coming Holocaust, sent her to Palestine in 1937. She recalled how when they came to say their farewells, and after her father had explained to Karol's father that the growing Polish anti-Semitism had forced them to leave, Karol was silent, too distressed to speak.

When she saw him, fifty years later at a gathering in St Peter's Square, she recalls how the Pope recognised her and inquired of her sister, Helen, and her mother. She told him that her mother had died at Oswiecim (Auschwitz) and her father had been killed in the Soviet Union: 'He just looked at me,' she recalled, 'and there was deep compassion in his eyes . . . he took both my hands and for almost two minutes he blessed me and prayed before me, just holding my hands in his hands. There were thousands of people in the Square, but for just a few seconds there were just the two of us.'

Regina also recorded of her neighbours: 'There was only one family who never showed any racial hostility towards us, and that was Lolek and his dad.'

There is also the story of a Polish Catholic family who were asked to shelter a Jewish child and whose parents were taken to the camps, never to return. They successfully concealed the child and after the war asked their young priest to baptise the boy. He asked about the child's origins and said that he should not be christened but brought up in his Jewish faith and allowed to make up his own mind when he matured. The boy eventually left Poland and is today a rabbi in Jerusalem. The young priest became bishop, archbishop, cardinal and then Pope.

Unsurprisingly, during Pope John Paul's pontificate Catholic–Jewish relations have been transformed, culminating at the very end of 1993 in the formal establishment of diplomatic relations between the Vatican and the State of Israel – forty-five years after its foundation.

From his childhood days, befriending and championing Jewish class-mates who were being subjected to anti-Semitism and bullying; to his involvement in underground groups which defied Nazism; to his repudiation and fierce condemnation of Communism, we see a man who refuses to acquiesce in the evils of the moment but steadfastly and staunchly upholds consistent values – values which throughout his life have been at variance with those of the world.

Catholics and Communism

One of the Pope's most attractive qualities is his ability not simply to oppose but his capacity to offer creative alternatives. His attitude towards Communism illustrates this.

After World War Two the Catholic Church in Eastern Europe found itself bitterly persecuted by Communist governments. No other nation was so devoutly Catholic as Poland and to some extent it had to develop its own unique system of co-existence. It was the diplomacy and the cat and mouse games of these years which helped form Karol Wojtyla. Cardinal Stefan Wyszynski was the Polish Primate during these difficult times, from 1948 until his death from stomach cancer in 1981.

Wyszynski was rabidly anti-Communist, as he had been anti-Nazi and also opposed to extreme nationalism. He was also very critical of the excesses of capitalism, a significant strain within the Polish Catholic Church. Understanding this background helps to explain the position which John Paul has consistently taken. His post-Communist ideas, which blend personal responsibility with an acute sense of social justice, are consistent with his Polish intellectual and spiritual formation.

Stalin died in 1953 but, if anything, the Polish regime became even more restrictive of Catholic publications, political and social activities, and travel. It tried to impose a siege on the Church. In the same year Wyszynski was arrested and theological schools closed.

There was a thaw in 1956 but the new First Secretary of the Party, Gomulka, soon capitulated to Moscow's demands for a tougher approach. Systematic harassment became the order of the day.

The Church, meanwhile, was updating its own thinking on questions of social justice. In 1962 John XXIII published *Mater et Magistra*,[10] which expanded on Leo XIII's famous social encyclical, *Rerum Novarum*[11] published in 1891. This became part of a powerful armoury which Catholic intellectuals, often led by Bishop Wojtyla, deployed against Socialism.

After his election in October 1978, he continued to deal with Communism at both levels: diplomatic and intellectual. His post-election Polish visit, in the spring of 1979, was a diplomatic triumph, galvanising the faithful and coining the phrase 'solidarity' which was to become redolent of Polish politics over the coming years. So concerned had the Kremlin become by November that the Secretariat of the Central Committee of the Soviet Communist Party drew up a six-point 'Decision to Work Against the Policies of the Vatican in relation with Socialist States'.

There followed three significant encylicals which were all central to the development of social ideas and combated

Socialism at an intellectual level. In 1981 *Laborem Exercens*[12] (On Human Work) railed against 'the people of today who lived in conditions of shameful and unworthy poverty'. He demanded 'relief and hope' for them. The same themes were reiterated in *Sollicitudo Rei Socialis*[13] (On Social Concern), in 1987, and in *Centesimus Annus*[14] (The Hundredth Year), in 1991, which commemorated the publication of *Rerum Novarum*. At the heart of these great letters to the Catholic community – and to those beyond it whom the Pontiff equally had in his sights – are the themes of dignity of work, the ethical value of putting wealth at the service of the poor and the need for the developed world to end the exploitation of the Third World.

In the space of 20,000 words *Sollicitudo Rei Socialis* scorns the West's 'superdevelopment' which 'makes people slaves of possessions and of immediate gratification, with no other horizon'. Although he clearly favours open and democratic societies, the Pope is scathing about the economic and social cultures which they have developed. In warning against the dangers of 'radical capitalist ideology' he undoubtedly sees Western culture as dominated by the personal sins of an 'all-consuming desire for profit' which he implies is the moral equivalent of totalitarian Communism's 'thirst for power, with the intention of imposing one's will on others'.

John Paul's Goal

What is his goal? Nothing less than the creation of a completely Christian alternative to the humanistic philosophies of the twentieth century – Marxism, materialism, structuralism and the atheistic ideas of the post-Enlightenment.

In a talk to Mexican businessmen in 1990 the Pope said it was wrong to claim that the Church's social doctrine condemned any particular economic theory. It was interested only in the effects of that theory when it violated or put in jeopardy human dignity. So, for instance, labour is not just a commodity which may be bought or sold; the only legitimate claim to ownership of the means of production can be that they are put at the service of labour. Businessmen must respond 'to the just requirements of the common good' and must not succumb to 'the grave danger' of striving for personal gain – 'usually linked to the thirst for power'.

As in all other matters we see here a man who is unconcerned about the way such uncompromising messages would be received by conservative governments, economists and businessmen. Central is his abiding belief that if the Church cleaves to a vision of society which is just, and ethically and morally consistent with the law of God, then the future of the Church will be secure. In a further effort to define this Christian approach to living he authorised the publication of the 691 pages of the *Catechism of the Catholic Church*.[15] This was the first such comprehensive document since the sixteenth century.

Trying to assess his impact and his contribution, the evangalist Billy Graham says, 'He'll go down in history as the greatest of our modern Popes. He's been the strong conscience of the whole Christian world.' *Time* magazine voted him their Man of the Year in 1994 saying that he has spread

through every means at his disposal a message not of expediency or compromise but of right and wrong; amid so much fear for the future, John Paul dared to speak of hope. He did not say what everyone wanted to hear, and many within and beyond his church took offence. But his fidelity to what he believes people need to hear remained adamant and unwavering.

There are echoes here of St Paul writing in I Corinthians: 'Woe to me if I do not preach the gospel!'

The Pope himself told *Time* that his beliefs 'always go back to the sanctity of the human being'. At the Beijing Conference on Women's Rights, perversely held in a country daily abusing women and human rights in 1995, at the Cairo Conference on Population in 1994, in his encyclicals and preaching, the Pope has never deviated one iota from his total and utter defence of life. At Cairo a 113-page document had been tabled committing $17 billion annually to curb global population growth. The Clinton Administration sought to include a statement that access to abortion should be available to all. The Vatican spokesman, Joaquin Navarro-Valls said that the Pope 'feared that for the first time in the history of humanity abortion was being proposed as a means of population control. He put all the prestige of his office at the service of this issue.'

For several days Vatican delegates lobbied and marshalled support among Latin American delegates, delegates from developing countries, and Islamic representatives. The Pope's team eventually succeeded in having inserted an explicit statement that 'in no case should abortion be promoted as a method of family planning'. Not altogether approvingly *The Tablet*, the British liberal Catholic periodical, commented that 'Never has the Vatican cared less about being popular than under Pope John Paul II.'

In the shifting sands of contemporary society, people increasingly understand that we have drifted too far from ethical certainties; and as a result lawlessness, anarchy and disintegration threaten civilisation itself. By being true to itself the Church can be a beacon of hope in such a society and no one has seen that more clearly than Pope John Paul II.

Notes

Chapter One

1. R. Muir, *History of Liverpool* (Liverpool University Press, 1907).
2. K. McAll, *Healing The Family Tree* (Sheldon, 1986).
3. G. Chandler, *Life of William Roscoe* (Liverpool City Library, 1953).
4. E. Rathbone, *The Disinherited Family* (Falling Wall, 1986).
5. E. Rathbone, *The Case for Family Allowances* (Penguin, 1940).

Chapter Two

1. R. Van de Weyer, *Island Vision: Prophets, Pastors and Pilgrims of the English Church* (Marshall Pickering, 1988).
2. J. Capon, *John and Charles Wesley: The Preacher and the Poet* (Hodder & Stoughton, 1988).
3. J. Pollock, *John Wesley* (Lion Publishing, 1992).
4. D. Alton, *Faith in Britain* (Hodder & Stoughton, 1991) and *What Kind of Country?* (Marshall Pickering, 1987).
5. T. Szulc, *Pope John Paul II: The Biography* (Scribner's, 1995).

Chapter Three

1. D. Selbourne, *The Spirit of the Age: An Account of Our Times* (Sinclair-Stevenson, 1993).
2. D. Selbourne, *Principle of Duty: An Essay on the Foundations of the Civic Order* (Mandarin, 1995).
3. J. Sacks, *Faith in the Future* (Darton, Longman and Todd, 1995).
4. D. Day in *The Chesterton Review*, Summer 1995.

5. J. Maritain, *Christianity and Democracy* (The Centenary Press, 1945).
6. J. Macmurray, *Persons in Relation* (Faber & Faber, 1995) and *Self as Agent* (Faber & Faber, 1995).
7. J. Sopel, *Tony Blair: The Moderniser* (Bantam Books, 1995).
8. J. Sacks, *Persistence of Faith: Religion, Morality and Society in a Secular Age* (Weidenfeld and Nicholson, 1992).
9. Sacks, *Faith in the Future*, op. cit.
10. J. Maritain, *Man and the State* (University of Chicago Press, 1951).
11. A. Solzhenitsyn, *East and West*
12. Pope John Paul II, *Evangelium Vitae* (Catholic Truth Society, 1995).
13. J. Maritain, *Freedom in the Modern World* (University of Notre Dame Press, 1990).
14. R. Sparkes, *The Ethical Investor* (HarperCollins 1995).
15. Pope John XXIII, *Mater et Magistra* (Catholic Truth Society, 1962).
16. Pope Paul VI, *Populorum Progressio* (Catholic Truth Society, 1966).

Chapter Four

1. Pope Pius X, *Acerbo Nimis* (Catholic Truth Society, 1905).
2. L. Rolfo, *James Alberione: Apostle for Our Times* (Alba House, 1987).
3. D. Agasso, *Thecla Merlo: Messenger of the Good News* (St Paul Multi Media Productions, 1993).
4. R. Parsons, *Sixty Minute Father* (Hodder & Stoughton, 1995).

Chapter Five

1. J. Sacks, *Faith in the Future* (Darton, Longman and Todd, 1995).
2. From a reported conversation with A. Solzhenitsyn in 1995
3. Lord Rees-Mogg, *The Times*, 23rd January 1995.
4. M. Craig, *Candles in the Dark* (Hodder & Stoughton, 1993).

Chapter Six

1. E. Duffy, *The Stripping of the Altars: Traditional Religion in England, 1400–1580* (Yale University Press, 1994).

Chapter Seven

1. O. Meinardus, *Monks and Monasteries of the Egyptian Desert* (The American University in Cairo Press, 1989).
2. *Human Rights Abuses: Egypt 1994* (Jubilee Campaign Publications).
3. *Human Rights Abuses: Turkey 1995* (Jubilee Campaign Publications).
4. The Jubilee Campaign is based in St John's, Wonersh, near Guildford, Surrey.

Chapter Eight

1. Jubilee Campaign and June 4th China Support, *Religious Persecution in the People's Republic of China* (Jubilee Campaign Publications, 1995).
2. Brother David, *Walking The Hard Road: Wang Ming Tao* (Marshall Pickering, 1990).

Chapter Nine

1. C. S. Lewis, *Mere Christianity* (Collins, 1983).
2. C. S. Lewis, *The Lion, the Witch and the Wardrobe* (Lion, 1950).
3. C. S. Lewis, *Prince Caspian* (Collins, 1990).
4. C. S. Lewis, *The Last Battle* (Lion, 1956).
5. C. S. Lewis, *Voyage to Venus* (Pan Books, 1960).
6. C. S. Lewis, *Out of the Silent Planet* (Pan Books, 1990).
7. C. S. Lewis, *That Hideous Strength* (Pan Books, 1990).
8. C. S. Lewis, *The Screwtape Letters* (Collins, 1993).
9. G. K. Chesterton in *The Chesterton Review*, September 1995.
10. *The Lewis Papers*, (Leeborough Press) Vol. 4.
11. C. S. Lewis, *A Pilgrim's Regress* (Collins, 1977).

12. C. S. Lewis, *Surprised by Joy* (Collins, 1986).
13. C. S. Lewis, *The Problem of Pain* (Collins, 1993).
14. C. S. Lewis, *Broadcast Talks* (Geoffrey Bles, 1942).
15. C. S. Lewis, *Christian Behaviour* (Geoffrey Bles, 1943).
16. C. S. Lewis, *Beyond Personality* (Geoffrey Bles, 1944).
17. J. Gresham, *And God Came In* (Lyle W. Dorsett, 1983).
18. C. S. Lewis, *The Four Loves* (Collins, 1963).
19. A. N. Wilson, *C. S. Lewis: A Biography* (Collins, 1991).
20. C. S. Lewis in *Atlantic Monthly*, January 1959.
21. B. Sibley, *Shadowlands: C. S. Lewis and Joy Davidman* (Hodder & Stoughton, 1994).
22. C. S. Lewis, *A Grief Observed* (Faber & Faber, 1966).
23. D. Watson, *Fear No Evil* (Hodder & Stoughton, 1994).

Chapter Ten

1. J. Pullinger, *Chasing the Dragon* (Hodder & Stoughton, 1980).
2. S. Kaplin, evidence given to the All-Party Parliamentary Drugs Misuse Group.

Chapter Eleven

1. E. Wilkie, *Pocketful of Dynamite* (Hodder & Stoughton, 1990).
2. Baroness Lockwood, House of Lords, Hansard 21/2/92 col. 1473.
3. A. Davis, SPUC (Society for the Protection of the Unborn Child) Conference, 1993.
4. House of Commons Debate 26/2/93 1177–1180.
5. N. P. Barry, *Welfare* (Open University Press, 1990).
6. A. Wohl, *Endangered Lives: Public Health in Victorian Britain* (Methuen, 1994).
7. P. J. Waller, *Town, City and Nation 1850–1914* (Oxford University Press, 1983).
8. 'China Adopts Law to "Improve" Babies', *Independent*, 28th October 1995.
9. F. Dikotter, 'China Moves to Ban Babies with Defects', *Sunday Times*, 5th February 1995.
10. 'China Reverses Birth Law', *Daily Telegraph*, 28th October 1995.

11. B. Wilson, 'Avoid Handicaps. Kill Babies', *Spectator*, 5th July 1995.

12. 'Pregnant Pause', *Nursing Times*, vol. 91, no. 1, 4th January 1995.

13. Dikotter, op. cit.

14. P. and T. Woods, letter to the editor, *Guardian*, 28th June 1995.

15. G. Himmelfarb, *The De-Moralization of Society: From Victorian Virtues to Modern Values* (IEA Health and Welfare Unit, 1995).

16. Wilkie, *Pocketful of Dynamite*, op. cit., pp. 188–9.

17. ibid. p. 188.

18. D. K. Smith and T. M. Marteau, 'Detecting fetal abnormality; serum screening and fetal abnormality; serum screening and fetal anomaly scans', *British Journal of Midwifery*, vol. 3, no. 3, 1995, pp. 133–6.

19. T. Marteau, 'Information on Antenatal Tests is Inadequate', *Nursing Times*, 21st June 1995.

20. Wilson, op. cit.

21. 'Abortion Advice over Infection "Is Wrong"', *Daily Telegraph*, 21st November 1994.

22. SPUC factsheet on Down's Syndrome.

23. 'Finding the Courage to End a Life', *Daily Telegraph*, 13th July 1995.

24. *Sunday Telegraph*, 21st October 1995.

25. Wilkie, *Pocketful of Dynamite*, op. cit., p. 48.

26. ibid.

27. B. Flannagan, *U2 At the End of the World* (Bantam Press, 1995).

Chapter Twelve

1. Pope John Paul II, *Evangelium Vitae* (Catholic Truth Society, 1995).

2. Pope John Paul II, *Ut Unum Sint* (Catholic Truth Society, 1995).

3. Pope John Paul II, *Tertio Millenio Adveniente* (Catholic Truth Society, 1994).

4. E. Arnold, *Why We Live in Community* (Plough Publishing, 1976).

5. Pope John Paul II, *Crossing the Threshold of Hope* (Alfred A. Knopf, 1994).

6. G. Austin, *Catholic Herald*, May 1995.

7. Pope John Paul II, *Evangelium Vitae*, op. cit.

8. T. Szulc, *Pope John Paul II: The Biography* (Scribner's, 1995).

9. G. F. Svidercoschi, *Letter To A Jewish Friend* (Hodder & Stoughton, 1994).

10. Pope John XXIII, *Mater et Magistra* (Catholic Truth Society, 1962).

11. Pope Leo XIII, *Rerum Novarum* (Catholic Truth Society, 1891).

12. Pope John Paul II, *Laborem Exercens* (Catholic Truth Society, 1981).

13. Pope John Paul II, *Sollicitudo Rei Socialis* (Catholic Truth Society, 1987).

14. Pope John Paul II, *Centesimus Annus* (Catholic Truth Society, 1991).

15. *The Catechism of the Catholic Church* (Geoffrey Chapman, 1994).